NORMAN F. BOURKE
MEMORIAL LIBRARY
CAYUGA
COMMUNITY COLLEGE
AUBURN, NEW YORK 13021

Technology Application Competencies for K-12 Teachers

Irene Chen
University of Houston Downtown, USA

Jane Thielemann
University of Houston Downtown, USA

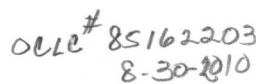

 **Information Science Publishing**

Hershey • New York

Acquisition Editor:	Kristin Klinger
Senior Managing Editor:	Jennifer Neidig
Managing Editor:	Sara Reed
Assistant Managing Editor:	Sharon Berger
Development Editor:	Kristin Roth
Copy Editor:	Angela Thor
Typesetter:	Michael Brehm
Cover Design:	Lisa Tosheff
Printed at:	Yurchak Printing Inc.

Published in the United States of America by
Information Science Publishing (an imprint of IGI Global)
701 E. Chocolate Avenue
Hershey PA 17033
Tel: 717-533-8845
Fax: 717-533-8661
E-mail: cust@igi-pub.com
Web site: http://www.igi-pub.com

and in the United Kingdom by
Information Science Publishing (an imprint of IGI Global)
3 Henrietta Street
Covent Garden
London WC2E 8LU
Tel: 44 20 7240 0856
Fax: 44 20 7379 3313
Web site: http://www.eurospan.co.uk

Copyright © 2008 by IGI Global. All rights reserved. No part of this book may be reproduced in any form or by any means, electronic or mechanical, including photocopying, without written permission from the publisher.

Product or company names used in this book are for identification purposes only. Inclusion of the names of the products or companies does not indicate a claim of ownership by IGI Global of the trademark or registered trademark.

Library of Congress Cataloging-in-Publication Data

Chen, Irene.
 Technology application competencies for K-12 teachers / Irene Chen and Jane Thielemann.
   p. cm.
 Summary: "This book is designed to strengthen understanding of the critical information in the framework for technology application competencies for K-12 teachers"--Provided by publisher.
 Includes bibliographical references and index.
 ISBN 978-1-59904-735-5 (hardcover) -- ISBN 978-1-59904-737-9 (ebook)
 1. Educational technology--Study and teaching. 2. Information technology--Study and teaching. 3. Teachers--Training of. 4. Teachers--In service training. I. Thielemann, Jane. II. Title.
 LB1028.3.C47 2008
 371.33077'5--dc22
                               2007007289

British Cataloguing in Publication Data
A Cataloguing in Publication record for this book is available from the British Library.

All work contributed to this book is new, previously-unpublished material. The views expressed in this book are those of the authors, but not necessarily of the publisher.

Technology Application Competencies for K-12 Teachers

Table of Contents

Foreword viii

Preface xi

Acknowledgment xvii

Section I:
Technology Applications Core

Chapter I
Technology Operation and Concepts for Teachers 1
    The Teacher Technologist 2
    A Brief History of Computers 2
    Computers in the Classroom 3
    Hardware 4
    Operating Systems 7
    Software 11
    WWW in Education 13
    Legal and Ethical Issues 15
    Equal Opportunity and Computers 17
    Emerging Technologies 20
    Final Words 21
    References 21
    Sample Questions 23

Chapter II
Teacher Productivity and Professional Practices 24
- *Teacher Productivity Software* 25
- *Computerized Data Analysis Tools* 26
- *Using a Variety of Productivity Tools* 50
- *Utility Software* 56
- *Software for Work and Home* 60
- *References* 61
- *Sample Questions* 62

Chapter III
Using Technology for Learning, Teaching, and Designing the Curriculum 64
- *Maximizing Student Achievement* 65
- *Technology Creates Opportunities for Learners with Special Needs* 72
- *Instructional Software* 78
- *Value Systems of Technology Integration* 79
- *Changes and Diffusion of Instructional Technology* 80
- *Educators as Life-Long Learners* 81
- *References* 82
- *Sample Questions* 85

Section II:
Digital Graphics/Animation and Desktop Publishing

Chapter IV
The Principles and Applications of Digital Design 88
- *Educational Relevance of Graphics and Animations* 89
- *Paint Programs* 91
- *Draw Programs* 92
- *Graphics from the Web* 96
- *From Clipart Collections* 96
- *Cameras* 97
- *Scan* 102
- *Other Graphic Sources* 104
- *Graphic Editing* 105
- *Animation* 107
- *Design Tips to Reduce File Sizes* 112
- *Final Words* 115
- *References* 116
- *Sample Questions* 117
- *Appendix: Technical Lingo for Media Effects* 118

Chapter V
Desktop Publishing for Schools 120
- *Educational Relevance of Desktop Publishing* 121
- *A Short History of Desktop Publishing* 122
- *Word Processing vs. Graphic Design vs. Desktop Publishing* 122

Choosing Desktop Publishing Software 123
Elements of Desktop Publishing Projects 124
Previewing 134
Printing 135
Final Words 137
References 137
Sample Questions 138

Chapter VI
Creating Multimedia for Special Audiences 140
Visual, Graphic, and Media Literacy in Education 141
Composition Principles 143
Using Colors to Appeal to the Audience 148
Using Lighting to Convey Meanings 152
Final Words 156
References 157
Sample Questions 158

Section III:
Video Technology and Multimedia

Chapter VII
School Multimedia Design Teams and Projects 161
Instructional Design Models 162
Managing Multimedia Projects for Education 163
Multimedia Project Life Cycle 166
Multimedia Design Team or Production Crew 167
Media Acquisition 169
Maintenance of Media 170
Final Words 171
References 173
Sample Questions 174

Chapter VIII
Video and Sound in Education 176
Educational Relevance of Audio and Visual Productions 177
Audio Use and Equipment 178
Specifications of Microphones 178
Video 184
Technical Lingo 196
An Interview Scenario 198
The Production Sequence 200
References 202
Sample Questions 203

Chapter IX
Design, Produce, and Distribute Educational Multimedia Products ... 205
Multimedia Authoring Programs 206

Hardware and Software Requirements 215
Help Your Students Create Projects 218
Evaluating Multimedia Projects 219
Multimedia Dissemination Formats 220
Concerns when Seeking Media Clips 224
Final Words 225
References 225
Sample Questions 227

Section IV:
Webmastering

Chapter X
Administration of Educational Web Sites 229
    District Technology Infrastructure 230
    WAN 231
    LANs 232
    The Internet of the Pre-Web Age 236
    The World Wide Web 237
    School Web Projects 240
    A Good Web Development Team 244
    Building an Educational Web Site 247
    Web Project Life Cycle 252
    References 255
    Sample Questions 256

Chapter XI
Web Design Tools for Educators 257
    School and District Web Pages 258
    Construction of Web Pages 258
    A Teachers Professional Homepage: A Scenario 259
    Common Web-Compatible Formats 263
    Web Page Tools 264
    Multimedia and Other Tools 275
    Navigation Schemes in Web Design 277
    Designing American Disability Act (ADA) Compliant Web Pages ... 278
    Print Design vs. Web Page Design 279
    Boosting a Web Site's Credibility 279
    Protecting Web Sites 280
    Wrap Up School Web Projects 281
    References 282
    Sample Questions 284

Chapter XII
Web Communications and Interaction for Teaching and Learning 285
    Virtual Learning Communities (or VLC) 286
    Distance Education/Learning 290
    Netiquette at School 293
    Ethical Issues 294
    References 297
    Sample Questions 299

About the Authors 301

Index 302

Foreword

Writing a worthwhile book on technology in education is not an easy task. In fact, the process of integrating technology that is both useful and beneficial into education is not an easy task. During the 1970s, when personal computers were emerging as a technical and then a social phenomenon, there were lots of false starts, blind alleys, and technical as well as pedagogical problems. I remember giving a talk at a conference in West Texas, and three worried teachers approached me during a coffee break. They wanted me to talk to their principal about his ideas for integrating technology into their elementary school. He had bought a computer for each of the teachers in May, and he wanted them to spend the summer developing teaching materials to be used with the computers. In the fall, the school would begin to use the computers in the classrooms.

At first, it sounded like a good idea, but the teachers quickly explained how they were to accomplish this worthy goal. At the time there were very few pieces of "educational" software, only one or two word processing programs, and precious few computers with anything but an ordinary cassette recorder for data storage. However, every personal computer came with an operating system and a version of the BASIC programming language. What the principal had in mind was for the teachers to spend their summer learning to program the computer in BASIC and then using their newly acquired knowledge to write computer programs for use in the classroom. The teachers had no idea how to begin this task and they were afraid to tell the principal.

The saying, "To someone with a hammer, the whole world looks like a nail" is an apt summary of those early days. We had a few drill and practice educational programs, a word processor or two, and the BASIC programming language. Hundreds of books, thousands of articles, and untold numbers of conference presentations, workshops, seminars, and panel sessions were devoted to helping educators place those three tools to use in the classroom.

A quick scan of the table of contents for the book Irene Chen and Jane Thielemann have written provides clear evidence that times have changed drastically. Programming in BASIC, which was a staple of computer literacy courses in the 1970s and early 80s, is no longer with us. Although word processing is still around, it has morphed into productivity software that includes both sophisticated text manipulation and multimedia applications. The use of computers in the classroom has grown exponentially from simple drill and practice math exercises to a wide array of methods and strategies involving multimedia technology and the use of the Internet for support teaching and learning.

The integration of technologies into education has come so far from those early beginnings that there are now national and state standards for what teachers, and students, should know and be able to do. This book is based on those standards, or competencies, and manages to address two different but related goals: to induct teachers into the sometimes mysterious and confusing realm of information technology hardware and software, and to help teachers see how that expertise can be successfully applied in the classroom. You might call the first goal "general computer literacy" and the second "profession-specific literacy." Few would argue with the assertion that today everyone needs to be computer literate. Educators need to be able to use routine tools such as word processors, databases, programs for creating multimedia materials, and the various packages, such as browsers and e-mail programs, for accessing and using the Internet. That is not enough, however. If you are a nurse, physician, lawyer, or architect, there are specialized programs and specialized uses of information technologies that apply specifically to that profession. Lawyers must be able to use case management software and the Lexis/Nexis database. Architects must master computer-aided design (CAD) programs such as AutoCAD. Members of professions must move beyond the ordinary computer literacy everyone needs and become proficient in the uses of information technologies that are particularly relevant to their work. That applies to education as much as it does to other professions. Chen and Thielemann have combined general and profession-specific literacy in this book, which was written specifically for the teaching profession, and they have combined hardware and software literacy topics with what I would call "professional skills." This book covers many of the professional tasks a teacher must be able to do with the help of technology, such as design instructional materials, perform professional jobs, and communicate and teach via multimedia materials delivered in many formats, from print to online. I commend the authors for their accomplishment. Chen and Thielemann meet an important need at a time when the potential for technology in the classroom is high, but we have not yet turned that potential into day-to-day practice. This book should help.

Jerry Willis, Professor
Louisiana State University

Jerry W. Willis *is professor for research in the College of Education at Louisiana State University. Dr. Willis has written more than 50 books, conference proceedings and software tutorials, the majority of these works related to teacher education, technology, and higher education. He is also the founding editor of the* Journal of Technology and Teacher Education (JTTE), *and the founder of the Society for* Information Technology and Teacher Education (SITE), *which will host its 18th annual conference in 2007.*

Preface

Since the federal Act of NCLB (No Child Left Behind) of 2001 was passed, stricter certification, higher expectations, and hiring policies for new teachers have been implemented by school districts across the state. NCLB requires teachers to meet the criteria of "Highly Qualified Status" in subjects they will be teaching. Record numbers of teachers in the traditional content areas of reading, social studies, math, and science desire to obtain additional certification in the area of technology. An analysis of the newly required technology competencies of a number of states reveals that emphasis lies with "classroom applications" rather than basic "computer literacy." Specifically, the areas of desktop publishing, audio, graphics, video, animations, multimedia creation, and Internet applications are now emphasized. Technology applications teachers also need to become familiar with ADA, assistive technology, diverse learning, ESL, digital divide, intellectual property, Internet security, and various ethical and social issues that involve the use of technology.

This study guide, written by faculty of a teacher preparation program, is designed to strengthen understanding of the critical information in the framework for technology application competencies for K-12 teachers.

Nationwide Demand

Many states now offer certification in the area of technology applications; however, very little preparation materials have been published to help teachers prepare for these exams. Many district technology administrators know that a host of certified teachers would like to pass new technology applications certification exams in order to teach computer-related courses.

This text can be used by preservice teachers enrolled in undergraduate computer literacy classes in teacher education programs. It may also aid professional development trainers for K-12 schools. It is believed that if preservice and in-service teachers receive instruction aligned to the new technology application competencies, they will better understand methods of integrating technology into classroom curriculum.

The authors anticipate that instruction in up-to-date technology competencies will aid preservice teachers enrolled in undergraduate programs better understand methods of integrating technology into the classroom curriculum. Instruction in up-to-date technology competencies will also help current teachers stay current with national trends in technology-assisted classrooms.

Keeping up-to-date with national and state technology competencies enables students to acquire the knowledge and skills needed to succeed in their chosen fields. Both preservice and in-service teachers need be highly competent in technology applications in order to enhance the opportunities for academic success for children and adolescents in inner-city schools. This is a critical time for faculty to update or retool their understanding of state technology requirement changes in order to ensure the "highly qualified" status required of all public school teachers.

Organization

The objectives of the book are aligned with National Educational Technology Standards for Teachers (NETS●T) for Teachers of International Society for Technology Education (ISTE). The organization of this text runs parallel with the sections and competencies of a number of states. The text is divided into four major sections. Each section covers one or more of the educator standards for this field. Within each section, the content is further defined by a set of competencies. The ISTE educator standards assessed within each section are listed for reference at the beginning of each chapter. These are followed by a list of key words, chapter content, and a number of sample questions testing the competencies.

The book is organized into 12 chapters. A brief description of the sections and chapters follows.

Section I

In **Section I, Technology Applications Core** (Chapters II through III), an overview of the technology-related concepts is presented, and the ethical practices for teachers about current technologies and their applications is discussed. Emphasis is placed on task-appropriate tools to synthesize knowledge, create and modify solutions, and evaluate results in a way that supports teachers' work.

Chapter I, Technology Operation and Concepts for Teachers, introduces task-appropriate concepts and tools for teachers in order to synthesize knowledge in a way that supports the work of individuals and groups in problem-solving situations. Specifically, the chapter focuses on ways for teachers to plan, organize, deliver, and evaluate instruction for all students that incorporate the effective use of current technology for teaching and integrating national and state technology standards into the curriculum.

Emphasis is also placed on the use of computers to complete routine tasks faster and more efficiently.

Chapter II, Teacher Productivity and Professional Practices, focuses on the software tools that can be used in the classroom to enhance a teacher's pedagogical productivity. In addition to word processing, other productivity tools such as electronic spreadsheets and database programs are also discussed. Emphasis is placed on helping the teacher use computers to increase classroom resources, thereby transforming the role of the teacher in the classroom.

Chapter III, Using Technology for Learning, Teaching, and Designing the Curriculum, discusses the essential conditions necessary to maximize student achievement in content areas.

Section II

Section II, Digital Graphics/Animation and Desktop Publishing, (Chapters IV through VI) introduces quantitative designs by discussing fundamental principles and applications of digital design. These chapters describe how desktop publishing and graphic design can be used in an education setting. Emphasis is placed on the basic principles of design that students and teachers should understand in order to help students with multimedia composition. The chapter also describes how to use technology to enhance students' creative projects and reports by incorporating graphics and animation. This chapter also describes how students can apply this enhanced technological knowledge to a wide range of projects.

Chapter IV, The Principles and Applications of Digital Design, focuses on the various uses of graphics and animations in today's classroom. Specific information is provided that details the use of digital cameras in schools. Specific examples of creative projects that incorporate graphics and photographs are also provided throughout the chapter.

Chapter V, Desktop Publishing for Schools, discusses how desktop publishing and graphic design can be used to enhance a document's visual appeal. Emphasis is placed on desktop publishing, and how it enhances visual communication and streamlines the process of disseminating information of all kinds. Specific details are also given to explain how desktop publishing can be integrated into English language arts, social studies, science, math, music, and other content areas.

Chapter VI, Creating Multimedia for Special Audiences, focuses on the use of multimedia in the classroom. Emphasis is placed on the importance of defining an audience. This chapter also describes color theory, basic lighting, and design and composition principles. Special emphasis is placed on specific technical issues, such as monitor selection, that may affect media design.

Section III

Section III, Video Technology and Multimedia, (Chapters VII through IX) begins with an introduction to school multimedia design teams and project management. An overview of the use of video and sound in education is also provided within these chapters. Information within this section helps technology teachers obtain a broad understanding of multimedia authoring programs.

Chapter VII, School Multimedia Design Teams and Projects, introduces the major instructional design models used in education. This chapter identifies the different roles and responsibilities involved in developing projects. This chapter also provides a detailed scenario of the design and development processes of multimedia design projects. Specific emphasis is also placed on the differences of audio and video media from other productivity tools. The procedures, hardware, software, and the technical language used in audio/video media are also discussed. Emphasis is placed on incorporating music into video and multimedia projects with regard to the aesthetics of selection of music, copyright considerations, and building original music. Downloading music from the Web, specific software for cut and paste music editing, and programs that allow for the instant creation of royalty-free music in custom lengths are also discussed.

Chapter VIII, Video and Sound in Education, provides an overview of the use of video and sound in school projects.

Chapter IX, Design, Produce, and Distribute Educational Multimedia Products, helps technology teachers obtain a broad understanding of multimedia authoring programs, with specific emphasis on input/output devices, project dissemination, viewers or plug-in software for multimedia projects, general design principles, and evaluations of multimedia projects.

Section IV

Section IV, Webmastering, (Chapters X through XII) addresses Web-editing tools, Web site management, and communicating information in different formats for diverse audiences online. Emphasis is placed on the role of the technology teacher and the knowledge and skills needed to teach the foundations for Webmastering. Specific emphasis is also placed on information acquisition, solving problems, and communication. The national and state technology standards are also discussed within these chapters.

Chapter X, Administration of Educational Web Sites, discusses the Internet of the pre-Web age, the World Wide Web, and School Web Projects. Emphasis is placed on the role of the school district in developing a wide area network (or WAN) to serve as the "backbone" that connects all local area networks (or LANs) and computers across the various sites and campuses.

Chapter XI, Web Design Tools for Educators, presents basic information about the construction of Web pages using common Web design tools. The common formats found on Web browsers are also discussed. Typical formats include HTML, Web graphics, scripts, Web-compatible files such as PDF, audio, video, and animations. Routine Web-editing processes used to create or test Web pages are also discussed. Emphasis is also placed on student participation in Virtual Learning Communities (or VLC) in order to span distances and link with others with similar interests or areas of expertise. Use of the Internet for professional communication among teachers is also discussed.

Chapter XII, Web Communications and Interaction for Teaching and Learning, discusses ways for teachers to monitor student activities carefully, as well as how to infuse lessons with information about "safe" online practices for students.

Disclaimer

Many states offer tests that measure the content knowledge required of an entry-level educator in the field of technology applications in public schools. This book is designed to guide the examinee's preparation by helping the test taker become familiar with the competencies to be tested, test item formats, and pertinent study resources. Educator preparation program staff may also find this information useful as they help examinees prepare for careers as educators.

When preparing for this test, emphasis should be placed on the competencies and descriptive statements, which delineate the content that is targeted for testing. A portion of the content is tested in the sample items that are included in this manual. These test questions represent only a *sample* of items. Thus, test preparation should focus on the complete content delineated for testing. There is no guarantee that the contents of this book will completely prepare an examinee for all questions on the test. Readers should consult technology textbooks, articles, experts, and Web sites for updates, extra resources, and verifications of information.

Acknowledgment

We would like to thank the many people involved in producing this book, especially Dr. Jerry Willis of Louisiana State University for always being inspiring and encouraging.

A special thanks to the graduate students at the MAT 6318 Advanced Educational Technology at University of Houston Downtown, Fall, 2006, who provided valuable feedback and usability testing on the text (Autry McMorris, MariaSol Gomez, Debra Laycock, Monica Jarisch, Candace Gilliam, James Newman, Lynn Shivers, Taronce Knight, Ayn Nys, Kanika Bass, Corey Casey, and Kimberly Sinclair).

We also appreciate the following reviewers for their input and suggestions: Drs. Gloria Stewart, Sue Mahoney, and Joe Kortz, all with the University of Houston Downtown.

Section I

Technology Applications Core

Chapter I

Technology Operation and Concepts for Teachers

ISTE NETS_T, I. Technology Operations and Concepts

Teachers demonstrate a sound understanding of technology operations and concepts.

ISTE NETS_T, VI. Social, Ethical, Legal, and Human Issues

Teachers understand the social, ethical, legal, and human issues surrounding the use of technology in PK-12 schools and apply those principles in practice.

Chapter Objective: *The teacher knows technology terminology and concepts; the appropriate use of hardware, software, and digital files; and how to acquire, analyze, and evaluate digital information.*

The Teacher Technologist

It is essential in the age of technology that teachers learn to appreciate and apply all that technology has to offer. It is becoming increasingly important that teachers of the 21st century learn to tap into this dynamic resource. In today's classroom, teachers must be able to incorporate technology in order to plan, organize, deliver, and evaluate instruction for all students. However, being a knowledgeable and competent technologist means much more than knowing how to use a word processor. The changing focus of technology in today's classroom requires that a teacher become competent in its use for enhancing instruction and student learning.

Over the past fifty years the educational system has experienced a drastic transformation with the advance of technology. The rapid changes and increase in technology require both students and teachers to familiarize themselves with the world of computers. All of the advances made possible by computers have created a more efficient and productive school environment. Computers are now widely used throughout primary and secondary schools and in colleges and universities, for both administrative and instructional purposes.

The beginning teacher is expected to be a teacher technologist in order to be effective in the classroom. This teacher will:

- Know basic technology terms and concepts.
- Understand the legal and ethical use of technology.
- Evaluate and help students evaluate technology and the information found there.
- Select the best technological tools and appropriate instruction to enhance learning.
- Communicate information to students and others with technology.
- Meaningfully evaluate students' technological products and projects.
- Understand the Digital Divide and how that applies to equity issues.

A Brief History of Computers

The history of computer development is often referred to in terms of the five generations of computing devices ranging from the early development of vacuum tubes to the more current development of artificial intelligence devices (Campbell-Kelly & Aspray, 1997).

- **First Generation** – 1940-1956: Vacuum tubes
- **Second Generation** – 1956-1963: Transistors
- **Third Generation** – 1964-1971: Integrated circuits
- **Fourth Generation** – 1971-Present: Microprocessors
- **Fifth Generation** – Present and beyond: Artificial intelligence

The development of the microprocessor ushered in the fourth generation of computers, as thousands of integrated circuits were built onto a single silicon chip. In 1981, IBM introduced its first personal computer running DOS. In 1984, Apple introduced the affordable Macintosh, computers that allowed the microprocessors to move out of the realm of the business world and into the arena of home and school (Campbell-Kelly & Aspray, 1997). Soon after, these small computers were linked together to form networks; thus began the early development of the Internet.

The development of dynamic artificial intelligence (AI) devices can be seen in the current or fifth generation of computing devices. Some AI applications, such as voice recognition software, are in widespread use today.

Computers in the Classroom

Since their first appearance, computers have proven to be invaluable resources for the classroom. Computers were first introduced into education in the late 1950s to be used by large universities for administrative work such as accounting, payroll, and student records. In the mid-1960s through the early 1970s the cost of computers decreased, while the availability of the machines increased (Impagliazzo & Lee, 2004). When computers were first introduced into schools, they were largely used for secretarial tasks and administrative purposes. Records of students and faculty could all be stored on a computer. Grades and attendance could be processed on a computer, which reduced miscalculations that might have occurred if records were kept by hand. Another administrative convenience introduced with computers was the ability to process and print for record-keeping purposes. For example, library books could now be managed through a computer system, monitoring the availability of books. Having computer access in schools was extremely beneficial for administrative purposes, but during these early years, it was still uncommon to see computers in classrooms. Computers did not begin to emerge in the classroom until the 1980s (Impagliazzo & Lee, 2004).

Following the administrative use of computers in the schools, computers were soon used to enhance classroom instruction. Computers provided teachers with many conveniences such as word processing to prepare lesson plans, worksheets, tests, and reports. Also, computers allowed teachers to easily calculate grades. Additionally, information about each individual student's progress could also be stored on a computer. Even in 1991, 98% of U.S. schools had at least one computer; one computer for about every 18 students. Today, the ratio is closer to 1 to 4 (Impagliazzo & Lee, 2004)

The integration of computers into schools brought exciting innovations and unavoidable changes to education. The increasing use of computers has required schools across the nation to alter the curriculum and has forced educators to vary their teaching methods. Today, computers are used more than ever in the classroom and a wide variety of software programs are now designed specifically for educational instruction. Instructional multimedia, games, tutorials, drills, and simulations are frequently used to help students learn.

Hardware

It is important for teachers to understand the major hardware components of a computer system and how they function and interact. The functions of a computer roughly follow these steps:

Step 1. Accept input data

Step 2. Perform calculations on the input data

Step 3. Output the result

Step 4. Repeat 1-3 until finished

A common analogy often used compares the operation of a computer to that of a manufacturing factory. Thus, the hardware of a computer falls into the following component categories when compared to a factory (Campbell-Kelly & Aspray, 1997)

Computer input unit

    The "receiving" department of the factory.

Computer output unit

    The "shipping" department of the factory.

Computer memory unit

    The low-capacity "warehouse" department of the factory. Intermediate parts of the product may be tentatively stored here.

Computer central processing unit (CPU)

> The "manufacturing" department of the computer; where the actual product is made. CPU is a microprocessor chip that is central to the entire computer.

Computer arithmetic and logic unit (ALU)

> This is part of the CPU, the "machinery" used to carry out the manufacturing process.

Computer secondary storage unit

> The long-term, high-capacity "warehouse" department of the computer.

The CPU performs the actual computations and controls all other hardware components. It is often referred to as the "brain" of the computer. Every CPU runs at a certain clock speed (Campbell-Kelly & Aspray, 1997). This, with respect to processing power, determines the number of calculations per second that a CPU can perform; it is expressed in Hertz (denoted as Hz).

Even though the CPU speed is an important factor to the overall speed of the computer, it is not the *only* important factor. A fast CPU will have to continually wait if it is equipped with slow memory. Modern computers make extensive use of memory to store data. Consequently, the speed at which the memory device operates is crucially important for the overall speed of the computer.

By far the most common kind of memory is a set of computer chips called random access memory (RAM). The CPU can store data in RAM by changing the value of data and storing it for present use. Computer memory can be compared to the short-term memory of the brain.

Often referred to as primary storage, RAM is volatile in the sense that its contents are erased when the power is switched off. Any information that the user wants to keep should be stored on something called *secondary storage*. This is the reason users should save work to the hard drives, jump drives, or floppy disks before turning off the computer.

Computer memory can also come in the form of ROM (for read-only memory). The difference between RAM and ROM is that the contents of ROM are fixed and cannot be changed by the CPU. ROM is often used to store software that is final where no further changes are needed.

Secondary storage can be compared to the brain's long-term memory. Today, two types of secondary storage are popular: hard disks, and CD-ROMs/DVDs and other newer devices. A CD-ROM is a plastic disc with microscopic pits pressed into it. This allows for storage of data up to 650 MB. A hard disk is similar to a CD-ROM, but it contains disks that are made of metal rather than plastic. Bits are stored on a hard disk by means of tiny magnets. The capacity of a typical hard disk is 40 GB.

Both primary memory and secondary storage have relative advantages and disadvantages. The main advantage of RAM is that it is much faster than secondary storage. Also, RAM and ROM are much more expensive than secondary storage. The newer computers also come with DVDs.

The motherboard of the computer contains all of the major components. Specifically, the motherboard contains the connections that allow the CPU to talk to the other hardware components. The motherboard contains a disk controller and a memory controller. It also provides access to, and control over, the various storage devices in the computer.

Modern computers are generally modular (Campbell-Kelly & Aspray, 1997). Most classroom-grade personal computers typically offer up to six expansion slots that allow a teacher to plug in expansion cards. These slots essentially connect the expansion card directly to the motherboard, thus enhancing the functionality of the computer. Two types of popular expansion cards are display cards and sound cards.

Other Input/Output Devices

Attaching an external device to the computer helps expand its functionality. An input device lets the user input data into the computer, whereas an output device allows the computer to communicate its results to the external world. Most of these devices provide a new way of either inputting or outputting data, and are therefore called input/output devices (also called I/O devices). Display and sound cards, both known as expansion cards, are two examples of I/O devices. Most peripheral external devices are optional. Teachers must decide which components are necessary for their classrooms and select accordingly.

A port is a connection for an external peripheral device. The various types of ports differ in technical specifications and in connector shapes. Most computers are usually equipped with both traditional serial and parallel ports. As a rule, ports are not interchangeable. When buying a peripheral component, the user should make sure that the component has a compatible connector. A type of port that is increasingly considered as the standard is the USB (abbreviation for "universal serial bus") port. The USB port is able to connect a wide range of devices to a computer. Most printers feature parallel port connectors and most modems feature serial port connectors.

When one thinks of technological resources today, students and teachers alike may erroneously categorize all of technology as "computer resources," but for clarity it should be noted that computer resources do not include all technology available to teachers. Teachers also need to recognize that some devices will become obsolete. For instance, some computers no longer have a floppy drive, and any material they want to keep will need to be transferred to newer mediums.

Avoid Failures

The cause of failure for most classroom technology devices usually occurs because of human error. Sometimes, factors in the school environment also cause a device to malfunction. These factors can include excessive buildups of dust, heat, or magnetism; viruses from the Internet or from shared files; static electricity shocks or power surges; carelessness such as spilling liquids or dropping the hard drive; incorrect installation of software; incorrect upgrades, or an incorrect setup of the PC's configuration.

The average user is not concerned with problems, until the problem actually occurs. Once a failure happens, repairs can be costly and time consuming. Therefore, it is important to become knowledgeable about the preventive measures that teachers should take to decrease the likelihood of computer failure.

Operating Systems

All computers use an operating system or OS. It may be a classroom desktop computer running Windows, a large district administrative mainframe computer running UNIX, or a handheld computer running Palm OS. All these systems need an OS to make sure the programs run smoothly (Campbell-Kelly & Aspray, 1997). An OS is a software program that enables the computer hardware to communicate with the software. Without an OS, computers would be useless. Currently, the most popular OS for PCs are DOS (disk operating systems), OS/2, and Windows, but others are available, such as Linux. An OS has three major functions: BIOS (or basic input/output systems), system resources, and networking.

BIOS. BIOS in a PC is the set of programs that is run once the computer first boots up. Often called the *ROM BIOS*, the BIOS is typically placed in a ROM chip that comes with the computer. On PCs, the BIOS contains all the code required to control the keyboard, display screen, disk drives, serial communications, and a number of miscellaneous functions. Without the BIOS, the computer would be unable to communicate. As extra input and output devices (peripherals) are added, then extra bits of software, which are called drivers, need to be loaded so that the computer can accept data input or send data output.

System resources. As the computer runs, programs save data to temporary storage areas in RAM and then load other pieces of data from memory. The OS has to make sure that the data is stored in proper sizes in the right place. In the same way, data stored to floppy, CD-ROM, or hard disk must be stored in a way that it can be found quickly in the storage.

Networking. Some operating systems have built-in functions that allow them to communicate with other computers in order to share data and programs. The OS ensures that different types of computers and hardware, such as printers and modems, can understand each other when connected. The other main job of the network OS is to offer system security to assign different levels of access security including passwords and filters.

Some people compare the operating system to a traffic cop, it makes sure that different programs and users, running at the same time, do not interfere with each other. It also ensures that unauthorized users do not access the system (Campbell-Kelly & Aspray, 1997). OS perform the following basic tasks:

- Recognizing input devices such as a keyboard
- Sending commands to output devices such as a display screen
- Keeping track of files and directories on the disk
- Controlling peripheral devices such as disk drives and printers

The OS provides a software platform on top of which other programs, known as application programs, can run. Users can then create documents and files using the application programs.

The term network operating system, abbreviated as NOS, is generally reserved for software that enhances a basic operating system by adding networking features. Several types of NOS include Novell Netware, Artisoft's LANtastic, and Microsoft Windows Server.

A Brief History of Operating Systems

The first personal computers, introduced in 1981 by IBM, ran DOS (disk operating system) as its OS. In 1985, IBM and Microsoft began the joint development of a system intended to replace IBM DOS (Campbell-Kelly & Aspray, 1997). This joint venture later became known as the Microsoft operating system or MS DOS. As late as 1990, the vast majority of PC applications were based on DOS.

In the 1990s, most PC users preferred Word Perfect for word processing, and Lotus 1-2-3 for spreadsheets. In the mid-1990s, Microsoft developed a suite of applications that ran within a new graphic environment. Users saw the advantages and switched to Word and Excel, respectively. Therefore, not only did Microsoft benefit from OS sales, but the company also gained a dominant market share in software applications.

On the other hand, Apple, incorporated in 1977, became the main manufacturer of a line of personal computers under the Apple Macintosh (Mac) brand name, peripheral components, and computer software. Apple introduced its OS System 1 in 1984. As of 2007, the latest Mac OS is X Leopard.

Other Options

In 1969, UNIX was developed based on the foundation laid out by Bell Lab, GE, MIT, AT & T, and DEC. Linux is a free version of UNIX still widely used. Cross-platform applications are programs executable with different operating systems. Cross-platform computers such as "Power" Macs let the user change to the PC mode, while "power" PCs can operate Macintosh software.

Directory File Structure

Directories and files are fundamental to most operating systems. A file system in most operating systems is a hierarchical structure (or tree structure) of files and directories. This structure, which graphically resembles an inverted tree, uses directories to organize data and programs into groups. A file system is a complete directory structure, including a root directory, with subdirectories and files beneath it. Some tasks are performed more efficiently on a file system than on the individual directory within the file system. For example, the user can perform management tasks such as backing up, moving, or securing an entire file system. Some of the most important system management tasks concerning file systems include

- Allocating space and monitoring space usage
- Making system files available to system users
- Backing up file systems
- Maintaining system files

Figure 1.1. A sample file system

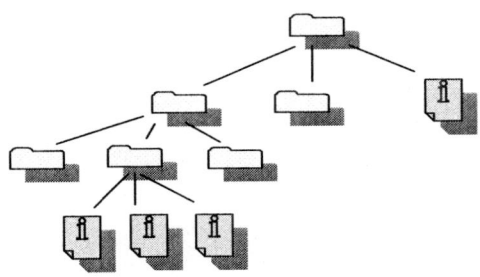

On Windows-based operating systems and Mac OS, directories are depicted as "folders"' and "folders within folders." Moving these around is accomplished by clicking on the icon and dragging it to the desired position.

Other useful features of OS are file extensions that can be found in the following format:

FileName.ext: The filename is "FileName"
The delimiter is the dot
The extension is "ext"

The extension defines the file "type," which can be either a text file, an executable file, a database file, or a graphic file. The file extension system is actually a remnant from old DOS filename limits. In practice, it shows that the combinations out of three letters are limited. It has proven its usefulness over the years.

An extension lets not only the user easily determine what sort of file it is, but even the OS or other programs can easily associate specific file extensions with specific programs; thus, the OS may start a certain application when the user clicks on a certain file. For example, mypresentation.ppt is more likely to be an MS PowerPoint file, and classbudget.xls is more likely to be in the Excel spreadsheet format.

Concerns Over Operating Systems

Unfortunately, with any computer program, errors are unavoidable. Errors in operating systems cause three main types of problems (Silberschatz, Galvin, & Gagne, 2004):

First, errors may cause the computer to work incorrectly with peripheral devices such as monitors. Second, security glitches found in some software errors leave a door open for the system to be invaded by unauthorized access to the computer system. Patching these flaws will keep a computer system secure. Third, a system may contain instabilities. A system crash is the act of a system becoming unresponsive, which would cause the user to have to reboot the computer. These can happen due to a software bug in the OS.

Software

In the classrooms of the past, students and teachers were unable to venture into many areas of learning because of the vast amount of effort required to navigate the system. Today, there are a number of ways to make technology work for teachers and students.

The types of software typically used in education include productivity software, authoring programs, reference software, groupware, and instructional software. The point in learning about the types of software is not to memorize each specific category, but to become versant in the features that are expected from various types of software.

Productivity Software

Productivity software is concerned with software tools. This includes any software that can be used as a tool and helps the user produce documents, spreadsheets, a database, or other products. MS *Word*, MS *Excel*, and MS *Access* are common productivity software packages used in schools. The Microsoft *Works* and the ClarisWorks are full-featured word processor, database, spreadsheet, graphics, and telecommunications packages published by Microsoft Inc. and Claris Inc., respectively.

Authoring Programs

Authoring programs are designed to help teachers and students produce courseware and programs. The term authoring suggests writing. These authoring programs help the user develop computer programs in computer languages that can be otherwise quite difficult to learn. *The Writing Center* is published by the Learning Company for Macintosh. With it, students' writing activities can combine desktop publishing with color illustrations. For example, *Bannermania*, published by Broderbund for Apple, Macintosh, and PC, produces professional looking banners, posters, and bumper stickers. The presentation type of authoring software is designed to help users compose dynamic electronic presentations with visual impact. It sometimes includes sound, pictures, graphics, video, text, and hypertext. *Slide Shop*, published by Scholastic for Apple and PC, also creates computer slides.

Electronic Reference Software

Electronic reference software is available in both CD and Web formats. Many encyclopedias, research journals, as well as geographic, medical, and educational references are now available for reasonable costs or through subscription. *Grolier's Multimedia Encyclopedia* and Microsoft *Encarta* are both electronic encyclopedias, including not only pictures, but sound and video as well. They also contain powerful key word searching capabilities.

Along similar lines, groupware type of productivity software is designed for groups of students. With this software, the computer is viewed by a group of students working in a cooperative group, or can be projected onto a screen for the entire class to view. For example, Tom Snyder Productions has created several software programs that can be used to stimulate discussions and debates.

Instructional Software

Instructional software can be used to enhance teaching and learning in myriad ways. The five most common courseware types include drill and practice, educational games, tutorials, simulation, and problem solving. For detailed information about instructional software, see Chapters II and III.

Sources of Software

Educational software for use in the classroom is available from a variety of sources; school district offices generally purchase software for classroom usage. Often, the school districts negotiate a site license with the software vendors. Teachers may purchase programs from vendors of educational software. Demo versions can usually be downloaded for a limited time.

A variety of educational software is available as shareware or freeware on the Internet. Freeware software is in the public domain, available for unrestricted use, and can be copied freely and even renamed and resold. Some programs, games, or utilities can be designed and distributed as shareware until the users pay to register. Shareware is a kind of "try before you buy" software. It is important to note that shareware authors retain full rights to the package. There is generally a limited period of use granted without paying a fee; commonly 30 or 60 days. After that period, the user pays a licensing fee to continue using the software. Today we have a growing number of software developers who offer their goods as shareware until the users pay to register. A teacher may download and install shareware onto her/his school computers for a free tryout, but once the teacher decides to keep using the software, she/he must pay as a registered user like anyone in the general public.

When problems occur while using computer systems, the term troubleshoot is usually applied when a problem is suspected to be hardware-related. The term troubleshoot can be defined as working to isolate a problem and fix it, typically through a process of elimination whereby possible sources of the problem are investigated and eliminated, beginning with the most obvious or easiest problem. On the other hand, if a problem is thought to be originating from the software, the term debug is more commonly used to address this type of problem. Educators must embrace the habit of maintaining the health and integrity of a system in order to prevent such problems and save money and time in the long run.

WWW in Education

In the mid-1960s, the Internet originated through the U.S. military's Advanced Research Projects Agency (ARPA). As universities and laboratories located across the nation were given research and development projects by the federal government, their staff and computers were granted access to a communications network known then as the ARPANet. The first portions of the experimental system went online at UCLA, Stanford Research Institute, and the University of Utah (Roblyer, 2004).

In 1972, the first e-mail program was created to send messages across the network. The term, e-mail, holds the title as being the first official Internet communications tool. In 1973, the first international connections to the ARPANET went online in Norway and England.

For almost 3 decades, the Internet existed for the exclusive use of government, research, and higher education. But that changed throughout the 1980s, as more and more people became aware of this incredible communications tool. In 1988, some K-12 schools in the United States were connected to the system, mostly to utilize the e-mail capabilities.

In the 1990s, when the government decided to reduce its funding, ARPANET ceased to exist, and the network, now officially referred to as the Internet, opened for commercial use.

Internet service providers (ISP), a new type of business, arose to meet the demands of the newly created Internet. By the end of 1991, dozens of ISPs offered Internet access to individuals, businesses, and schools. At the same time, leading commercial online services like America Online (AOL), Prodigy, and CompuServe opened gateways to the Internet, which gave thousands of people access to the Net.

In 1992, the World Wide Web (also WWW, or the Web) was created by a research facility in Switzerland. By the end of 1994, advertising, and mass marketing found their way online. In this early stage of development, nearly 3 million computers were connected to the Internet, and 140 countries could be reached via e-mail. By the end of 1994, the number of total Internet users increased exponentially to 14 million (*Netizens: An anthology,* 1996). As of 2002, more than 98% of America's public schools had Internet access. A recent survey by the Pew Internet & American Life Project found that 94% of students between the ages of 12 and 17 accessed the Web for research (Minkel, 2002).

Never before, in the history of education, have teachers and schools had the means to communicate both nationally and internationally so easily. Today, e-mail functions as a communication system between teachers and the office for sharing ideas, information, and documents, with the goal of reducing paperwork and the need for time-consuming meetings. Disseminating information throughout a district is also important, because teachers can be given instantaneous announcements. E-mail communication can also link parents and teachers. Furthermore, teachers can participate in electronic discussion groups to enhance their professional development. Most important, the Web serves as an important equalizer, giving teachers, in rural or urban settings, connections to professional information and organizations.

Some schools have used access to educational technologies as a reward for exemplary achievement. Furthermore, using the computer as a communication and information-gathering device has opened up a whole new realm of expectations that must find a place within the curriculum. Because electronic communication is relatively new, guidelines and expectations for use have to be developed as well. For example, some schools request students' caregivers to let schools know whether they give permission for their children to access the Internet, or have their names or photographs placed on the Internet. For safety, teachers who put students' work on a Web site also have to obtain permission, and students' names should still not be posted.

A new requirement from many states is that teachers understand procedures for acquiring information. It is important for educators to understand how search engines are used on the Web. Without the use of search engines, it would be virtually impossible to locate anything on the Web without knowing a specific Web address. Not every search engine uses the same algorithm, or determined pathway, to search through the Web. There are three major types of search engines: those that require users to type in keywords; those that require users to type in natural languages; and those that function as a Web directory or yellow pages of the entire WWW.

Most search engines allow the user to type in a few key words, and then search for the occurrence of the specific words within the database. Each search engine has a predetermined method of deciding what to do about approximate spellings and plural variations. Some search engines use a kind of "fuzzy" logic in searching for the AND of multiple words as well as the OR of the words.

The algorithm that uses terms such as AND, OR, NOT is called a Boolean expression. Google and Alta Vista both use the Boolean algorithm to conduct keyword searches for information. For example, when a teacher looks for a lesson plan on the solar system, she is likely to type in "solar AND "lesson plan"" as a Boolean expression. Most current search engines have separate advanced search forms where the user types in keywords in the blanks without typing in complex Boolean expressions.

A search engine, such as Ask.com, accepts natural language when searching for information. Natural language is a human language such as English, French, and Chinese, in contrast to computer languages, such as FORTRAN and COBOL. For example, when using Ask.com, a teacher can search for a lesson plan on the solar system by typing in the question, "Where can I find a lesson plan on the solar system?" Many elementary teachers reported that students were more efficient with search engines using natural languages.

Other types of search engines function as a Web directory or the yellow pages of the entire WWW. Yahoo, a Web directory type search engine, divides the Internet into a wide variety of categories such as Arts & Humanities, Business & Economy, Computers and Internet category, and Education. Using the same example provided previously, teachers who are looking for a lesson plan on the solar system can select the proper category and then search for a good lesson plan on the solar system.

Legal and Ethical Issues

Every teacher should be concerned about the legal issues surrounding the use of computers in the classroom. Traditionally, under the "Fair Use" guidelines, teachers have taken great liberty with duplicating copyrighted materials, so long as it has been for classroom use. The rules of Fair Use with computers, however, have changed with the advancement of technology. Secondary students must be educated in determining what constitutes information found in the public domain and what does not. When students work on desktop publishing or multimedia projects, they may want to use easily recognized logos such as a famous record label or a sports team logo. Students must be taught that this information is copyrighted, and thus they are not allowed to copy such material and place it into their projects. Many students may think that if no money is involved in copying, no harm is done, but from the creator's perspective, some commercial value of the property is lost. Also, there exists the possibility that others might see a logo and popular company name or slogan and assume that it is "the real thing."

The use of music or audio clips with multimedia presentations is also subject to Fair Use guidelines (Torrans, 2003). If the music is in the public domain, for example, "Twinkle, Twinkle, Little Star," the student may use it. If the music is newer than 50-years old, it is most likely not in the public domain. The best rule regarding the integration of music is to check the copyright on the recording itself.

Students must also be taught that pictures in magazines are also protected; scanning in pictures from magazines for Internet posting is not allowed. Just because it is posted on the Internet does not mean that it is public domain, for the use of anyone who wants it. Also, copying others' work in its entirety is never considered Fair Use. Normally, Fair Use gives a person the right to copy just enough to make a point, such as in a parody, critique, research, proving a point, and reporting news (Torrans, 2003). Derivative stories or other works, except with parody, are also not allowed. An example might be the creation of Harry Potter stories or stories using computer game characters.

The Fair Use provision of Copyright Law generally applies when using copyrighted work for in-class use (Fishman, 1997). In the past, teachers referred to the Fair Use provision of Copyright Law to answer questions raised when using copyrighted elements in student and teacher multimedia projects. The following are not copyrighted and may be freely used (Fishman, 1997):

- Logical, comprehensive compilations (such as the telephone book)
- Unoriginal reprints of public domain works
- Materials or reprints of materials in the public domain (all prior to 1923; most between 1923-1963)
- Freeware (not shareware)
- Most U.S. government materials (some items created by contractors for the government might be copyrighted)
- Facts
- Ideas, processes, methods, and systems described in copyrighted materials

When using images, sounds, video in K-12 student samples or actual K-12 student projects that will only be seen in the classroom, students must be taught that citing sources is required (copyright information and full bibliographic description at the end including author, title, publisher, and place and date of publication/Web address.) In these cases, teachers and or students do not need to ask for permission to use the copyrighted work. However, if the student is going to use more than the recommended percentages/quantities, or if the work ends up with a larger audience (such as on the Web), the student must be taught to e-mail a request for use permission.

When using images, sounds, and video on a home page, such as a teacher's home page that will be uploaded to a school Web site, citing sources is required. However, it is important to note that just citing the source is not enough (Fishman, 1997). Correct citing should include a full bibliographic description at the end (including author, title, publisher, and place and date of publication/Web address.) Teachers need to check the Web site from which the material was obtained in order to determine if there are restrictions on using any of the materials. Unless there are specific directions that the images (or other content) can be used without permission, the teacher needs to e-mail the Webmaster requesting use permission.

Teachers must also remember that posting actual student work or presentations, or pictures of students on the Web, requires parental permission. Student handbooks provided by school districts usually attach permission-request letters for parents to sign and return to the school file. This introduction to using copyrighted material is easily learned when the teacher provides a model.

It is also important that students learn netiquette. Netiquette involves teaching students the proper use or "manners" involved with using the Internet. For example, netiquette forbids the perpetuation of flame wars, which are a series of angry letters from one small group of users directed toward each other. Flaming is what people do when they express a strongly held opinion without holding back any emotion (*The Core Rules of Netiquette*, 2004). This type of misuse can dominate the tone and destroy the camaraderie of a discussion group. This behavior is unfair to the other members of the group. And while flame wars can initially be amusing, they get boring very quickly to people who are not involved in them and become an unfair monopolization of bandwidth.

One reason to use the computer as a communicator is to ensure quick communication in order to save everyone's time. However, certain types of communication expend needless amounts of time. Under the rules of netiquette, spam, the term for e-mail junk mail, should not be forwarded; furthermore, chain letters should never be forwarded (The Core Rules of Netiquette, 2004).

Other proper netiquette procedures include using summarization skills for quick communication, and using a salutation and a closing signature identifying oneself. Furthermore, students should be taught not to forward the e-mails of others without permission; such action is considered a breech of privacy. E-mails are seen by many as copyrighted, so permission to forward should be sought. Students should also be taught to be cautious of inadvertently passing viruses. Finally, students should be taught to be aware of predators on the Internet. Students should be cautioned never to give their full names, phone numbers, or addresses, and to report "techno strangers" to adults if anyone asks for that kind of information (The Core Rules of Netiquette, 2004).

Equal Opportunity and Computers

The digital divide refers to a gap between those who have access to technology tools and those who do not. A 1998 National Telecommunications and Information Administration report, *Falling through the Net II: New Data on the Digital Divide,* indicated that, although more Americans now own computers, certain groups are still far less likely to have computers and Internet access (1998). Lack of such access affects the ability of students and adults to learn valuable technology skills, and the ability of families to benefit from online connection.

Lack of access means more than inconvenience, it means lack of educational opportunities. Research has shown that four groups do not enjoy equity regarding computer and technology use and, thus, in time may not reap the benefits of a technology-based economy (Roblyer, 2004):

- Students from low-income homes and schools
- Minority students
- Students with special needs
- Girls

Warren-Sam's (1997) booklet, *Closing the Equity Gap in Technology Access and Use*, describes three major areas in which inequities can arise: access, types of use, and curriculum. The result of not having equal access can be far reaching for all of these groups. For instance, those learners who are not able to grow up playing and learning with computers can be less comfortable using them and may develop feelings of helplessness or develop negative beliefs about technology. Many fields in the sciences and mathematics rely on computers or other technology, so when students reach upper levels in high school, they may not be comfortable enough to take courses that employ abundant technology. This reluctance in middle and high school, in turn, blocks access to similar classes in college and later in the job market.

Organizations such as the Technology Access Foundation have been leading a movement to close the Digital Divide. The Technology Access Foundation collaborates with community and corporate partners to create programs that teach kids not only to be users of technology, but also to be providers of content and technological creators. Purchasing the hardware teachers need for day-to-day needs, including e-mail and Internet connection, is an important step towards this goal.

Another type of Digital Divide arises from physical challenges that some people face. Potential students and instructors may have mobility, visual, hearing, speech, learning, and other disabilities that could influence their participation in courses as they are currently designed. The Americans with Disabilities Act (A.D.A.) of 1990 delineates and projects the civil rights of people with disabilities. Computer software and hardware vendors are required by the law to comply to A. D. A. Section 305 of the Telecommunications Act 1996 that mandates captioning on almost all television programming in the U.S. (Lidwell, Holden, & Butler, 2003).

As far as schools are concerned, video clips and interactive television programs are required to provide captioning for students with all types of disabilities. Adaptive technologies for low vision and blind users are also available. Also available are screen-reading software programs that convert text, navigation, and graphic "alt tags" into a Braille output or a voice output through a synthesizer; screen enlargers, and magnifiers; scanners that convert text into synthesized speech or a Braille printout; voice recognition software; Braille or enlarged keyboards; and Braille display. Teachers must also be aware of adaptive technologies for students with physical disabilities and repetitive strain injuries (RSI). These technologies may include devices such as a modified mouse (in various styles—head mounted, foot operated, eye-tracking system, joysticks, etc.), and voice recognition software. Adaptive technologies for the hearing disabled also include closed captioning, show sounds that translate nonspeech audio into a visual manifestation, and telecommunications devices for the deaf (TDD). Educators must also be aware that the process called "universal design" exists to assure that a course is accessible to students and instructors with a wide range of abilities and disabilities (Lidwell et al., 2003). Although not all courses must comply with these standards, the "universal design" guidelines provide a good model for the design of accessible materials:

- **Electronic communications:** Text-based resources, such as bulletin boards, e-mail, and distribution lists, are fully accessible to students with disabilities, regardless of the assistive technology they use.
- **Videos:** Ideally, captioning should be provided for those who have hearing impairments, and audio description of the visual content should be provided for those who are visually impaired.
- **Web pages:** Web pages are accessible to students and instructors using a wide variety of assistive technology. Developers have to either avoid certain types of inaccessible features or formats, or create alternative methods for accessing the inaccessible content.

It is important for teachers to note that gender bias is a concern in employing technology in schools. Gender bias, like the literature of the past, may be evident when motivating software excludes girls in its programs. Stereotyping may send a message that women use computers for clerical jobs. Another group, the lower-achieving students, may be stereotyped by the type or use of their allocated computer time, mainly for skill-and-drill use.

Student's use of technology in the classroom must be allocated equally and fairly by the teacher, whether from a multicultural perspective, a special needs perspective, or when considering tolerance and bias. Vigilant teachers need to ensure that traditional biases and inequities that have been evident in the education system of the past are not infiltrated into the realm of educational technology. It is important to note that teachers should not create unequal situations in their classroom by assigning homework related to computer work that would create unequal grading situations for students who do not have easy access. Finally, it is most important that teachers ensure that all students have equal work time, higher-level activities, and "play time" on the computers.

Emerging Technologies

In the book, *Information Anxiety 2*, Wurman, Sume, and Leifer (2000) estimate that today's college grads have spent 10,000 hours playing video games, 20,000 hours watching TV, 20,000 hours talking on the phone, not to mention countless hours listening to music and surfing on the Web, and using Instant Messenger, chatrooms and e-mail (2000). At the same time, these students have only spent 5,000 hours reading and 11,000 hours attending school.

In his text, *The new basics: Education and the future of work in the telematic age*, Thornburg (2002) suggests that because students live in a technological age, classroom instruction has to evolve in order to mirror this type of learning. Thornburg suggests that learning in the classroom should move at a fast pace so the student can receive information quickly. Students prefer step-by-step instruction and random access, hyperlinked, and just-in-time learning experiences. Students also like less text, and more pictures, sounds, and video wherever possible. Thornburg (2002) purports that in order to meet the needs of the students, teachers should provide opportunities for multitasking, networking, and interactivity.

Norton and Sprague (2001) described three apparent trends of emerging technology found in the education arena:

1. **Emerging development in artificial intelligence (AI):** The capabilities of AI can be found in designing more intelligent computers and software, robotics, voice recognition software, and intelligent tutoring systems (Chen, Nath, & Parker, 2005).
2. **Emerging development in virtual reality (VR):** VR can be described as a computer-generated three-dimensional environment that gives the user an illusion of being immersed in a real world. The users may have to wear data gloves, headphones, goggles, and other devices to interact with the synthetic system (Chen, Nath, & Parker, 2005).
3. **Emerging development in distributed learning:** Wireless technologies will continue to decrease in cost and increase in speed. Personal digital assistants (PDA) will keep on evolving. These bring in flexibility in classroom organization and configuration. Handheld systems will be used more as a portable extension of a traditional personal computer (Chen et al., 2005).

It is important for technology teachers to keep abreast of emerging technologies that are on the horizon of development. Since these technologies are constantly changing as scientists define new limitations and capabilities, bringing technological developments in a state of development to classrooms is not without controversy. However, emerging technologies have the potential to impact learning of the new generation.

Final Words

In sum, it is important that teachers realize that the integration of computers into schools has resulted in unavoidable changes in the way teaching and learning take place. The increasing use of computers has required schools across the nation to alter their curriculum and has forced educators to vary teaching methods. Today, it is pertinent that teachers become familiar and comfortable with computers, since they will play an increasingly larger role in modern education. When examining technology education in the broader sense, most educators agree that the primary objective of computer literacy for teachers should be to make students comfortable with learning using computers. In accomplishing this task, technology application teachers should understand their operations and applications of computers, and become knowledgeable of their ethical use.

References

Campbell-Kelly, M., & Aspray, W. (1997). *Computer: A history of the information machine.* New York: HarperCollins Publishers.

Chen, L. I, Nath, L. J., & Parker, E. M. (2005). *Using technology in the middle school and high school classroom.* In J. Nath & M. Cohen (Eds.), *Becoming a middle school or high school teacher in Texas* (pp. 309-350). Belmont: CA: Wadsworth/Thomson Learning.

Falling through the Net II: New Data on the Digital Divide. (1998). Retrieved June 18, 2007, from http://www.ntia.doc.gov/ntiahome/net2/falling.html

Impagliazzo, J.. & Lee, J. A. N. (2004). *History of computing in education.* New York: Springer.

Lidwell, W, Holden, K., & Butler, J. (2003). *Universal principles of design.* Gloucester, MA: Rockport Publishers.

Minkel, W. (April, 2002). Web of deceit. *School Library Journal.* Retrieved June 18, 2007, from http://slj.reviewsnews.com/index.asp?layout=article&articleid=CA202848

Netizens: An anthology. (1996). Retrieved February 11, 2006, from http://www.columbia.edu/~rh120/

Norton, P., & Sprague, D. (2001). *Technology for teaching.* Boston: Allyn and Bacon.

Roblyer, M. D. (2004). *Integrating educational technology into teaching* (3rd ed.). Upper Saddle River, NJ: Merrill, Prentice Hall.

Ryan, K., & Cooper, J. (2006). *Those who can, teach.* Boston: Houghton Mifflin Company.

Silberschatz, A, Galvin, P., & Gagne, G. (2004). *Operating system concepts* (7th Ed.). Hoboken, NJ: John Wiley & Sons.

Thornburg, D. (2002). *The new basics: Education and the future of work in the telematic age.* Alexandria, VA: Association for Supervision & Curriculum Development.

Torrans, L. A. (2003). *Law for K-12 libraries and librarians.* Westport, CT: Libraries Unlimited.

Warren-Sams, B. (1997, June). *Closing the equity gap in technology access and use.* Portland, OR: Northwest Regional Educational Laboratory.

Wurman, R. S., Sume, D., & Leifer, L., (2000). *Information anxiety 2.* Indianapolis, IN: Que Publishing.

Sample Questions

1. What is the best method to use when conducting a keyword search for information on a Web search engine?
   a. Boolean
   b. Natural language
   c. Wildcard
   d. Complete sentence

2. Which of the following is a task of a computer operating system?
   a. Allocate memory resource
   b. Database
   c. Software driver
   d. Input

3. When installing a new scanner to the class computer, a teacher needs:
   a. a router
   b. a graphic program
   c. a software driver
   d. a video card

4. What is one requirement placed on teachers by the rapidly changing nature of technology?
   a. Need to analyze and develop personal knowledge webs.
   b. Need to become effective at designing distance learning.
   c. Need to read technical and educational publications
   d. Need to become knowledgeable of technological advances.

5. The Internet became accessible to many more business and educator users during mid-1990 due to the following factor:
   a. E-mail
   b. Search engines
   c. WWW
   d. Security

Answers: (1) A (2) A (3) C (4) D (5) C

Chapter II

Teacher Productivity and Professional Practices

ISTE NETS_T, V. Productivity and professional practice
Teachers use technology to enhance their productivity and professional practice.

ISTE NETS_T, VI. Social, ethical, legal, and human issues
Teachers understand the social, ethical, legal, and human issues surrounding the use of technology in PK-12 schools, and apply those principles in practice.

Chapter objective: The teacher knows how to use technology tools to solve problems, evaluate results, and communicate information in a variety of formats for diverse audiences.

Teacher Productivity Software

In the classrooms of the past, students and teachers could not venture deeply into many areas of learning because of the limitations of standard classroom materials. Today, thanks to the development of technology, teachers and students are able to explore learning in innovative ways. This innovative method of learning, known as information technology, supports learning in two ways: by enhancing productivity and by improving professional practice. Specifically, when teachers use computers to complete routine tasks faster and more efficiently, productivity can be greatly enhanced. Similarly, when a science teacher uses computer simulation to illustrate to students how DNA works, professional pedagogical practice is enhanced.

In today's classroom, a word processor is the most commonly used productivity tool for teachers (Roblyer, 2004). Most school districts have a site license for a productivity package like Microsoft *Office* or *WordPerfect Office,* that lets schools pay one fee and use the computer software on all the computers in the school or district.

Teachers routinely use a word processor to create, edit, and print documents. Of all the uses for computers in education, word processing is the most common one. To perform word processing, a teacher must have a computer, a word processing program, and a printer. With a word processor, a teacher can create documents, store them electronically on a disk, display the documents on a screen, or modify them using the program's commands and options. When modifications are complete, the teacher can then view the final draft, or print the final version of the document by sending the document to a printer.

The great advantage of word processing over the obsolete method of using a typewriter is that microprocessors allow a person to make changes without retyping the entire document (Roblyer, 2005). If a mistake is made, the writer can simply back up the cursor and correct the mistake. Furthermore, if a paragraph needs to be deleted, the writer can simply remove it without leaving a trace. It is equally easy to insert a word, sentence, or paragraph in the middle of a document. Word processors also make it easy to move sections of text from one place to another within a document, or between documents. After a writer has made all the changes, the file is then sent to the printer in order to obtain a printed hardcopy.

In addition to word processing, other productivity tools include electronic spreadsheets and database programs. These additional program tools can be used in the classroom to enhance a teacher's pedagogical productivity.

Computerized Data Analysis Tools

Electronic Spreadsheets

A good analogy for an electronic spreadsheet is an accountant's ledger sheet. Spreadsheet contains an array of rows and columns displayed on the computer screen (Gipp, 2005). Spreadsheet is used for completing calculations and setting up financial balance sheets, necessary procedures for accountants and managers. Two well-known electronic spreadsheet programs include Microsoft *Excel* and *Lotus 1-2-3*.

One of the best uses for spreadsheets in the classroom is for numerical applications (Gipp, 2005). Many effective lessons in the middle and secondary grades require data collection, representation, and interpretation. Technology using spreadsheets and databases can be easily integrated with mathematics, social studies, earth science, and other content areas. For example, weather observations will generate data, and a variety of technologies can be used to organize, display, interpret, and finally evaluate weather patterns in the local area. Using spreadsheets and other productivity tools in the classroom will provide a way for the teacher to integrate technology into the classroom and create lessons in which the students are actively engaged in learning. This will allow the teacher to meet the following goals of enhancing instruction through the integrating of technology into the classroom by:

- Delivering inquiry-based lessons and content
- Developing models for integrating appropriate technology, spreadsheets, and databases
- Assuming the role of a guide and facilitator of student learning by providing the resources and questions
- Demonstrating to students the capabilities of using technologies to search for information, including scientific investigations
- Aiding student understanding of how different subjects interact (integrated curriculum) and work together (e.g., science, mathematics, and technology)

Simple Spreadsheet Templates

A spreadsheet template is a blank form consisting of cells organized in rows and columns. In a spreadsheet, the cell is defined as the space where rows and columns intersect. The generic name or address of a cell is its column letter and row number. For example, B12 and AZ23 can all be cell names or cell addresses.

In the spreadsheet template in Figure 2.1, all the cells have been defined but no data has been entered. A spreadsheet allows a person to store, manipulate, calculate, and analyze data. The data is stored on a worksheet and several worksheets will constitute a workbook. In MS *Excel*, each workbook is saved as one separate file. Each cell can be filled with text (labels), number data (constants), and/or formulas (mathematical equations). Labels are text entries that do not have a value associated with them. A person typically uses a label to identify the data. Constants are used to enter number data. Constants are entries that have a specific fixed value. If someone asks how many students are in the class, a specific answer can be provided. Other teachers may have different answers, but a fixed value exists for each teacher. Once entered into the cell, the numbers can be displayed as different formats such as currency, fractions, and percentages. A list of formats is available within MS *Excel* under the menu Format – Cells – Number.

Formula

Formulas are mathematical equations that can be used to calculate the value to be displayed within a cell. A list of the mathematical functions available within MS Excel can be found under the menu Insert – Function. When working with formulas, the numbers are not entered; instead, an equation is entered. The equation will be updated upon the change or entry of any data that is referenced in the equation.

The example provided in Figure 2.1 is from a grade book program created with Microsoft *Excel*. In the grade book example, as shown on Figure 2.1, the average for Exam I for the hypothetical class of 5 is 92.4. The number "92.4" was not entered through the keyboard. The formula that was typed into cell B9 of the spreadsheet was:

=Average(B3:B7).

Figure 2.1. A sample grade book

	A	B	C	D	E	F	G
1							
2		Exam I	Exam II	Homework 1	Homework 2	Homework 3	Total
3	Amy	89	89	92	79	91	
4	Bob	95	91	89	77	93	
5	Cindy	93	78	92	89	88	
6	David	94	89	100	89	77	
7	Emily	91	94	93	92	90	
8							
9	Average	92.4					

Once the formula was entered, the built-in average function calculated the average of the specified data. This simplifies the procedure for the teacher. The program automatically adds all of the indicated cells together and divides by the total number of cells. The syntax is as follows:

=Average (first value, second value, etc.)

Text fields and blank entries are not included in the calculations of the Average Function. In figure 2.1, the Exam I scores of the hypothetical class are displayed from Column B Row 3 (B3) through Column B Row 7 (B7). The sum of all students' Exam I scores (89 + 95 + 93 + 94 + 91 = 462) was divided by 5 because there are 5 students in the Example class. Dividing by 5 will provide an average score of Exam I of 92.4.

In MS *Excel*, formulas or functions must begin with an equal sign (=). It is important to enter the cell where the data is stored and not the data itself. It is also important to type in the reference to the constants instead of the values. Had "462/5" been entered into the cell, the formula would only work for that particular set of data. If the exam scores from this set were changed, the average would not change. When entering formulas into a spreadsheet, it is important to make as many references as possible to existing data. If the information is referenced, then it does not have to be typed in again. More importantly if other information changes, then the equations do not have to be changed. For instance, in the hypothetical class previously mentioned, if Amy's Exam I score is 97 instead of 89, what is the class average for Exam I going to be? Once "97" is entered into B3, the Exam I average is updated to 94 in cell B9.

Examine the equation that is found in cell B9:

= Average(B3:B7)

= (89 + 95 + 93 + 94 + 91)/5

Both of these equations produce the same answers, but one is much more useful than the other. It is important to determine which is more useful and why.

It is best if the data is referenced as much as possible as opposed to typing data into equations.

The last example is useful for educators; it contains students' exams and homework scores and average scores. Once a teacher creates a working spreadsheet, then it can be saved to use at a later time. If each of the actual cells is referenced (instead of users typing the data into the equation), the entire spreadsheet can be updated by typing in the new student names and scores; then the work is quickly finished!

Spreadsheets have many built-in mathematical functions. One of the most popular functions in any spreadsheet is the SUM function. The Sum function takes all of the values in each of the specified cells and totals their values. The syntax is:

=SUM(first value, second value, etc.)

Other basic operations for educators are the standard average, maximum, minimum, multiply, divide, add, and subtract. These operations follow the order of operations, just like algebra.

Study the following examples that show how a typical function can be used. Use Table 2.1 for this exercise. Notice that in A4 of Table 2.1, there is a TEXT entry. This has no numeric value and cannot be included in a total.

Using the cell values in Table 2.1, and applying the formula in the operation column in Table 2.2, the following calculations shown in the answer column of Table 2.2 were determined.

Table 2.1. A generic spreadsheet of 4 cells with data

	A
1	93
2	79
3	82
4	Test Score

Table 2.2. A table that shows different types of operations

Example	Operation	Cells to operate on	Answer
Example 1	=sum (A1:A3)	A1, A2, A3	254
Example 2	=sum (A1:A3, 100)	A1, A2, A3 and 100	354
Example 3	=sum (A1+A4)	A1, A4	#VALUE!
Example 4	=sum (A1:A2, A2)	A1, A2, A2	251
Example 5	=average(A1:A3)	A1, A2, A3	84.67
Example 6	=max(A1:A3)	A1, A2, A3	93
Example 7	=min(A1:A3)	A1, A2, A3	79

Figure 2.2. The formula is entered in cell G3.

	A	B	C	D	E	F	G
1							
2		Exam I	Exam II	Homework 1	Homework 2	Homework 3	Total
3	Amy	97	89	92	79	91	90.16667
4	Bob	95	91	89	77	93	
5	Cindy	93	78	92	89	88	
6	David	94	89	100	89	77	
7	Emily	91	94	93	92	90	
8							
9	Average	94					

Cell reference: G3 =B3*0.25+C3*0.25+ AVERAGE(D3:F3)*0.5

Continue using the hypothetical grade book scenario for the problem that follows. Assume that a teacher needs to calculate each student's semester total grade. In the formula, each exam counts for 25%, and the three homework assignments combined together count for another 50% of the entire semester's grade. In most cases, the teacher will build the formula for the first student in cell G3 as shown in Figure 2.2.

Notice the formula entered into G3 is as follows:

=B3*0.25+C3*0.25+ AVERAGE (D3:F3)*0.5

The * (asterisk) sign is used to indicate multiplication in spreadsheets. Specifically, the formula is asking for Amy's Exam I score times 0.25 plus Amy's Exam II score times 0.25 plus the average of her three homework scores times 0.5. An important note here is that when the formula is applied, it may be wise to double-check the answers with an electronic calculator.

Care should be taken to avoid circular reference. Circular reference happens when a formula is entered that includes functions that refer back to the cell in which the formula is contained. If this mistake occurs, then an error message will appear referring to circular reference.

Relative and Absolute Addresses

In this scenario, in order to complete the electronic grade book, the teacher should repeat the same formula for the other four students. In spreadsheets, the copy and paste commands can be used. The cell locations in the formula are pasted relative to the position from which they were copied.

A cell's information is copied from its relative position. In this grade book scenario, in the original cell (G3), the equation was (=B3*0.25+C3*0.25+ AVERAGE (D3: F3)*0.5). When the function is pasted for the second student, Bob, it will occur in the next row. So the equation pasted into (G4) will be (=B4*0.25+C4*0.25+ AVERAGE (D4:F4)*0.5). And the equation pasted into (G5) will be (=B5*0.25+C5*0.25+ AVERAGE (D5:F5)*0.5).

Cell addresses may be either absolute or relative. In this example of relative addresses, when a formula is used for a range of cells, it is automatically adjusted to be relative to the cells to which it refers. Therefore, for the second student, Bob, the formula for his total score reflected this dynamic change.

An absolute address is used when it is necessary to maintain a certain position that is not relative to the new cell location. This is possible by inserting a dollar sign, $, before the column letter or a $ before the row number, or sometimes both. This is called absolute positioning or absolute address. The dollar signs lock the cell location to a fixed address or position. When copied and pasted, it remains exactly the same.

In our grade book scenario, let us assume the teacher decides to add 2.877 to everyone's total score "to curve." The number 2.877 is entered into cell B11. The effective formula to make the adjustment for the first student is as follows:

=G3+$B$11

Instead of typing 2.877 for everyone, the absolute address $B$11 is used. The absolute address of $B$11 constantly refers to the number 2.877. In case the teacher changes her mind to another number, she only has to change the value in B11

Figure 2.3. The absolute address "=G3+$B$11" is entered into H3

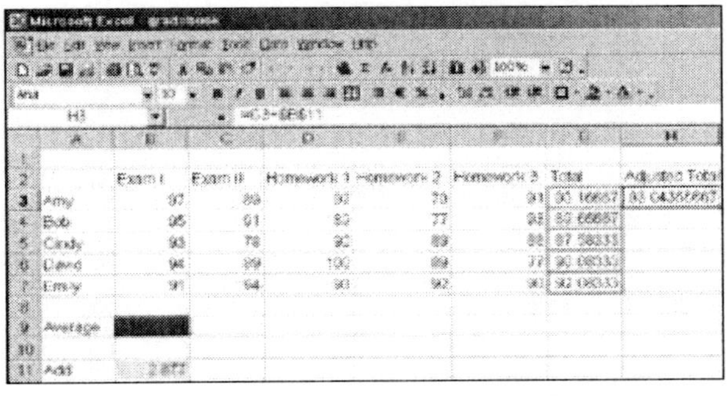

Figure 2.4. Displays the selected range of cells G3 through H7 and the number tab from the format menu

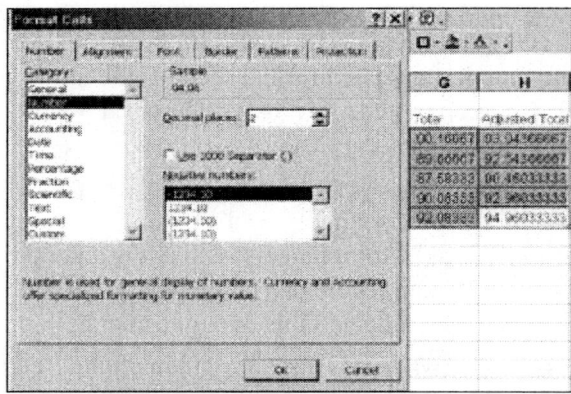

instead of changing the data in several places. Again, it is advised that the teacher double-check with a calculator before copying and pasting the formula with absolute address to cells H4 through H7, as displayed in Figure 2.3.

As mentioned in the previous section, a teacher may need to format the numbers in order to display the appropriate number of decimals, dollar signs, percentage, negative numbers, and so forth. It is best to keep numbers describing similar items as uniform as possible.

For example, in Figure 2.3, if the number 90.16667 was used, then we would probably have to make the column wider, thus wasting space. It is advised to set the number of decimal places to match what is important. Since this is a class grade book, in most cases, the number will be 90.17.

Another example provided in Figure 2.4 displays what would be seen if the range of cells G3 through H7 were selected and if the number tab was selected from the format menu.

Charts

It has been said that a picture reveals a thousand words. Visual literacy and graphic literacy are relatively new phrases amid the rising wave of multimedia technology. Personal computers and the Internet have become standard modes of learning within schools, and students now learn highly innovative skills such as how to manipulate digitized images, film and edit digital movies, make presentations, and create sophisticated animations.

Visually pleasing, accurate charts enable users to easily and quickly find relevant/critical data or recognize important relations between data. It is important to note that visual literacy/graphic literacy skills can be found in all content areas in K-12 schools. Currently, most state and national standards promote and link technological literacy with the study of science, social studies, and other content-area subjects.

Teachers have found it important to integrate graphic literacy (or "graphicacy") throughout the curriculum in order to address the issue of teaching students how to "read" and interpret images and technical information. Students must be taught to develop their visual literacy skills in order to become better critical thinkers.

Within the classroom, teachers may use graphics technologies to achieve the following objectives:

- Promote effective use of graphics to communicate scientific and technical information.
- Support conceptual and theoretical problem solving through an inquiry-driven design format
- Allow visualization of both quantitative and qualitative data.
- Support National Standards in Technology, Science, and Mathematics.
- Promote positive attitudes toward technology.

An effective means of teaching students to develop their technical visualization skills is through the use of graphic functions (Gipp, 2005). The graphing function of many spreadsheet programs can represent numbers quickly to a large audience in an image format such as a diagram, chart, or graph. The Chart Wizard of *Excel*, which is built into its main program, will guide users through the steps and create a chart from the answers.

Many types of charts exist that can help students develop their technical visualization skills. It is important that teachers model for students how to match the appropriate chart with the data. The most commonly used charts include the line chart, the bar chart, the column chart, and the pie chart.

Line charts are best used when a variable has more than five data points and it is important to emphasize continuity over time. The slope of the line displays the direction of the data trends to the viewer (see Figure 2.5).

Bar charts and column charts are best used when a need exists to compare data displayed by the lengths of different bars or columns to each other. Bar charts are often the best way to compare a set of individual items or several sets of related items. The bar's length corresponds to its ranking; the bar label identifies the item (see Figure 2.6).

Figure 2.5. The slope of the line displays the campus growth to the viewer

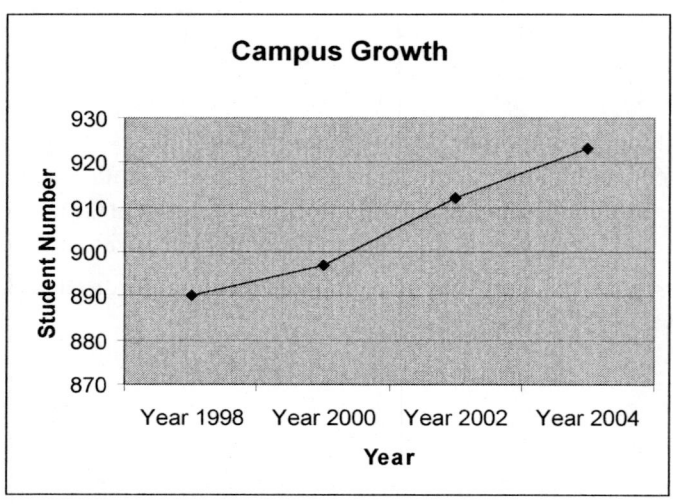

Figure 2.6. A student used the bar's length to correspond to its ranking; the bar's label identifies the item

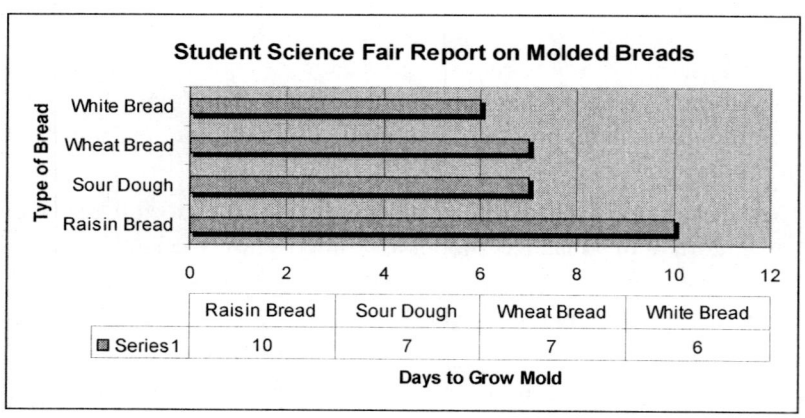

A pie chart is usually used to determine what makes up the whole, as well as highlights a part or parts of the whole. For example, a pie chart would best illustrate the proportion of state government budget spent on education. Another example is a pie chart that displays the class budget and the percentages of dollars spent on each category such as field trips, project supplies, and party supplies. It is important to note that when using a pie chart, the number of pie slices should not be more than five, and each slice should be easy to view and interpret.

Another visual graphic commonly used in the classroom is a frequency polygon. The purpose of a frequency polygon (or histogram) is to graphically summarize the distribution of a data set. The most common form of the histogram is obtained by splitting the range of the data into equal-sized bins (also called classes). For each bin, the numbers of points from the data set that fall into each bin are counted. In the example in Table 2.3, 50 students were asked how many hours they had studied last weekend and the responses were recorded in a frequency polygon.

Table 2.3. A frequency table showing the number of hours studied of 50 students

Number of Hours Students Studied		
HOURS	FREQUENCY	PERCENT
18	1	2
17	0	0
16	0	0
15	1	2
14	0	0
13	2	4
12	1	2
11	3	6
10	5	10
9	4	8
8	5	10
7	11	22
6	4	8
5	2	4
4	3	6
3	4	8
2	2	4
1	1	2
0	1	2

Figure 2.7. A frequency polygon/histogram displays the frequency and hours studied by students

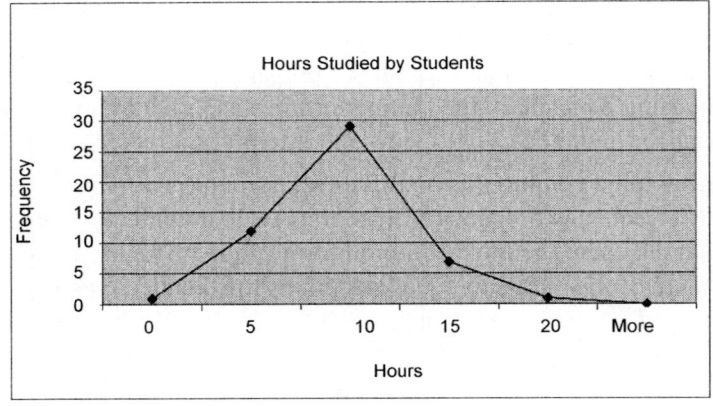

Table 2.4. Displays the number of hours studied and the grades of 5 students

Hours Studied	Test Grade
0	52
10	95
6	83
8	71
6	64

The shape of this distribution is unimodal because it has one main peak. This distribution is positively skewed, although slightly. The distribution is close to being symmetrical.

Data can also be visually displayed in order to plot one variable against a second variable using a scatterplot. In this example, the instructor asked five students how many hours they had studied for an exam. In Table 2.4 are the numbers of hours studied and the students' grades.

A scatterplot can be created for this data in order to visually display the data of the first variable in relation to the data of the second variable. The plot shows a very strong, but certainly not a perfect relationship between these two variables. It is important to note that scatterplots should be constructed when the relationship between two variables is of interest.

Another commonly used form for visual representation of data includes organizational charts. Organizational charts display functional relationships found within an organization. The data can be displayed using a flow chart to show the diagram of process and using a Gantt chart to show the duration of different tasks.

Figure 2.8. Scatterplot showing the relationship between hours studied and the test scores of five high school students

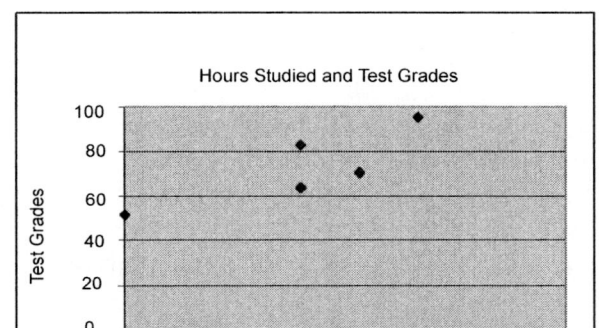

These charts are easily created with spreadsheet software such as MS *Excel*. With a few simple keystrokes, the user can change bar width, color, type size, and other elements.

In addition, legends can be added to reveal titles, percentages, and the change that will make the charts more informative. It is important to note some of the basic guidelines that can be used for designing graphics generated from electronic spreadsheet programs (Gipp, 2005):

1. Make the chart easy to read. Label the X and Y axes and label the lines, bars, or pie wedges. Make the most important text largest.
2. Check for accuracy.
3. Always start a numerical axis at zero.
4. Compare only like variables.
5. Eliminate all unnecessary details. Avoid details unless they relate to the message.
6. Use no more than four colors per visual.
7. To focus attention, use color, shading, or arrows to highlight key words or concepts.
8. Write in upper and lower case to make texts easy to read.
9. Use all data, not only the ones that fit the assignment's expectations.
10. Use common units (e.g., not miles when kilometers are the common unit)
11. If appropriate, add labels.

Macros

Many advanced users of productivity tools, such as Microsoft *Office*, use macros to simplify repetitive tasks. A macro is a set of directions for the program that does a particular task. For example, writers can use MS *Word* macros to automate the creation of references for papers. Specifically, a macro is a way to automate a task that users perform repeatedly. It is a series of computer actions that can be saved and run whenever the users need to perform the task. Users can record or build a macro, give it a name, and then play it to automatically repeat the series of commands.

A macro recorder is a built-in feature of many spreadsheet programs, such as MS *Excel,* and it is a simple way to create a macro. In *Excel* the first step is to open up the desired electronic spreadsheet or workbook. Then click on Tools, select Macros, and then click on Record new macro from the menu. The Record Macro dialogue box should then pop into view.

When recording a macro, as displayed on Figure 2.9, it is important to provide four types of information:

- **Name:** Type the name of the macro.
- **Shortcut key:** Choose a letter from the keyboard. For example, if the letter "t" is chosen, then the macro will run every time the CTRL key and the "t" key are pressed.
- **Store macro in:** The macro is normally stored in the current workbook being used, but macros can be saved in a personal macro workbook so it will be available in any of the spreadsheets or workbooks created.
- **Description:** Give a description of the macro for easy reference.

Figure 2.9. A screen capture showing the Record Macro pop-up window

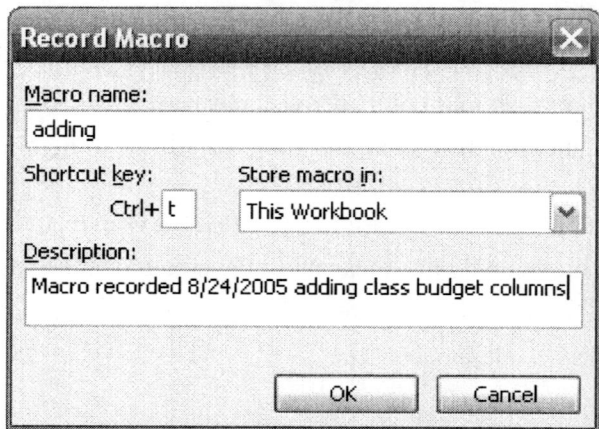

Recording the macro. When finished filling in the information click the OK button to start the macro recorder. From now on, every move taken in the workbook will be recorded by the computer. It is important to manually go through the process that is desired for the macro to recreate, for instance, adding up the class budget column. When finished, stop recording by clicking on macro recording box again. Double-check the sequence by playing the macro back.

Run the macro. Click on tools, hover the mouse over Macro, then select Macros. The Macro dialogue box, similar to that shown in Figure 2.9, will pop up and the macro should now be ready to use. To use the macro simply select it and then click the Run button.

If there is an assigned keyboard shortcut to the macro, then at this time, run it by holding down the CTRL key and pressing the associated letter.

A series of recorded macros can be played back to improve the speed and accuracy of spreadsheet work. The features of spreadsheets can be integrated to achieve advanced functions.

Electronic Databases

An electronic database management system (or DBMS) can be best visualized as an electronic file cabinet from which it is easy to access, retrieve, and investigate (query) data. In corporate America, large-scale DBMS, such as SAP, Oracle, and PeopleSoft, are applied in administration, accounting, operation, finance, and many other business divisions (Rob & Coronel, 2006). In most school districts' central offices, the data retrieval and query features of an electronic database make it an efficient tool to maintain and manipulate data, such as demographic data, sports and health records, and test result analysis. In classrooms, databases can be used as task-appropriate tools for elementary, middle, and secondary teachers to synthesize knowledge, create and modify solutions, and evaluate results in order to support the work of individual students and groups in problem-solving situations and project-based learning activities (Mills & Roblyer, 2006).

MS *Access* is among the most popular DBMS in schools today. The MS *Access* program has numerous built-in features to assist teachers.

Data Hierarchy

Often times it is important to investigate and display data hierarchy. Examine the data hierarchy example below involving a student council organization comprised of teachers and students. Before examining the hierarchical data, it is important to note the keywords involved in this process: database file, table, record, field, and data-type.

- **Database file:** This is the main file that encompasses the entire database. When users save to the hard-drive or floppy disk, they save the entire database file. Example: StudentCouncil.mdb
- **Table:** A table is a collection of data about a specific topic. There may be multiple tables in a database. Examples: Student table, Teacher table, and so forth.
- **Record:** A record is a collection of fields about a specific person, object, event, place, idea, or item. There can be multiple records in a table. Example: Students.
- **Field:** Fields are the different attributes within a record. A record usually contains multiple fields. Examples: Studentnumber, studentlastname, studentfirstname.
- **Data-types:** Data-types are the properties of each field. A field only has one data-type. Examples: Field: Studentnumber (data-type: numeric); Field: Studentlastname (data-type: text).

The following example (in Figure 2.10) reveals the concept of data hierarchy by revealing the structure of the database of a school student council that involves both teachers and students.

Most database systems allow users to switch views from the Datasheet View (spreadsheet view) to the Design View and vice versa. The Datasheet View displays the view that allows users to enter raw data into the database table, while the Design View allows the user to enter fields, data-types, and descriptions into the database table.

Figure 2.10. The hierarchy of the student council database

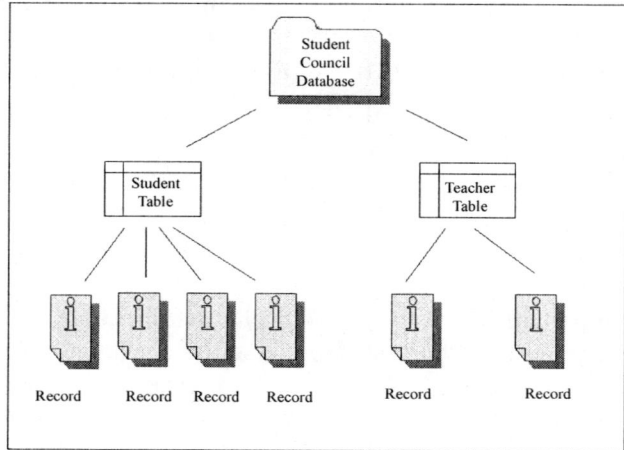

Define a Table

Each database management system has rules for naming fields, choosing data-types, and defining other properties for fields. The data-type determines what field values the user can enter for the field (Mills & Roblyer, 2006).

The specific attributes of a variable or field determine what kind of data it can hold. There are 10 data-types available in MS *Access*. The Text and Memo field data types allow the field to store either text or numbers, but the Number data type limits the field to store numbers only. Number data type fields store numerical data that will be used in mathematical calculations. The Currency data type will display or calculate currency values. Other data types may include: Date/Time, Yes/No, Auto Number, OLE (object for storing pictures), hyperlink, or lookup wizard.

For example, Figure 2.11 shows an example of a Student table consisting of five fields: studentnumber, studentlastname, studentfirstname, studentgrade, and dateofbirth. In the student council database, the student table will include a studentnumber field and a studentgrade field, each of which will store number values; the user of the database management system will assign the number data-type to this field (see Figure 2.11). It is important to note that the MS *Access* program will allow only numbers as values in the studentnumber field. Moreover, the studentnumber field should be designated as the primary key of the database in that it does not accept duplicate values, so a unique student number should be entered for this field. On the other hand, the studentlastname and studentfirstname fields are defined as text fields, and the data entered should match accordingly. Finally, the dateofbirth is defined as a Date/Time field. Following these procedures will ensure that all five fields in the Student table are clearly defined.

In a similar manner, the Teacher table, teacherid, teacher gradelevel, teacherroomnumber, and teacherphone are defined as numerical fields, while teacherlastname, teacherfirstname, and teachere-mail are defined as text fields. Figure 2.12 shows an example of a Teacher table consisting of seven fields.

Figure 2.11. Data-types found within the Student table

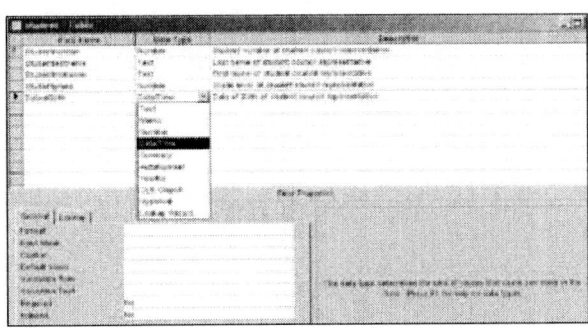

Figure 2.12. Data-types found within the Teacher table

Field Name	Data Type
Teacherid	Number
Teacherlastname	Text
Teacherfirstname	Text
Teachergrade	Number
Teacherroomnumber	Number
Teacherphone	Number
Teachere-mail	Text

Setting Up A Primary Key

In the example of the student council database, the studentnumber field is the primary key, meaning that every student has a student number and no two numbers are the same. It is important to note that the Index feature should be turned on because this speeds up searches and sorting on the field, but may slow updates. Also note that the primary key does not allow null values and must always have a unique value. The primary key is used to relate a table to important keys (foreign keys) in other tables. Also, one or more fields in a table can be designated as a primary key, whose value or values uniquely identify each record in a table.

If a primary key is not defined, MS *Access* prompts the user to create one when the table is being saved. Even though the user does not have to define a primary key, it is usually a good idea. It is important to note that in the MS *Access* table, the field that is designated as the primary key of the table is denoted with a key icon.

Data Entry

In order to enter data into the student table, click on the datasheet view and simply start by entering the data into each field. Before starting a new record, the studentnumber field must have some value (texts or numbers) in it, because it is the primary key and designated as required. If the user does not set a primary key then it is fine to leave it blank. It is important to note that due to its field definition, the system will only accept unique (no duplicate) student numbers.

Continue entering data as follows:

- To add a new row, drop down to a new line and enter the information.
- To update a record, select the record and field, and then change its data.
- To delete a record, select the entire row and hit the Delete key on the keyboard.

Additional advanced features include:

- Assigning a field a specific set of characters (e.g., making a social security number field that only allows 9 characters by defining the field size).
- Formatting a field to look a specific way (e.g., formatting a phone number that starts with the area code (xxx) xxx-xxxx using the Input Mask Box feature).
- Selecting a value from a dropdown box with a preselected set of values. This saves the user from having to type it in each time. This feature helps the user avoid unnecessary data-entry errors (e.g., choose a city from a list through the use of the Lookup tab in the Design View).

It is also important to note that using a separate table for each topic ensures that the data is stored only once; this leads to efficiency and error reduction. For this reason, tables are organized visually into columns (fields) and rows (records).

An example of a field can be seen in Figure 2.13. Note that each field in the Student table contains the same type of information for every student representative, such as student's number.

An example of a record can be seen in Figure 2.13. Each record in the Student table contains all of the information about the student representative, such as Last Name, First Name, Grade Level, and Date of Birth. Figure 2.14 shows a screen capture of the Teacher table with three entries.

Figure 2.13. Data organization for a student council table

	Studentnumber	Studentlastname	Studentfirstname	Studentgrade	Dateofbirth
	90335	Farish	Rose	3	06/18/96
	90378	Alpine	David	3	03/01/96
	91221	Trudel	Brian	4	04/28/95
	91299	Wix	Emily	4	11/20/95
	93345	Elm	Annie	5	06/01/93

Five Fields — Five Records

Figure 2.14. A screen capture of the Teacher table

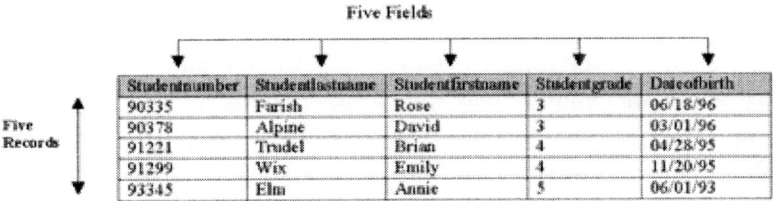

Field Name	Data Type
Teacherid	Number
Teacherlastname	Text
Teacherfirstname	Text
Teachergrade	Number
Teacherroomnumber	Number
Teacherphone	Number
Teachere-mail	Text

Relationships

Sometimes, information is scattered throughout many tables. For example, in the hypothetical Student Council database, students' information is stored on the **Student** table while supervising teachers' information is stored on the **Teacher** table. It is important to note that in order to retrieve information from more than one table, table relationships must be established in order to be used.

After multiple tables in the MS *Access* database are set, users need a way of telling the DBMS how to integrate the information together again. The first step in this process is to define the relationships between the tables. After establishing the table relationship, users can then create queries, forms, and reports to display information from more than one table.

A relationship works by matching data in key fields found in each table. In most cases, these matching fields are the primary key from one table, which provides a unique identifier for each record, and a foreign key in the other table. For example, teachers can be associated with the student representatives they are responsible for by creating a relationship between the Teacher's table and the Student's table using the teacherid field.

In our example of the Student Council database, let us assume one teacher is assigned to supervise several student representatives of the same grade. Through the studentgrade field in the Student table and the teachergrade field in the Teacher table, the two tables can be joined together in one relational database (see Figure 2.15).

In order to create relationships between tables, the following steps must be followed.

1. In the Database Window view, at the top, click on Tools ---> Relationships.
2. Select the tables to be linked together (i.e., Student table and Teacher table) by clicking on them and selecting the Add Button.
3. Drag the studentgrade field in the primary table (Student in this case), and drop it into the teachergrade field in the child table (Teacher in this case).
4. Click Create
5. Save the Relationship.

Create Filter and Query

It is important to differentiate a filter from a query. On one hand, a filter allows the application of a set of selection criteria and/or sorting instructions to the records in a table. It is a quick mechanism that is created for one-time use in the context of a particular table. On the other hand, a query is reusable. When a database is closed,

Figure 2.15. Through the studentgrade field in the Student table and the teacher-grade field in the Teacher table, the two tables are joined together in this relational database

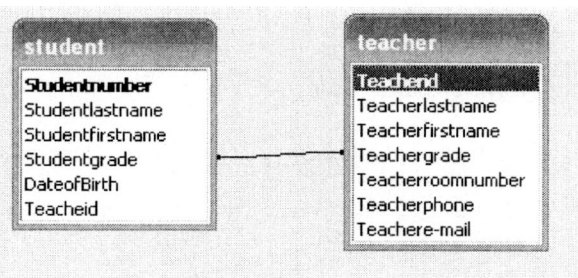

the selection criteria and/or sorting instructions will be wiped out. Therefore, in order to retrieve the same records again, the filter has to be recreated. However, a query allows the selection criteria and/or sorting instructions to be saved and reused. Moreover, queries are capable of performing the functions of filters, namely adding selection criteria and sorting instructions.

To create a filter, open the selected table; then, click the **Edit Filter/Sort** button in the toolbar or go through Records→Filter→Advanced Filter/Sort. Next, enter the selection criteria and sorting instructions in the filter window. In the following exercise, the school principal requests information on all of the student representatives in the Student Council with grade levels greater than fourth, sorted in ascending order of grade levels and last names.

In general, there are two types of queries: a select query and an action query. A select query gathers, collates, and presents information in usable forms. An action query makes changes in specified records of an existing table, or creates a new table. In addition, queries allow calculation of new fields.

Figure 2.16. The figure reveals the results of the filter/sort: all the student representatives in the Student Council with grade level greater than 4 are shown, sorted in ascending order of grade levels and last names

Student Number	Studentlastnam	Studentfirstnam	Studentgrade	DateofBirth	Teacherid
91221	Trudel	Brian		4/28/1995	3214
91299	Wix	Emily	4	11/20/1995	3214
93045	Elm	Annie	5	6/1/1994	3321
0			0		0

Figure 2.17. Requested student information for the Student table

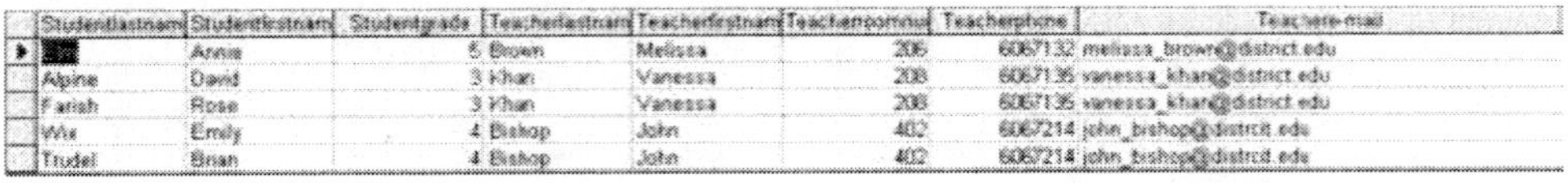

Figure 2.18. Users go through View→Design view and set the criteria of student-grade to equal 3

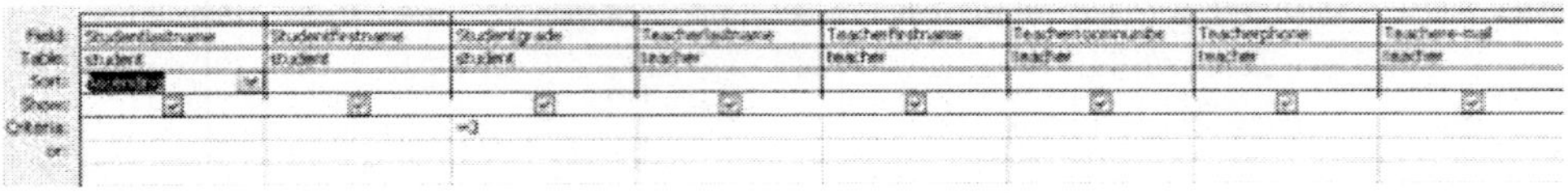

Figure 2.19. The correct query results displays all of the student representatives in the third grade in addition to the information requested about their supervising teacher

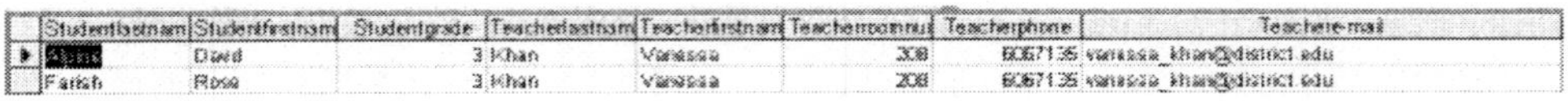

In the following exercise, the principal requests information on all of the student representatives in the third grade. The principal also requests information on the student's supervising teachers. In order to find this information, it is important to follow these steps:

- Click the Query button and then the **New** button in the Database window.
- Select Simple Query Wizard.
- From the Student table, select studentlastname, studentfirstname, and student-grade.
- From the Teacher table, select teacherlastname, teacherfirstname, teacher-roomnumber, teacherphone, and teacher-mail.
- The resulting table (see Figure 2.17) displays the requested fields for all students in the Student table.

Forms

A form is a graphic representation of a table. For most users, a form allows for friendly data entry. The user can add, update, and delete records in a table by using a form. A form built from a table can manipulate the same information as that found in the table. It is important to note that if the user changes a record in a form, the resulting data change will be viewed in the table as well.

Teacher Productivity and Professional Practices 47

A form is very convenient for data entry when the user has numerous fields in a table. Rules can then be embedded into the form to validate data. By using a form, all the fields can be viewed on one screen; whereas, in the Datasheet View, the user would have to keep scrolling down to get to the fields at the end of the list.

It is easy for most users to create a form using the Form Wizard. The following steps are needed to create a basic form:

1. From the Database Window, click on the Forms button on the left side of screen.
2. Double click on Create Form Using Wizard.
3. On the next screen select the fields from the table to view on the form.
4. Select the layout.
5. Select the style.
6. Provide a name for the form.
7. Select Finish.

After following the steps described, the form should then appear on the screen (see Figure 2.20). To adjust the design of the form, click on the design button and customize the form accordingly. Once the overall look is decided, some teachers may choose to place the school logo on the form, adjust the width of each field, change the captions for the fields, or give the field that is designated as the primary key a special color.

Figure 2.20. A data entry form for the Student Table in the student council database

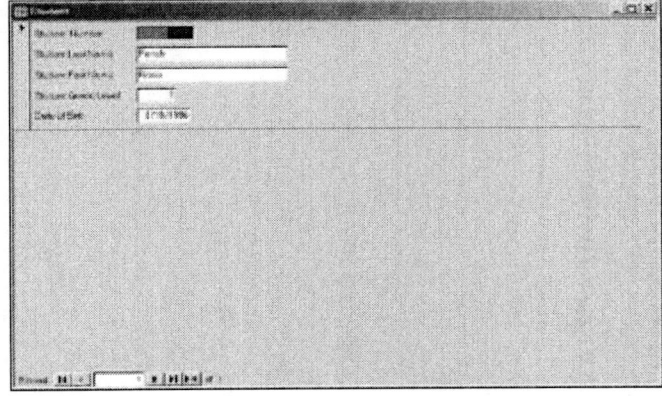

Copyright © 2008, IGI Global. Copying or distributing in print or electronic forms without written permission of IGI Global is prohibited.

Reports

A report is an effective way to present data in a printed format. When creating a report, users have considerable control over the size and appearance of the data found within the report.

As with the Form, most users create a report using the wizard. The following steps are needed to create a report using the Report Wizard of MS *Access*:

1. From the Database Window, click on the Reports button on the left side of the screen.
2. Select Create Report Using Wizard.
3. Select the desired fields to view on your printed report.
4. Decide how to group the records.
5. Select the desired layout, paper orientation, and style.
6. Give the report a name, and select Preview the Report.
7. Select Finish.

After these steps are followed, the report should then appear on the screen (see Figure 2.21). To adjust the design of the report, simply hit the design button and adjust the report accordingly. One useful feature of the report is to allow some information (such as report title) to remain the same, while the details change from page to page.

Figure 2.21. The report displays student council representative in the ascending order of the grade fields

Student

Studentgrade	Student Number	Studentlastname	Studentfirstname	DateofBirth
3	90335	Farish	Rose	6/18/1996
3	90378	Alpine	David	3/1/1996
4	91221	Trudel	Brian	4/28/1995
4	91299	Wix	Emily	11/20/1995
5	93345	Elm	Annie	6/1/1994

Discussions of Computerized Data Analysis Tools

Whatever the instructional area, it will be beneficial for teachers to investigate the classroom applications of spreadsheet and databases (Roblyer, 2005). The typical application for these applications is as follows:

- Information retrieval
- Recognition of patterns and trends
- Analysis of relationships
- Testing of hypotheses
- Interpretation of data
- Critical thinking
- Format of retrieval information
- Sorting features
- Type of data, for example, text, numerical, graphic, video, sound
- Organization of data

Becoming familiar with data analysis tools, such as spreadsheets, will allow teachers to understand the application of these programs in the classroom. Some of the applications include showing students how to (Fewell & Gibbs, 2006):

- Create and read a graph
- Evaluate graphs of experimental data
- Draw a conclusion from data
- Analyze charts about science/math data
- Apply an understanding
- Relate causes and effects of physical changes
- Associate a situation with a science/math concept
- Make prediction with current data

Specific examples for classroom application, provided by Ryan and Cooper (2006), include teaching students (with age-appropriate information) to use spreadsheets as a tool for forecasting and predicting trends; using databases to create more personal categories for class, school, or home collections; and using a word processor to revise personal work.

Using a Variety of Productivity Tools

It is important that teachers help students match the outstanding feature of each program type to their needs (Fewell & Gibbs, 2006). In spite of most word-processing programs' ability to handle images, tables, and databases, they are best used for word processing. Similarly, electronic spreadsheet programs can handle text, but are best used for manipulating data. Likewise, electronic database management systems are more powerful than spreadsheets in calculations and other advanced data analysis functions. It is important to note that for complex tasks, students should learn to match the task to the program features. For example, when a student is writing a document in a word-processing program and then finds that he needs to use a complex table, he can then create a worksheet in an electronic spreadsheet program and embed the worksheet into his word processing document. When students learn to use the various productivity tools to meet their needs, then the computer application to the classroom becomes very effective.

Exchanging Data Between Electronic Spreadsheets and DBMS

In both electronic spreadsheet programs and DBMS, queries can be run to sort and filter data, run calculations to derive the desired information, generate reports, view reports in different formats, use forms to add, change, delete, and navigate data easily, connect to external data, and import data from external databases and other file types.

Both programs organize data in columns that store a particular kind of information. One difference in terminology is that a row in an electronic spreadsheet program is called a record in DBMS.

More and more data files are now available for classroom teachers on the WWW, and many of these files are in special text formats that are easily imported into spreadsheet or database programs. Files created with spreadsheets or DBMS programs can also be exported and viewed by a Web browser and/or can be saved as text or other formats. However, some file types are easier to import and export than others. For example, both *Excel* and Access can save simple data files in tab-delimited, space-delimited, or comma-delimited formats. The export and import procedures make exchanging database and spreadsheet files easier.

The following steps are needed to import MS *Excel* spreadsheet data to MS *Access*:

1. Make sure the MS *Excel* data is in the list format and each column has a label in the first row and contains similar facts, and there are no blank rows or columns within the list.

2. Close the *Excel* workbook that contains the data needed for use in MS *Access*.
3. In *Access*, open the database in order to copy the *Excel* data.
4. On the *Access* File menu, point to Get External Data, and then click Import.
5. In the Import dialog box, click Microsoft *Excel* in the Files of type box.
6. In the Look in list, locate the file needed for import, and then double-click the file.

Embedding and Linking Objects

An embedded object is a document or part of a document stored within another program's document. In most word-processing programs, teachers can easily show students how to embed objects, such as charts, diagrams, sounds, and videos, into their work. The only requirement is that the program that creates the object is installed on the student's computer.

In the following example (see Figure 2.22), the teacher would like to insert the class budget (created as an electronic worksheet illustrated in Figure 2.23) into the following word processing document.

To embed the class budget worksheet into the memo, in the word-processing program, the following steps should be followed.

1. First, click on Insert→Object, which displays a dialog box with two tabs that lets the user either create a new object or create from an existing object.
2. Since the user desires to insert from an existing spreadsheet, the user must click on the Create from File tab, then browse to the folder with the file of the object to be inserted, as shown in Figure 2.24.
3. Figure 2.25 shows the finished memo with linked object from an existing spreadsheet file.

Figure 2.22. A memo in regular word-processing format

```
Memo

To:   Rita Johnson
From: Marion Nash
Date: 11/21/2005

Subject:

Please review the class budget and give me your comment.
```

Figure 2.23. A worksheet to be embedded into the memo

	A	B	C
7		The 5th Grade Class of Ms. Nash	
8			
9	Expenses		
10		Materials for Science Project	$23.21
11		Field Trips	$108.75
12		Volentine's Day Event	$12.89
13			
14	Total		$144.85
15			

At first glance, an embedded object looks just like something created with the word-processing program. When the user double-clicks on the linked object, however, the worksheet is opened in Microsoft *Excel*, as illustrated in Figure 2.26. When the user clicks on the "table" area, the entire table is selected, with sizing handles surrounding the worksheet. When the user double-clicks the worksheet, he can now work on individual cells. Even though the document now has MS *Excel* toolbars replacing the MS *Word* toolbars, upon examining the title bar, it is evident that the user is still in MS *Word*. This action is known as embedding.

Figure 2.24. A dialogue window to insert an object from an existing file

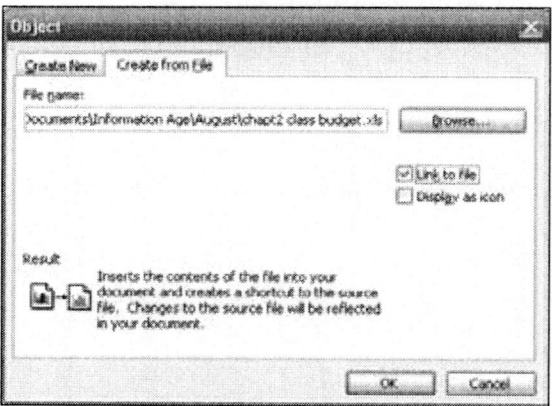

Figure 2.25. The memo with linked object from an existing spreadsheet file

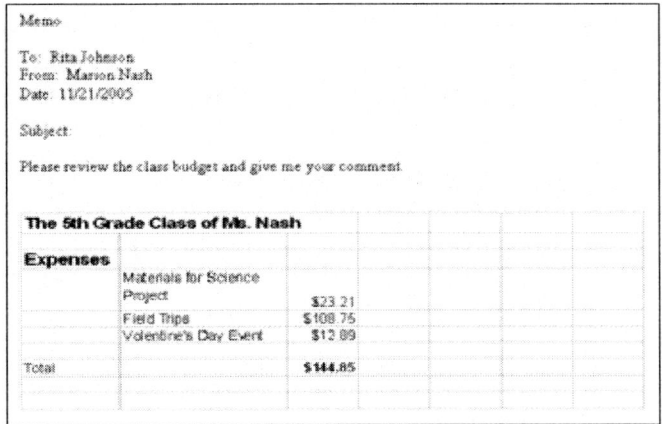

Figure 2.26. MS Excel toolbars within the MS Word document

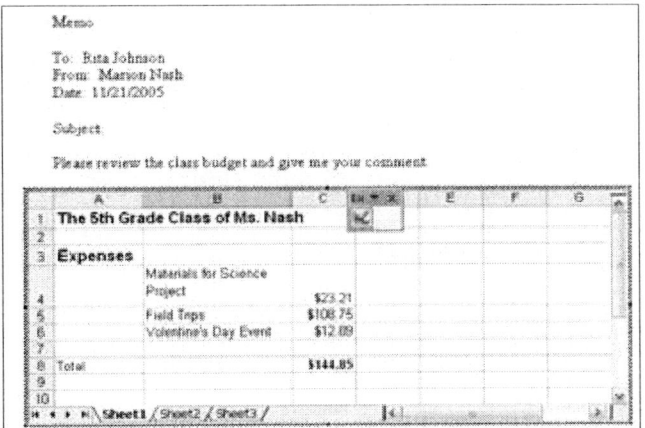

Linking a Worksheet Object to its Source

It is important to note that once an object is embedded, if the user makes changes to the original worksheet, the changes would not be reflected in the MS *Word* document with the embedded object. The changes would be reflected only if the user links the object to the source file. When linked, the system inserts the latest version of the object into the document every time the document is opened. In this example, in order to link the memo with the class budget spreadsheet, the user must first select and copy the range of needed data from the spreadsheet, then (from the memo file) click on Edit → Paste Special.

Figure 2.27 displays the Paste Special dialog box with its Paste Link button checked and Excel Worksheet Object highlighted to link the object to its source file. Following these procedures ensures that the object is reinserted into the document every time the document is opened, and that the most recent version of the object is used.

Teachers can help students embed or link numerous types of objects (other than worksheets) into their work including:

- A media clip
- A video clip
- A sound file
- Another Word document
- Microsoft Paint bitmapped image
- MS PowerPoint slide

Classroom Productivity Tools

A wide variety of technological materials and resources for teachers are now available for increasing productivity within the classroom. For example, in the science classroom or lab, more and more scientific probeware can now be used with a desktop, laptop, or handheld computer to collect and analyze data for experiments

Figure 2.27. The Paste Special dialog box with its option button to link the object to its source file

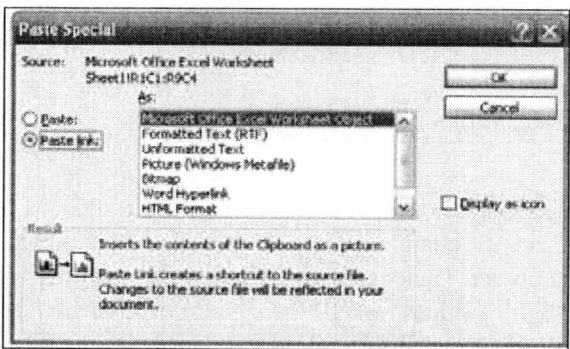

that require scientific measurement. Probeware measures real-life phenomena such as temperature, light, distance, motion, pH, and force. Middle-grade science teachers teaching earth systems, marine science, and energy are the first group of teachers to include activities related to the use of temperature, light, and voltage probeware and other probe-based activities. With probeware, a portable data collecting system now puts the power of a complete laboratory at the students' fingertips and replaces time-consuming data-collection tasks with the excitement of hands-on scientific experience.

Some productivity tools can be used by all classroom teachers. In some school districts, the grade book has become obsolete. Some school systems have automated everything from electronic absentee submission, to lesson plans file transfers, to grading. These automated grade book systems may either be available on the Web through secured local district servers or come as computer software to be installed on teachers' computers.

When using such tools, it is important that new teachers ask appropriate questions about the district privacy policy (FERPA) and about the specific reporting system that the district uses. Furthermore, teachers should become aware of any other additional systems used by school districts that aid teacher-student communication, such as an electronic homework system that allows students to contact teachers at home via e-mail.

Additional electronic teacher productivity tools may include (Chen, Nath, & Parker, 2005):

- Graphing calculator
- Language translator
- Electronic thesaurus
- Classroom management tools
- Database manager
- Daily/monthly planner
- Electronic evaluation tool
- Time liner
- Test generators
- Seating charts generators
- Worksheet and puzzle generators
- Question banks
- Portfolio assessment management tools
- IEP (Individual Educational Plan) software management for exceptional students

- Concept-mapping tools
- Poster and banner utilities
- Time management tools
- Certificate or award software
- Lesson-planning software
- WebQuest templates
- Grant-writing software
- Plagiarism detection tools

Schools and districts usually purchase a site license for specific software to install on all institutional computers. Sometimes the licenses are extended to cover even teachers' home computers. However, it is important that teachers check with their district before installing school software on their home computers to avoid copyright violations and other potentially illegal activity.

Utility Software

System Tools

System tools are intended to make the computer system faster and more stable (Silberschatz, Galvin, & Gagne, 2004). Some system tools, such as defragmenter or back-up utilities, may come with an Operating System. These system tools are used to scan and fix registry and hard disks for system and file inconsistencies.

Some system tools provide comprehensive cleaning of a PC. These tools can find and delete junk files and clear up space on the hard drive. Some special system tools, called history eraser software, ensure privacy by wiping Internet history from the computer. Another special system tool called a defragmenter allows the user to defragment files on the hard drive and directories. Other system tools can coordinate e-mail account folders, messages on Palm computers, bookmarks, address book, and cookies.

Memory managers or RAM boosters allow users to enhance the efficiency of RAM when a system slows down, thus enabling efficient uses of computer memory.

Additional system tools allow the user to monitor operation of accessory devices such as power, battery, or hard disk space consumption.

One specific type of system tool is a file management utility system, which may serve several functions including (Silberschatz et al., 2004):

- Finding and deleting duplicate files
- Displaying directories within current path with its sizes and file counts
- Some permanently wipe files, disk drives, and unused disk space so that no recovery is possible, while some recover the corrupted file.
- Backup, Security, and encrypt files and directories
- Undelete to recover deleted files.

Antivirus Tools

Teachers need to become knowledgeable of the various types of viruses before they can understand antivirus tools. Microsoft Corporation (2006) explains that basic viruses typically require unwary computer users to inadvertently share or send them. Some viruses that are more sophisticated, such as worms, can replicate and send themselves automatically to other computers by controlling other software programs, such as an e-mail sharing application. Certain viruses, called Trojans (named after the fabled Trojan horse), can falsely appear as a beneficial program to coax users into downloading them. Some Trojans can even provide expected results while quietly damaging a system or other networked computers at the same time.

A worm is a self-propagating computer virus. A Trojan is a program, similar to a virus, that is disguised as something harmless, like a computer game. Some types of virus, such as the famous "I love you" virus that propagated by e-mail, were disguised as a file attachment. That is the reason why users should not open an attachment they are unsure of. Some of the more cunning recent viruses have disguised themselves by naming the virus-laden attachment as LOVE-LETTER-FOR-YOU.TXT.VBS in the hope of tricking naive users.

Hoaxes usually arrive as e-mail messages and purport to warn the user of a new virus that is on its way. They usually urge the user to spread the warning around. They can also come in the form of an e-mail chain letter. Hoaxes are not specifically destructive, but they do frighten naive users. More seriously, they can disrupt network traffic by jamming the communication channels.

Word macro viruses, which mushroomed in 1996, spread via the MS Word files. The original one, which seemed to strike everywhere at some time, was the "Concept" virus.

It is important to note that to date, no known viruses have the ability to damage computer hardware such as hard drive motherboards.

To counteract viruses that may harm computers, antivirus software programs have been developed. Antivirus software programs are antidote utilities created to detect, eliminate, and protect a computer from viruses, worms, and Trojans. The antivirus program typically contains an engine, a resident virus shield, virus databases or DAT files, a task scheduler, an e-mail scanner, and an update manager.

The engine is the core of the antivirus program. It is important for teachers to understand that virus databases or DAT files have to be updated regularly. The resident virus shield found within the antivirus program protects current data against new threats while the computer is operating. The task scheduler, found within the antivirus program, schedules unattended checking activities. The e-mail scanner scans incoming and outgoing mails. Finally, the update manager connects to the antivirus software company's DAT Web pages for the latest updates.

An antivirus program can guard against computer viruses by lurking in memory and checking everything that is run on the computer while it is being used. The virus shield can also check the files on the disks at a time the user specifies.

If after installing the antivirus software program problems still exist, sometimes computer users have to install different software as a solution for firewall, pop-up blockers, and antispy ware.

What is important is that teachers keep school computers current with the latest antivirus tools, stay current of recent virus threats, and follow a few basic precautionary rules when downloading files and opening attachments. Teachers should train students to use good practices to avoid virus problems as well as backing up data regularly and dealing with potential issues early, before the virus checker is required to do any work.

In many schools, file exchange has caused serious virus damages to school computers. It is good practice to train students not to open any zipped or .exe files that are received by e-mail without virus checking carefully first, particularly .exe, .zip, .bvs, .pit, .html, and .doc (MS Word) files. It is also good practice to teach students not to send unsolicited attachments unless they first ascertain that the addressee really wants to receive it.

Some software companies maintain Web pages for new critical security updates that address severe vulnerabilities affecting their products. From the software company Web pages, readers can read virus alert, protection strategies, or download updates and patches to their computers.

Compression Tools

Compression is the process of reducing a file's size, this is also known as "zipping" or "archiving." The compressed (zipped) file can originate from a large file or can originate from several files that have been reduced into a single file. This many-to-one compression feature makes file group identification, copying, and transporting easy. Compression software can be configured to create executable files with .exe extension. This ensures that the file will self-extract when clicked.

The word "extracting" is used here to describe the process where software is decompressed to its original size. Usually compression (zipping) software also contains a decompression (unzipping) tool to allow users to open the compressed files on their computers. Some special purpose compression tools compress and virus check outgoing e-mail attachments for e-mail simultaneously. Other compression software focuses on special functions, such as compressing and backing up messages from an entire e-mail account, and reducing the sizes of graphics or video files. Popular archived files formats are .zip, .cab, .rar, .ace, InstallShield CAB, .tar, and .jar.

Device Drivers

Most devices, whether peripheral or not, require a software program, called a device driver, that converts general commands from an application into specific commands that the device understands. For example, when a teacher buys a new printer for the classroom, it is necessary to load special printer driver software in order to enable the operating system to communicate with the new hardware. In most cases, the drivers for scanners, fax/modem, digital cameras, DVD drives, sound blasters, and printers are packaged in the CD-ROMs provided by original manufacturers. Software drivers are frequently updated to improve performance, quality, and enable new features. Teachers should stay current with the latest drivers in order to download them as they become available. Most hardware manufactures allow for free download of drivers from their corporate Web sites. However, some generic drivers can be shared by devices that meet a specified industry standard.

When removing (uninstalling) a program from a system, it is important for teachers to understand that they cannot simply delete its folder, because almost all programs make changes to various parts of the operating systems. Teachers should be aware that many software drivers come with a special uninstaller, which should be used if it exists. Otherwise, teachers can uninstall programs from the Control Panel if the computer is running on the Windows operating system.

Format Converter

Teachers should understand the use of file format converters. To date, there are hundreds of file formats used to describe text formats, graphic formats, audio samples, music notation, video formats, and more.

Text converters convert between various text file formats such as RTF (rich text format, a generic text format), .DOC of MS *Word*, .WPS of MS *Works* document, and .WKB of *WordPerfect for Windows* document.

Graphics converters convert between various graphic file formats such as .bmp, .png, .jpg, .pcx, and .gif.

Audio converters convert a variety of different audio file formats including WAV, MP3, OGG, FLAC, AAC, WMA, AU, AIFF, and MSV. Audio files usually contain information about the included audio waveform's characteristics and how it is stored.

Video converters convert between various video file formats such as VGA, NTSC, and PAL.

Multimedia

For detailed information on multimedia, please see Chapter IX.

Network

For detailed information on networks, please see Chapters X, XI, and XII.

Software for Work and Home

Some school districts have acquired site licenses from software vendors in order to provide unlimited copies of diverse software onto the district-owned computers and networks. In this case, the software may be disseminated to teachers on floppy disks or CD-ROMs from the local area network. It is important that teachers understand that if the school district does not have a site license, then teachers cannot legally download software onto their computers. In conjunction with a technology plan, school and district planners frequently develop an AUP (or acceptable use policy), which addresses how students, staff, and community members may use school-provided software programs and the Internet. It is important that teachers read and understand their district's AUP; these policies will help to define acceptable behaviors of information systems.

Teachers should monitor students carefully to ensure that they adhere to these policies. Finally, teachers should conduct management and Fair Use lessons in order to instill good practices and usage habits into their students as they use electronic materials.

References

Chen, L. I, Nath, L. J., & Parker, E. M. (2005). Using technology in the middle school and high school classroom. In J. Nath & M. Cohen (Eds.), *Becoming a middle school or high school teacher in Texas* (pp. 309-350). Belmont: CA: Wadsworth/Thomson Learning.

Fewell, P. J., & Gibbs, W. J. (2006). *Microsoft Office® for teachers* (2nd ed.). Upper Saddle River, NJ: Merrill Prentice Hall.

Gipp, J. (2005). *Spotlight on spreadsheets.* Boston: Course Technology.

Mills, S. C., & Roblyer, M. D. (2006). *Technology tools for teachers: A Microsoft Office® tutorial* (2nd ed.). Upper Saddle River, NJ: Pearson Merrill Prentice Hall.

Rob, P., & Coronel, C. (2006). *Database systems: Design, implementation, and management* (7th ed). Boston: Course Technology.

Roblyer, M. D. (2005). *Integrating educational technology into teaching* (3rd ed.). Upper Saddle River, NJ: Merrill - Prentice Hall.

Ryan, K., & Cooper, J. (2006). *Those who can, teach.* Boston: Houghton Mifflin Company.

Silberschatz, A, Baer Galvin, P., & Gagne, G.(2004). *Operating system concepts* (7th ed.). Hoboken, NJ: John Wiley & Sons.

What is a computer virus? (2006). Retrieved June 18, 2007, from Microsoft Web site: http://www.microsoft.com/athome/security/viruses/intro_viruses_what.mspx

Sample Questions

1. A large elementary school decides to computerize its family information. Which of the following type of applications will best support this task?
    a. Word processor
    b. Database
    c. Project management
    d. Spreadsheet

2. Which of the following should be considered when a school district purchases grade book software for teachers?
    a. The number of students and assignments that can be stored on the software
    b. The type of school computer network
    c. The type of information to be stored on the software
    d. All of the above

3. In order to import text into a spreadsheet, it is best to:
    a. Use only numbers
    b. Set up proper delimiters
    c. Use only texts
    d. Set up the same column width

4. When will a student mostly likely need to export from a database?
    a. To share data with a word processor
    b. To share data with a spreadsheet
    c. To share data with a desktop publishing application
    d. To output data to a video format

5. A math teacher thinks a shareware tutorial software program that he used in class can be helpful for a group of disadvantaged children that he volunteers to mentor after school in a community center. In order to follow Fair Use policy, what do you suggest him to do?

   a. Request to purchase an individual copy of the software to be installed on several computers in the community center.

   b. Use the school software CD to install a copy for the community center.

   c. Download a free copy of the shareware and install for the community center. He doesn't have to pay for the software since his school has paid for his use.

   d. Request to purchase as many individual copies of the software as needed in the community center as required by the software company.

Answers: (1) B (2) D (3) B (4) B (5) D

Chapter III

Using Technology for Learning, Teaching, and Designing the Curriculum

ISTE NETS_T, II. Planning and designing learning environments and experiences

Teachers plan and design effective learning environments and experiences supported by technology.

ISTE NETS_T, III. Teaching, learning, and the curriculum

Teachers implement curriculum plans that include methods and strategies for applying technology to maximize student learning.

ISTE NETS_T, IV. Assessment and evaluation

Teachers apply technology to facilitate a variety of effective assessment and evaluation strategies.

Chapter objective: The teacher knows how to plan, organize, deliver, and evaluate instruction that effectively utilizes current technology for teaching.

Using computers to increase classroom resources is both an impetus for and outcome of transforming the role of the teacher in the classroom. Once known as the sole disseminator of information, teachers now identify themselves as facilitators whose roles are to motivate students and engage them in learning and reflection. Most states expect technology applications teachers to demonstrate knowledge and skills in the following areas:

- to plan and implement instruction that allows students to use technology applications in problem-solving and decision-making situations.
- to plan applications-based technology lessons using a range of instructional strategies for individuals and small/whole groups.
- to develop and facilitate collaborative tasks and teamwork among group members.
- to perform administrative tasks.
- to use a variety of instructional strategies to ensure students' reading comprehension.
- to help students learn how to locate, retrieve, analyze, evaluate, communicate, and retain content-related information.
- to evaluate student projects and electronic portfolios using formal and informal assessment methods.
- to use assessment results for gauging student progress and adjusting instruction.

Maximizing Student Achievement

Recently several researchers have suggested that technology serves as a catalyst for change in the content areas and for enhancing students' ability to learn specific content. Statham and Torell (1996) have identified the essential educational conditions that are necessary to maximize student achievement with technology:

- **Better access to technology:** In order to become an integral part of students' learning, computers need to be available for individual student use during extended periods of time. Currently, student access to computers is estimated to be less than 4% of total instructional time. The success of technology depends on having significant critical access to hardware and applications that are appropriate to the learning expectations of the activity. Electrical and communication systems must be updated in order to maximize the benefits of computer technology. Best practice indicates that one computer for every four to five students is necessary if students are to be able to use technology in a manner that will yield significant improvements in learning.

- **Learning environments:** Computers must be viewed as learning environments with multiple capabilities to support and enhance student learning as an important medium for instruction. The success or failure of technology involves seeing it as a valuable resource. This requires determining where it can have the highest payoff and then matching the design of the application with the intended purpose and learning goal. The success or failure of technology-enabled learning experiences often depends on whether the software design and instructional methods surrounding its use are congruent.

- **Professional development:** Teachers must be provided with instruction and practice in integrating the curriculum with the technology and become familiar with hardware and software. The success or failure of technology is more dependent on human and contextual factors than on hardware or software. The extent to which teachers are given time and access to pertinent training, to use computers to support learning, plays a major role in determining whether or not technology has a positive impact on achievement. Students of teachers with more than 10 hours of training significantly outperformed students whose teachers had 5 or fewer hours of training.

- **Age and grade appropriateness:** In addition, best practices suggest that teachers also have to understand the developmental stages of their elementary, middle, and secondary students, and know that students need both structured and unstructured lessons. During the planning phase of every lesson, teachers should consider whether or not any technology or technological materials would be useful and appropriate for the lesson and for the age level and, if so, which materials would be best. As early as kindergarten or first grade, students are capable of searching for information, writing a letter to a friend, or using a drawing program to illustrate their stories. As they enter middle schools and high schools, students learn to make informed decisions about technologies and their applications through the study of technology applications foundations, including technology-related terms, concepts, and data input strategies. The efficient acquisition of information includes the identification of task requirements; the plan for using search strategies; and the uses of technology to access, analyze, and evaluate the acquired information. Most middle-grade elementary students enjoy working on electronic slide show presentations. The teacher must remember that in secondary schools, students seem to learn more when they initiate activity.

The Center of the Curriculum: The Students

Teachers should be aware that the technology needs and competence of children changes, over time, on a growth sequence. Children pass through several stages on their road to becoming literate consumers of technology.

Early Childhood to Primary Grades

Market researchers tracking software trends found that the largest software growth has been in new titles and companies serving the needs of early childhood education. Researchers suggest that computers can be used with children in kindergarten, preschool, or childcare settings; the computer should be one of many activity choices children can explore.

For example, a computer center may be one of several activity options in the room. Young children frequently use computers for short periods and then become interested in other activities. Researchers found that children 3- to 5-years of age spend about the same time at a computer as they do on other activities. For this age group, the value of the computer is in its open-ended use, not in creating a product. The teacher's role is to create an environment in which children become aware and explore, and then act to support a child's exploration and inquiry. Software programs for this age group should be appropriate for children's skill level and the intended use (Clements & Nastasi, 1992).

Some parents see computer competencies as a way for a young child to get a competitive jumpstart on their peers. Preparing a child to be computer capable is essential in the twenty-first century. Competency for students in lower grades might include basic skills such as starting up the computer and shutting it down, using the mouse, clicking on the appropriate icons, and following print instructions. The term "lapware" is used to describe the programs that teach young children the alphabet and spelling using sound, pictures, and video clips (Roderman, 2002). These products imitate early learning experiences, such as matching shapes and learning the alphabet.

Effective image use depends on knowing what images will be "readable" or understandable by those receiving them. Effective use means finding an image that contributes to making a point. In some cases, the visual image may be the only "word" on the page or screen and must do all the work. In some cases, the image may have just one word or one sentence with it. This is common with early reader books and advertising targeted to all ages.

In the primary grades, 5 to 8 years of age, as children become more able to read and write on their own, they are not limited to icons and pictures on the screen for understanding. More opportunities for independent use become available with increasing language and literacy skills. For example, simple word processors can now become important educational tools as children experiment with written language.

A study conducted at the Children's Digital Media Center of Georgetown University examined the effect of user control on content retention of 53 preschool-aged children using an online storybook (Calvert, Mahler, Zehnder, Jenkins, & Lee, 2003). Researchers found that when children controlled the mouse and progressed through the story, there was never a significant drop in attention. By contrast, children's attention declined when the adult controlled the mouse. In addition, researchers found that boys remembered visually presented content more than girls, and boys made more efforts to control the activity than girls did, particularly when adults were controlling the progress of the story (Calvert et al., 2003). These results suggest that control is an engagement feature that pulls children into an activity.

Adolescent Students

As students enter middle or high schools, their computer experiences continue to broaden along with developing reading and writing skills. The increasing curiosity, attention span, memory, and developing logic and problem-solving skills make for an increasingly more independent experience (Chen, Nath, & Parker, 2005). Students can remain focused with an activity longer, remember more about where things are and how to get where they want to go in a program, and they can enjoy a broader range of subjects and activities. Students now have the capacity to move from simple cause and effect experiences to lessons requiring problem-solving skills, creating illustrated stories and multimedia clips and graphics, and even using visual reference programs.

As student's cognitive skills develop, the text-heavy Internet becomes more comprehensible, and as their sense of the world broadens, e-mail and correspondence with children from far away places becomes both comprehensible and exciting.

Adolescent students should be able to use instructional software in several content areas, understand basic computer vocabulary, and show skills with paint and draw software and logical thinking programs. Secondary students' ability to follow longer multistep procedures allows them to use more complicated production programs to make slideshows, multimedia productions, even animations (Chen et al., 2005). The facility with the printer and other input and output devices gives them control over a wide range of creative "productions." Older students can compare all the media at a glance. They can discuss how real-world companies and organizations might decide on a particular media for their products or the information they wish to leave out. Older students can examine how the medium and the content work together to draw the audience in or leave the audience wondering, and so forth.

In the 1980s, industry trainers and vocational educators viewed educational technology as vocational training. They believed that an important function of school learning is to prepare students for the work force in which they use technology. They also believed that vocational training can be a practical means of teaching all content areas such as the 3Rs. This perspective of educational technology, also known as "technology education," has brought about a curriculum change in K-12 vocational education to technology education courses taught with high-technology computer work stations such as desktop publishing, electronic word processing, and computer-assisted drawing (CAD).

In secondary classrooms, the teacher's role is to set up a supportive learning environment and activities, matching software and hardware use to the curriculum as well as to the students' special needs and interests. The teacher is less involved in directing the activities, and more involved in monitoring and intervening, as necessary, to guide and pose questions that encourage thinking (Chen et al., 2005).

Creating and Using Age Appropriate Computer-Based Projects

When creating or using multimedia products, if the software is not age appropriate, students are likely to become frustrated and associate the computer with failure. Students with access to software that is not age appropriate may be exposed to negative influences such as violence, strong language, or over-stimulation from fast-action graphics.

To allow children to reap the greatest benefits from using technology, multimedia programs must be developmentally appropriate, that is, in line with the student's developmental learning stage, and must be able to support or extend the curriculum.

Multimedia development projects are often successful in that they involve students and faculty in the information creation cycle. The student plays the double role of active information producer and consumer. Table 3.1 summarizes students' technology skills as producers and consumers at key developmental points.

The International Society for Technology in Education (ISTE) has released a set of national standards by which educators can measure students' technology skills at key developmental points (Carroll & Witherspoon, 2002). Across the country, ISTE standards are adopted as competency standards. The NETS for Students were

Table 3.1. A summary of students' multimedia skills as producers at key developmental points

	Ages 4-7	Ages 8-11	Ages 12-14	Ages 15-18
Use simple multimedia programs	x	x	x	x
Downloading pictures and graphics for school reports		x	x	x
Putting together multimedia reports such as slideshows		x	x	x
Using graphic software to display data and extract quantitative relationships			x	x
Selecting and using appropriate technology devices		x	x	x

released by ISTE in June 1998, NETS for Teachers in June 2000, and NETS for Administrators (TSSA) in November 2001. As of 2002, at the state level, 49 of the 50 states have adopted, adapted, aligned with, or otherwise referenced at least one

Table 3.2. A summary of students NETS for Pre-Primary (Early Childhood)

	Pre-Primary (Grade K)
Terminology/Component-	• Use appropriate terminology to describe parts of computer and other technologies, (calculators, printers, scanners, VCRs) • Use appropriate terminology to describe parts of computer (mouse, keyboard, monitor)
Keyboarding-	• Participate in teacher-directed exploration of keyboard layout and keyboard concepts
Word Processing-	• Execute and utilize text within an appropriate program for an age-appropriate activity
Graphics-	• Use age-appropriate graphics software for a simple activity
Research -	• Participate in teacher directed exploration of primary reference programs (My First Picture Dictionary)

Table 3.3. A summary of students NETS for Primary—Grades 1, 2

	Primary -Grades 1, 2
Terminology/Component-	• Use appropriate terminology to describe parts of computer and other technologies (calculators, printers, scanners, VCRs) • Use appropriate terminology to describe parts of computer (mouse, keyboard, monitor)
Care/Operations-	• Demonstrate the proper care and safe use of equipment • Demonstrate use of keyboard and mouse functions • Demonstrate proper startup and closing procedures for a software package • Identify potential abuses to and proper care of hardware
Keyboarding-	• Participate in teacher-directed exploration of keyboard layout and keyboard concepts • Demonstrate understanding of keyboard layout.
Word Processing-	• Execute and utilize a word-processing program for an age-appropriate activity • Create, edit, and print a simple document

continued on next page

Table 3.3. continued

Graphics-	• Use age-appropriate graphics software to complete activity. • Produce an age-appropriate project using graphics or desktop publishing software
Multimedia-	• Produce an age-appropriate project using a multimedia program (ClarisWorks, HyperStudio, Kid Pix) that may include the following: text, graphics, sound, video, or simple animation
Research-	• Use CD-ROM or Internet-based primary reference sources • Use a teacher-chosen Internet site to locate information • Demonstrate use of online catalog system

Table 3.4. A summary of students NETS for Intermediate—Grades 3-5

Intermediate- Grades 3-5	
Terminology/Component-	• Use appropriate terminology to describe parts of computer and other technologies, (calculators, printers, scanners, VCRs) • Use appropriate terminology to describe parts of computer (mouse, keyboard, monitor) • Know difference in terms of hardware and software
Care/Operations-	• Demonstrate proper care and safe use of equipment • Demonstrate use of computer peripherals (printer, scanner, video in/out) • Demonstrate use of data storage practices (saving to floppy disk, zip disk, or network)
Keyboarding-	• Improve touch keyboarding speed and accuracy skills on home-row, numeric, and alphabetical keys
Word Processing-	• Use formatting procedures in word processing such as font type, font size, bold, italics, and so forth. • Use word processing features such as spell check, thesaurus, and copy/paste features
Graphics-	• Combine graphics into a word-processing document • Produce an age-appropriate project using a presentation program, a desktop publishing program, or a graphics program
Multimedia	• Produce an age-appropriate project using a multimedia program (ClarisWorks, HyperStudio, KidPix) that may include the following: text, graphics, sound, video, or simple animation • Produce an age-appropriate project using multimedia equipment as available (CD-ROMs, digital camera, scanner, or laserdiscs)

Continued on next page

Table 4. continued

Care/Operations-	• Demonstrate proper care and safe use of equipment • Demonstrate use of computer peripherals (printer, scanner, video in/out) • Demonstrate use of data storage practices (saving to floppy disk, zip disk, or network)
Problem Solving-	• Determine suitable software for projects • Determine computer and/or software suitability between platforms (Mac/Windows)
Research-	• Use of electronic primary reference sources • Use general electronic reference sources-dictionaries, encyclopedias, local and wide area networks, to access information from electronic databases • Demonstrate use of online catalog system • Use Internet addresses to access and bookmark appropriate Internet sites • Use search engines on Internet for classroom topics • Properly cite Internet resources (bibliography, footnotes, etc.) • Import Internet resources (graphics, sound, or video) to produce a research project.

set of standards in their state technology plans, certification, licensure, curriculum plans, assessment plans, or other official state documents. Tables 3.2, 3.3, and 3.4 contain summaries of ISTE recommended students' multimedia technology skills at key developmental points (n.d., 2000, 2002).

Technology Creates Opportunities for Learners with Special Needs

The terms "universal design" and "inclusive design" are sometimes used interchangeably in the literature. To find the subtle differences in meanings, universal design can be defined more narrowly than inclusive design to denote accessibility issues for people with physical, cognitive, or perceptual disabilities. Inclusive design, on the other hand, takes a user-centered approach, encompassing factors such as age, gender, experience, and ethnicity. Inclusive design is important for marginalized groups, such as learners with special disabilities, and language and cultural minority students, and it will end up benefiting all learners.

New access technology for special needs students will arise from the fast-paced development of innovative devices and technologies. Visual, kinesthetic, and audio activities dominate the education especially in the areas of spelling and grammar. Multimedia systems should eventually produce affordable and useful systems and services for people with special needs. Multimedia is of inherent interest to those with disabilities for two reasons:

It allows them to perceive what they might not otherwise be able to since it can gather information in a sensory modality in which they are impaired and deliver it to one where they are not.

Multimedia technology has to be adaptable to the individual senses and capabilities of the user if it is to provide a satisfactory illusion of reality. This means that well-designed multimedia products are inherently adaptable to a wide range of individual needs.

Key applications are shown, with respect to the impairment to which they apply, where multimedia can make a significant contribution to the development technology for people with special needs.

Visual Impairment

Most traditional curricula force students to read and write in every subject. Technology derived from multimedia, such as sophisticated forms of auditory and tactile imaging, may help people with visual impairments see and use computing systems. This could could be accomplished by providing an alternative access method for the GUIs that are increasingly found on modern personal computers. Vision correction devices can electronically process an image derived from a head mounted camera before delivering it to the eye. This can enable objects to be magnified, edges to be given higher contrast, or important information to be delivered to unimpaired parts of the visual field. Images can be relayed to a sighted person at a remote location, if necessary.

According to most researches, more than 8% of the male and about 0.04% of the female population have some sort of color anomaly or deficiency. Most visual impairments have physiological causes (Gage, 2000). Those individuals who show drastic deficiencies in their ability to discriminate colored stimuli are called colorblind, although this term is too strong for most of the deficiencies.

Recent ADA legislation in the United States (the Americans with Disabilities Act) requires high contrasts between light and dark colors on all signage, so that the visually disabled can see the information.

Hearing Impairment

With multimedia, speech can be represented as gesture or text; other sounds can be represented graphically. Ideally, captioning should be provided for those who have hearing impairments and audio description of the visual content should be provided for those who are visually impaired. Automated recognition of 3-D gestures, such as the sign language used by deaf people, can be used to aid communication by providing translations from gesture to speech or vice versa. Video images of people gesturing can be converted into simpler formats before being transmitted over a relatively low bandwidth link. By removing unnecessary information from the signal, the remaining data can be displayed with higher resolution.

Motor Impairment

Some special needs students struggle with fine motor skills. Multimedia techniques can also be used through compensation of motor and sensory deficits, allowing a disabled person to explore and manipulate learning or new environments. It therefore has the potential to be used as a learning tool and training aid for skills such as spatial coordination and orientation. For instance, VR environments could be used to aid physiotherapy in areas such as the teaching of balance skills, throwing and catching, and so on.

Cognitive Accessibility for Students with Intellectual Impairment

Universal design aims to create products and environments that are accessible to people with cognitive challenges, as well as physical ones. Cognitive accessibility is the super layer of strategies and methods that help any learner or user understand or cognitively integrate and interface with the content (Roberts, 2004).

Intellectual Impairment

Students with all types of learning styles or learning difficulties can be helped by multimedia, which can remove the complexity often found in the initial stages of learning. For example, to help visual learners, new abstract concepts, such as written words, can be paired with realistic representations of the real-world objects or events they represent. Multimedia techniques, such as VR environments, can be combined with knowledge-based systems to help those who have problems with cognitive tasks such as remembering events and names.

The applications vary substantially in terms of their technical difficulty and in terms of the degree to which they are suitable for providing access to telecommunications services. Most of the applications of virtual reality that have been proposed for people with special needs could potentially be networked.

Cultural and Language Minorities

Culture has a huge impact on learning because culture pervades learning, with respect to factors such as language and semantics, learning style differences, and educational values. Learners who are from a different culture than the dominant Western perspective may experience a variety of difficulties in learning situations. McLoughlin (2001) classifies cultural minority students' learning problems into three categories: sociocultural adjustment, language issues, and teaching and learning issues relating to different expectations and perspectives on learning. They may be self-conscious of language differences, and therefore reluctant to participate in oral discussions.

As stated previously in this chapter, colors have different meanings in different cultures. The Eurocentric notion of the study of science, something to be dissected, segmented, measured, analyzed, deduced, and recorded, is different from an Aboriginal view of nature: holistic, and to be understood through experience (King, 1991). Children's software sometimes personifies animals, which is culturally insensitive to Muslims. Reeves (1997) advocated collaborating with members of the intended audience to prevent cultural insensitivities in instruction. Designing culturally sensitive material is not easily accomplished, though. Multimedia designers can unintentionally use something culturally inappropriate.

Advantages of Using Technology for Learning

Most teachers hold the general perception that computers have improved the climate for learning, especially by increasing student motivation. Moreover, technology seems to increase students' confidence in writing and creative initiative in art and music (Howard & Taylor, 2005). According to Roblyer (2005), many educators recognize and use technology applications and see the powerful capabilities they offer to enhance classroom learning:

Motivation: One of the most important characteristics of educational computer software is its ability to encourage students to be proactive learners. Computer software offers such varied options that most students seem to enjoy using them. Students who frequently struggle to complete a project on paper often will tackle computer projects enthusiastically. Technology-based approaches are effectively used to gain learner attention, engage the learner through production work, and increase learners' perception of control.

Unique instructional capabilities: Teachers can now offer learners a vast array of learning tools through a variety of educational software. Educational software offers the student diverse ways to learn, and provides opportunities for choice and control during the learning process. With hyperlinks and the World Wide Web, learners can be linked to information sources as never before. Software and hardware, such as simulations, virtual reality, and problem-solving tools, help learners visualize problems and solutions. In addition, intelligent tutorials and testing programs can be used to track learner progress.

Support for new instructional approaches: As education changes to reflect new social and educational needs, teaching strategies have changed accordingly. Educators have now begun to use technology to support the active learning initiatives found within cooperative learning, shared intelligence, problem solving, and higher order thinking.

Problem solving: Technology should be used by the teacher as a facilitating tool. Computer skills should be taught within the context of what students are learning in order to enhance the meaningfulness of the learning process. When students understand how technology can enhance their content area knowledge or skills in some way, the rationale for learning technology becomes self-evident. Therefore, it is important for teachers to incorporate technology in problem-solving and decision-making situations. Educational software packages can be found that address both of these views through games, simulations, puzzles, and so forth. This software can also be found by searching keyword descriptors, such as critical thinking, higher-order outcomes, decision making, problem solving, and thinking skills, on the Internet. Of course, this type of software should be reviewed to ensure that it is age appropriate and that it matches the specific concept or skill being taught. Roblyer provides several helpful suggestions for helping to integrate problem-solving software within the classroom (2005):

1. Allow students sufficient time to explore and interact with the software, but provide some structure in the form of directions, goals, a work schedule, and organized times for sharing and discussing results.
2. Vary the amount of direction and assistance, depending on each student's needs.
3. Promote a reflective learning environment; let students talk about their work and the methods they use.
4. Stress thinking processes rather than correct answers.
5. Point out the relationship of courseware skills and activities to other kinds of problem solving.
6. Let students work together in pairs, whole group, or small groups.
7. Use alternatives to traditional paper-and-pencil tests; incorporate authentic assessment measures.

Teachers can also encourage problem solving and exploration when students have computer dilemmas. For example, teachers can "come to the rescue" whenever a student asks for help in finding tools or manipulating the computer in some way, or they can encourage students to search for themselves, experiment a bit, and/or use the internal computer or online help. However, teachers should remember that young people can sometimes become easily frustrated and should be monitored carefully.

Teachers recognize that technology should be a facilitating tool. Computer skills that are taught in context with what students are learning are always more meaningful to the learning process. When students understand how technology can enhance their content area knowledge or skills in some way, the rationale for learning technology becomes self-evident. Therefore, teachers should incorporate technology in classroom problem-solving and decision-making situations. Teachers can locate software packages that address both of these views through games, simulations, and puzzles, and so forth, or by descriptors such as critical thinking, higher-order outcomes, decision making, problem solving, and thinking skills. Of course, this software must be reviewed to ensure that the keywords listed on a package really match the skill(s) in which they are interested in teaching, that it is a match with the curriculum, and that it is age appropriate. Roblyer suggests that teachers implement problem-solving courseware in these steps (2005):

1. Allow students sufficient time to explore and interact with the software, but provide some structure in the form of directions, goals, a work schedule, and organized times for sharing and discussing results.
2. Vary the amount of direction and assistance, depending on each student's needs.
3. Promote a reflective learning environment; let students talk about their work and the methods they use.
4. Stress thinking processes rather than correct answers.
5. Point out the relationship of courseware skills and activities to other kinds of problem solving.
6. Let students work together in pairs or small groups.
7. For assessments, use alternatives to traditional paper-and-pencil tests.

The philosophy of technology integration directs teachers to provide a restructured technology setting that includes problem solving. Grabe and Grabe (2000) explain this restructured setting by describing the role of learner and the instructor. In this setting, (a) students will create personal knowledge by acting on content provided by teachers, media resources, and personal experiences. (b) The teacher functions as a facilitator, guide, and learner, (c) students work cooperatively, (d) assessment of knowledge is through application, and (e) technology is used as a source of information for interpretation and original knowledge creation.

Instructional Software

The instructional software can be integrated into the classroom to enhance teaching and learning in many ways. The followings are five common courseware categories (Simkins, Cole, Tavalin, & Means, 2002):

Drills and practice: Drills and practices is software designed to allow the user to practice a skill that has already been acquired or taught. A common type of drill and practice software involves practicing math skills such as multiplying two-digit numbers. There are thousands of drill and practice programs that teach everything from math facts to foreign languages and many other basic skills.

Educational games: Computer games are a type of direct instruction program that can be adapted for use as a preparatory activity. Many types of interesting games are available. They generally involve a scenario such as saving a planet or discovering a treasure through knowledge and understanding of some skill. There are some collaborative efforts by scientists, educators, and professional video game and educational software developers who have come together to do research on and develop teaching materials that integrate games and computer-based explorations with learning. Their research activities focus on the human-computer interaction issues associated with learning in an electronic game environment. Specific topics include studying which game formats (fast-action, simulations, puzzles, etc.) can be used to carry math-science educational content, formats that are most attractive to students, and formats that are most conducive to learning. These researchers are also studying how to integrate electronic game learning with more traditional classroom learning environments, the effect of collaborative play, how collaborative work can be incorporated into electronic games, and the role of mediation by teachers.

Tutorials: Whereas drill and practice software is designed to provide a way to practice a skill that has already been learned, tutorial software is designed to teach the skill initially by direct instruction methods. While tutorial software may include elements of drill and practice and assessment, it is unique in that it presents new information and may even provide an independent teaching environment without a teacher. In its purest form, tutorial software is the embodiment of the "teaching machine." The software takes the learner through a sequence of steps by presenting a new idea, concept, or task; providing feedback on the student's response; and finally, directing the learner to a different sequence based on his or her performance.

Simulations: Simulations can be described as imitations of life, often using materials and roles to help participants experience as well as understand the dynamics of a complex situation (Alessi & Trollip, 2001). The computer can act as the simulation controller, scheduling the events to occur and providing the outcomes based on actions the role players take. Because of this, the game can be played in regulated time or in real time. There are many simulations where playing in real time rather than accelerated time would be beneficial to enhancing the realism. Because people can interact at a time of their own choosing, a computer-based simulation can extend over days, weeks, or months.

Problem solving: Problem solving is a relatively sophisticated mental ability that is difficult to learn. This software teaches specific steps for solving certain problems, thereby, encouraging students to learn problem-solving skills, in general.

Fortunately, many Web sites cater to problem solving for middle and secondary students. The inquiry-based format of WebQuest is a new alternative to the traditional lesson plan format.

Value Systems of Technology Integration

Research shows that among teachers who use technology in traditional ways, such as direct instruction, drill-and-practice programs are still in the majority (Howard & Taylor, 2005). However, it is important to remember that a worksheet is a worksheet, be it on paper or the computer.

Jones, Valdez, Nowakowski, and Rasmussen (1995) suggested three distinct phases in technology uses and expectations: print automation, expansion of learning opportunities, and data-driven virtual learning:

In **Phase I**, instruction was characterized by the use of behavioral-based branching software that relied heavily on drill and practice to teach segmented content and/or skills.

During **Phase II**, computers became tools for learner-centered practices rather than content delivery systems, helping teachers move from largely isolated learning activities to applications that involved working in groups.

Phase III carries with it the additional expectation of making schools more effective through the use of data-driven decision making of a much more sophisticated nature than previously expected. Ideally, both teachers and students have access to data and use it to meet accountability expectations.

Whereas traditional categorizations, such as the three phrases discussed are descriptive, Maddux, Johnson, and Willis (2001) claimed the Type I and Type II clarification system that they propose "embodies an educational value system judgment" (p. 99). Since the 1980s, Maddux, Johnson, and Willis have attempted to categorize all educational computing as either Type I or Type II applications (Eastmond & Granger, 1998).

Maddux, et al. defined Type I application as software that is designed to make it easier, quicker, or otherwise more efficient to continue teaching topics in the same ways they have always been taught. Type I applications include the use of technology for drill and practice, tutorials, assessment, as well as administrative tasks, and computer-managed instruction.

In contrast, Type II applications make available new and better ways of teaching, and are treated as more important and more significant ways to use technology in education (Maddux et al., 2001). Type II applications include word processing, electronic spreadsheets, database management, programming language, simulations, problem solving, computers as prosthetic aides for the handicapped, and telecommunications. Type II applications can function as intellectual partners with the learner, in order to engage and facilitate critical thinking and higher-order learning. Effective Type II applications are also generalizable computer tools that are intended to engage and facilitate cognitive processing. Virtually all the examples given for Type II applications can be used in ways that are much more traditional and standard, in other words, Type I uses.

Changes and Diffusion of Instructional Technology

Recently, several researchers have suggested that technology can serve as a catalyst to change content area teaching and for enhancing students' ability to learn specific content. The literature indicates that technology influences content areas in the following ways (Jones et al., 1995).

- Hypertext and hypermedia add depth, elaboration, and interactivity to content through associative, audio, dynamic visuals, and video texts that affect the nature of reading and writing across the curriculum.
- Interactivity of computers allows for adapting content to meet individual student needs.
- Computer-mediated communication patterns differ from verbal face-to-face communication patterns traditionally found in disciplinary discourse about information, more widely disseminating the locus of control from the teacher to students.

- Telecommunications and the Internet provide access to emerging disciplinary and interdisciplinary databases, real-time phenomena, and social communities not accessible through print-based curricula.
- Computers and ancillary electronic devices facilitate the manipulation of data and the visualization processes invisible to the human eye or beyond human memory capacity, which assists with experimenting and understanding actual, futuristic, and hypothetical concepts, principles, relationships, and probabilities.
- Computers in classrooms can be used as "an alternative pencil and paper" or as "a true cognitive tool" to engage and enhance thinking and manage information in ways that allow users to think more clearly, creatively, and critically; thus allowing users to organize information in new ways, in order to evaluate and construct personally meaningful representations.

Educators as Life-Long Learners

Technology innovations increase the demand for reforms in teaching and learning approaches that, in turn, have a significant impact on technology-use expectations for teachers. Most educators agree that the primary objective of computer literacy for teachers should be to make people comfortable with computers. Technology application teachers should be able to operate them, know their applications, and understand the ethics involving the use and misuse of computers.

Technology innovations also make it important for teachers to keep current with the latest instructional technology through journals, trade shows, and conferences. Through these means, teachers can also collaborate with others on how to best use online support systems such as the Global SchoolHouse. Sponsored by Microsoft, the Global SchoolHouse (http://www.gsh.org/) offers a wide variety of opportunities for educators to stay current with the use of technology in the classroom. Global SchoolHouse offers listservs and tasks for educators to learn in electronic communities or self-directed activities. Among the popular topics sought after by educators are:

- How to help students and peers learn to use a "library without walls."
- How to provide help with topics beyond the student or teacher's range of knowledge.
- How to communicate with colleagues throughout the country and world.
- How to design and manage collaborative classroom projects on the Internet.
- How to use the Internet to solve problems in a team setting.

- How to expand knowledge and retrieve information in areas of interest.
- How to use the tools of the Internet.
- What are the ethics of access, copyright, network structures, and censorship?

Overall, the literature addressing how technology enhances and/or changes disciplines or content areas indicates that teachers and students will need to know how to select and use electronic resources that provide (1) the core content for a given curricular area, (2) the interactive supports that adapt content to the individual's developmental and/or learning style needs, and (3) open-ended tools that allow teachers and students to modify content for contextual purposes (Lee & Owens, 2000). It is common for teachers to keep current with the latest instructional technology through reading journals, attending conferences and workshops, or by subscribing to relevant listservs.

The integration of computers into schools has resulted in far-reaching, innovative changes. The increasing use of computers now requires schools across the nation to alter the curriculum, and has forced educators to vary teaching methods. Today, it is pertinent that teachers become knowledgeable about the innovative ways that computers can enhance education, since they play a large role in modern society.

References

Alessi, S. M., & Trollip, S. R. (2001). *Multimedia for learning: Methods and development* (3rd ed.). Boston: Allyn and Bacon.

Calvert, S. L., Mahler, B.A., Zehnder, S.M., Jenkins, A., & Lee, M. (2003). Gender differences in preadolescent children online interactions: Symbolic modes of self-presentation and self-expression. *Journal of Applied Developmental Psychology, 24*, 627-644.

Carroll, J., & Witherspoon, T. (2002). *Linking technology and curriculum: Integrating the ISTE NETS standards into teaching and learning* (2nd ed..). Upper Saddle River, NY: Merrill Prentice Hall.

Chen, L. I, Nath, L. J.. & Parker, E. M. (2005). Using technology in the middle school and high school classroom. In J. Nath & M. Cohen (Eds.), *Becoming a middle school or high school teacher in Texas* (pp. 309-350). Belmont, CA: Wadsworth/Thomson Learning.

Clements, D. H., & Nastasi, B. K. (1992). Computers and early childhood education. In M. Gettinger, S. N. Elliott, & T. R. Kratochwill (Ed.), *Advances in school psychology: Preschool and early childhood treatment directions* (pp. 187-246). Hillsdale, NJ: Lawrence Erlbaum Associates.

Eastmond, D., & Granger, D. (1998). Using Type II computer network technology to reach distance students. *Distance Education Report, 2*(3), 1-3.

Gage, J. (2000). *Color and meaning: Art, science, and symbolism.* Berkeley: University of California Press.

Grabe, M., & Grabe, C. (2000). *Integrating the Internet for meaningful learning.* Boston: Houghton Mifflin.

Howard S., & Taylor, L. (2005). *The implementation guide to student learning supports in the classroom and schoolwide: New directions for addressing barriers to learning.* Thousand Oaks, CA: Corwin Press.

International Society for Technology in Education (n.d.). *NETS_T: Educational technology standards and performance indicators for all teachers.* Retrieved June 18, 2007, from http://cnets.iste.org/teachers/index.shtml

International Society for Technology in Education. (2000). *National educational technology standards for teachers and students: Connecting curriculum and technology.* Eugene, OR: ISTE.

International Society for Technology in Education. (2002). *National educational technology standards for teachers: Preparing teachers to use technology.* Eugene, OR: ISTE.

Jones, B. F., Valdez, G., Nowakowski, J., & Rasmussen, C. (1995). *Plugging in: Choosing and using education technology.* Oak Brook, IL: North Central Regional Educational Laboratory. Retrieved June 18, 2007, from http://www.ncrtec.org/capacity/plug/plug.htm

King, C. (1991). Indian world view and time. In E. J. McCullough & R. L. Calder (Eds.), *Time as a human resource* (pp. 183-187). Calgary: The University of Calgary Press.

Lee, W. W., & Owens, D. L. (2000). *Multimedia-based instructional design: Computer-based training, Web-based training, and distance learning.* San Francisco: Pfeiffer.

Maddux, C., Johnson, D. L., & Willis, J. (2001). *Educational computing: Learning with tomorrow's technologies* (3rd ed.). Needham Heights, MA: Allyn and Bacon.

McLoughlin, C. (1999). The implications of the research literature on learning styles for the design of instructional material. *Australian Journal of Educational Technology, 15*(3), 222-241.

Reeves, T. C. (1997). An evaluator looks at cultural diversity. *Educational Technology, 37*(2), 27-31.

Roberts, S. (n.d.). *Instructional design and accessibility: Cognitive curb cuts.* Retrieved June 18, 2007, from http://www.aect.org/Divisions/roberts.htm

Roblyer, M. D. (2005). *Integrating educational technology into teaching* (3rd ed.). Upper Saddle River, NJ: Merrill - Prentice Hall.

Roderman, L. (2002). *Technology and the very young: Lapware, smart toys, and beyond.* Retrieved June 18, 2007, from http://www.cpsr.org/prevsite/essays/2002/2ed11.html

Simkins, M., Cole, K. Tavalin, F., & Means, B. (2002). *Increasing student learning through multimedia projects.* Alexandria, VA: Association for Supervision & Curriculum Development (ASCD).

Statham, D. S., & Torell, C. R. (1996). *Computers in the classroom: The impact of technology on student learning.* Boise, ID: U.S. Army Research Institute and Boise State University.

Sample Questions

1. A teacher decides to integrate the WWW into his finance & math class. One desirable feature of the integration is:
   a. Self-grade function of the Web site
   b. Strong problem solving support of the Web site
   c. The Web site gives plenty of examples
   d. The Web site provides a working calendar

2. Of the following, which is the best way for teachers to keep current with the latest instructional technology?
   a. Journals
   b. Trade shows
   c. Buying new software
   d. Request new hardware

3. How can teachers determine if technology is integrated effectively into the curriculum and classroom activities?
   a. Students seem pleased and satisfied with the work they are doing.
   b. Students spend more time on the task than they otherwise would have.
   c. It would be difficult to do the activity if the technology weren't there.
   d. Computer activities are clearly separated from noncomputer ones.

4. Of the following, which resource helps support students' understanding of scientific concepts by allowing them to engage in scientific phenomena that otherwise would be difficult to visualize?
   a. Simulation
   b. Database
   c. Avatars
   d. Controlled disc-read over medium

5. Which of the following is NOT a characteristic of effective teacher training with technology?
    a. Having instructors who model the technology methods they are teaching
    b. Allowing teachers to select the desired computer platform for their training
    c. Assuring that teachers have access to technology resources after training
    d. Providing technology training over time rather than just once or twice
    e. Distribute CD-ROMs with tutorials

Answers: (1) B (2) A (3) C (4) A (5) E

Section II

Digital Graphics/Animation and Desktop Publishing

Chapter IV
The Principles and Applications of Digital Design

ISTE NETS_T, II. Planning and designing learning environments and experiences.

Teachers plan and design effective learning environments and experiences supported by technology.

ISTE NETS_T, III. Teaching, learning, and the curriculum.

Teachers implement curriculum plans that include methods and strategies for applying technology to maximize student learning.

Chapter objective: The teacher demonstrates knowledge of the principles of design and their application to digital graphics/animation products.

Educational Relevance of Graphics and Animations

In today's world, visual communications are everywhere. It is important for educators to have knowledge of how to use and produce visual graphics. The use of graphics and animations in schools can range from producing district bulletins and reports to posting a school bulletin board to the middle school Web site. Teachers must also help students learn to use a wide range of technological equipment. In schools, students use a variety of cameras—from tiny digital cameras that replace the traditional 35-mm film cameras to larger and more sophisticated digital cameras the local paper uses to capture graduation ceremonies and football victories for tomorrow's edition. This chapter focuses on the various uses of graphics and animations in today's classroom. Specific information is provided that details the use of digital cameras in schools. Specific examples of creative projects that incorporate graphics and photographs are also provided throughout the chapter.

It is important in today's classroom that students learn to enhance their learning through creative projects and reports that incorporate graphics and animation. Students can apply this enhanced technological knowledge to a wide range of projects. A few types of student projects are listed as follows:

- **Neighborhood life:** Student organizations can take pictures that capture life in the neighborhood: or they can create a map or a guidebook illustrated with photographs of important landmarks that show the things a visitor should not miss. The images can then be incorporated into a printed publication or integrated into a Web site the entire community can view.
- **Role models and career projects**: Students can explore a career that interests them by investigating the work of a role model. Interviews and visits to offices and worksites can be documented with digital pictures as well as diagrams, charts, and other types of illustrations. The results can be a visual display, a report, or a Web site.
- **Nature study:** Students may want to capture digital images of the animals found within their neighborhood, or images of their school campus. They can use the images to create a printed or electronic guidebook to the recorded plant or animal life.
- **Changes over time studies:** How do things change over time? Photographic studies using time-lapse digital photography are a great way to study everything from the sprouting of a butterbean, the emergence of a caterpillar, the growth of an infant, the flooding of a river, or the change of seasons. Students are able to view how quickly an image they are studying can change over time by taking pictures at regular intervals to record the change.

- **Digital storytelling:** Students may wish to take a series of photos that tell a story without words.

Graphics can also be used to enhance student learning. Graphic images, used in student presentations, multimedia projects, or Web pages, can be used to enhance learning and increase student interest. Graphics can originate from a variety of sources such as:

- Painting programs
- Drawing programs
- Graphics from the Web
- Clipart collections
- Digital camera images
- Scanners

With access to a range of computer software programs, teachers can show students how to incorporate different types of images into documents and presentations, and create their own or change existing graphics. Students can be taught to import both digital images and photographs into computer programs, edit the images for slideshows, presentations, Web sites, or printed documents, make high quality color prints, or export the graphic files to a CD or DVD. Any image in a computer, or from a scanner, or from a digital camera, is a potential candidate for inclusion in lessons ranging from rain forests to the Battle of Gettysburg. Digital files are files that a computer can manipulate. Images have to be "digitized," a process that converts the image into tiny dots or "picture elements" (pixels) represented in the computer by numbers. It is important to note that many computer programs have been developed just for creating, editing, and manipulating digital image files.

Teachers also need to help students understand the difference between "still images," (images that are static and do not change) and animated images. For example, an animated drawing can begin with a drawing of a set of parts strewn around a workshop, but changes as each part of the car drawing moves quickly into place. The final image of a completed automobile culminates as an animated drawing.

The effect of animation is accomplished by creating a series of individual images (known as frames or panels) and stringing them together in a timed sequence to give the appearance of continuous motion. CAD (computer-aided design) and CAM (computer-aided manufacturing) programs are just two of the many types of programs that create animation. These motion files can be either in 2-D or 3-D formats. Animation software enables the user to transform still images smoothly from one shape to another. This technique offers tremendous potential for artistic expression and helps foster the development of visual literacy skills. In general, animations attract more "wows" from the audience than most other multimedia effects. There are many methods for adding animation to images. Some animations are created specifically to run on Web sites, others are designed to be embedded in online documents, and still others will be part of an animated cartoon or movie.

Recently, *Time* magazine included a set of pictures on the cover that came from a program that took the pictures of young male and female Americans from different ethnic groups and showed how their child might look. These images of the child were created with a "morphing" program, which is a special form of animation program that takes two images and morphs them into a third image. Morphing is also used in sophisticated animation programs to allow artists to specify the beginning and end images, and then lets the software create a short animation that goes from the beginning to ending. Many television advertisements today use this type of animation. In schools, animation programs can create many types of graphics files with names like GIF, PNG, JPG, and so on. There are also many types of animated graphics files; the most popular type is animated GIF, a new type of file called rich media animation.

Paint Programs

Students need to know that when working with graphics programs, the first step should involve planning. There are a number of sources for images, and there is no substitute for first creating a rough sketch of the graphics to be used and the page layout desired for a project. Still images can be imported into many types of projects, from a PowerPoint presentation on the life of Shakespeare to an ad announcing parent's night for the school newspaper.

There are two fundamentally different ways of creating and storing graphical information on a computer. These two ways are similar to painting and drawing with paint brushes and drawing pens. One common feature for both paint and draw programs is the use of toolboxes with a palette of action buttons. Some of these tool palettes are tear-off palettes that can be moved by the mouse to a convenient spot on the monitor. The action buttons on the palettes let the user perform a number of functions very simply; other programs require the user to wade through endless dialog boxes to achieve the same results. An example of a paint program on the Widows Operating System is *PaintShop Pro,* found in the MS *Paint* of Windows operating system. Other similar programs can be found in *Appleworks* and *Clarisworks* on the Macintosh operating system.

Four shape tools are common with most Paint programs: rectangle tools, polygon tools, ellipse tool, and the rounded rectangle tool. Shape tools are all very similar in features and can draw three types of shapes: outline, filled with outline, and filled without outline. The interior of the outline shape is transparent, whereas the filled types fill the shape with a background color.

An advantage of paint programs is that they make it easy to extract a piece of an image for use elsewhere, as an object in a draw program. The products of paint programs can also be saved as bit maps. Bitmaps are one of the most commonly compatible types of image formats. With bit maps, images are laid out in pixels, much like dots of paint on a canvas. As such, bitmap objects are not independent entities, which can be singled out for manipulation, but patterned series of dots. Simply stated, bit maps are stored patterns of colored dots (pixels on the screen). They are not resizable without degradation of image quality. It is best to always use bit map graphics at their original size. Bit maps potentially require a lot of storage space because of the number of pixels involved. Images stored this way can be compressed with techniques. Bitmap graphics created with paint programs can be stored in the formats with file extensions such as .bmp or .jpg. Other file formats include: imb, dib, fig, mtx, pcx, tif, tga, wpg, and cur.

Draw Programs

There are inescapable complexities in the world of graphics. Work with graphics requires both a paint program and a draw program. Paint programs provide the user with the ability to work with the single picture elements, the pixels. Users get fine control, but changing size forces an approximation. Draw programs avoid this problem by working with shapes. Users can freely change the size of a square, circle, or line because these shapes are stored as "formulas." Even letters like "A" and "a" are stored as "formulas" and can be resized.

Another distinct feature for paint or draw programs is layering. Layering is a must when creating complex drawings. Most high-end draw programs support multiple-layer control, or layering. This feature lets users place objects or groups of objects on separate layers so that they can show and hide the objects or work on them separately.

An advantage of draw programs is that they make it easy to create compact yet resizable graphics. The products of draw programs can be saved as vector graphics. Vector graphics are stored as mathematical descriptions of sets of lines, triangles, squares, circles, and so forth, with defined line thickness, line colors, and fill colors. Vector graphics consist of objects, each of which can be separately manipulated, such as sized, moved, grouped or ungrouped, and positioned to the back/front. The graphic components are calculated; hence can be sized without distortion. Because vector graphics are stored as mathematical objects, they are resizable and will always be displayed neatly whatever the user's screen resolution or browser window size. They will also print out in nice quality on higher resolution printers.

There is no separate draw program that is shipped with the Windows Operating System. A drawing component is available, however, through the Drawing tool bar in MS *Word* and MS *PowerPoint*. To display the Drawing toolbar in MS *Word*'s pull-down menu, go through View then Toolbars. The Drawing Toolbar with MS *Office* provides many commands for creating and editing graphics. The toolbar can be activated by selecting View -> Toolbars -> Drawing from the menu bar.

Separate images have their own set of selector handles. With grouping, images can be grouped together so they become one image and can be moved together, or the same formatting changes can be applied to both at once. To select all the images that will be grouped, hold down the SHIFT key and click once on each image. Then select Group from the Draw menu. The images can be ungrouped by selecting Ungroup from the same menu.

The order of overlapping images can be changed using the Order feature on the Drawing toolbar. The Send Backward command can be used to move the image below the next image. Send Backward and Bring Forward will move elements by one layer. Send to Back and Bring to Front moves the element to the back or top of a series of several overlapping graphics.

WordArt can create special effects on text from either the Insert ->Picture->WordArt menu or by a mouse click on the Insert WordArt Drawing toolbar icon. Select a WordArt style from the dialog box of premade shapes to apply in your document. The Edit WordArt Text dialog box will open in order for the user to enter the text or make changes.

Besides rectangle, ellipse, and other basic shapes, there are additional shapes available on the AutoShapes menu. To access these shapes, click AutoShapes from the Drawing toolbar, position the mouse on a category, and click the desired shape.

Here are additional interesting features on the Drawing toolbar:

- **Shadow:** Select a text box to add shadow to text or choose an object to add a drop shadow.
- **3-D:** Add a three-dimensional effect to text and objects.
- **Nudge:** Use the nudge actions to move an object slightly in one direction.
- **Align or Distribute:** Select a group of objects and choose one of the commands from the Align or Distribute menu to change the position of the objects in relation to one another.
- **Rotate or Flip:** Rotate an object 90 degrees or flip the object.

Many commercial applications of the paint or draw concepts create bit maps and vector images. Some industry standard vector-based drawing programs include FreeHand, Illustrator, and Photoshop from Adobe, and Fireworks from Macromedia. Professional-grade graphic editing software may be needed for more sophisticated graphic editing tasks.

Professional grade graphic editing software uses a palette system to control the behavior of tools. Here is a list of commonly used palettes:

- **History:** The History palette records and displays individual changes made to an image and allows users to undo them. Every time a change is made, the software saves the changed state of the image in the History palette. Users can also delete unwanted changes and view the state of the image before and after the change.
- **Swatches:** The Swatches palette displays the color table for the image file that is currently open. To add a new color to the Swatches palette, use the eyedropper tool to select a color from the Color palette or from the image.

Selecting the exact area of an image to edit is of primary importance. Once the user makes a selection, only the area within the selection can be edited; areas outside the selection are immune to change. There are four commonly used selection tools with professional-grade graphic editing software programs:

- The marquee tool allows users to select rectangular or elliptical areas in an image.
- The lasso tool allows users to draw a freehand selection area, with either curves or straight lines.
- The move tool allows users to move a selection marquee or objects on a single layer.
- The magic wand tool allows users to select parts of an image based on color similarities of adjacent pixels.

In addition to the different output file formats, layering is another distinct feature for paint or draw programs. Paint programs provide a single image layer. If images are placed over other images, they replace the original images. An advantage of paint programs is that it is easy to cut or extract a piece of an image for use elsewhere, often as an object in a draw program. Fortunately, when using this feature, images that do not appear to be in layers often were composed in layers. Sliding an upper layer to one side can reveal composition parts that were once hidden. When working in this manner, each layer is treated as an object. Each new image element brought into a composition becomes the topmost layer until the user rearranges the layers in the stack. A draw program can overlap and rearrange (reorder the stack) any number of layers from a paint program in addition to creating additional layers on its own. The dialog box allows the user to set the initial opacity of the layer, which controls how much of lower layers are revealed. It is important to note that each layer really only forms a part of the final image. The final image will be composed of all of the layers within the image depending on the order of the layers and the transparency levels that are set for each layer.

Most collage images were created using this concept. For example, all the elements displayed on *PowerPoint* slides are also objects in layers, but this seldom is noticeable

Another important feature is that users can work on each object as if it were an independent image without interference from any graphical elements on other layers. Since an adjustment layer does not make permanent changes to the underlying image pixels, the image can be modified a number of times without degrading image quality. The objects can be hidden or discarded at any time, or moved up and down in the layers palette. When users achieve the desired on-screen result, the image can then be merged or flattened into a single image in order to compress the size; this also makes exporting easier.

Generally, in order to use an image file in an environment outside of the original programs, it must be flattened and saved as a GIF, JPEG, or other file type. Vector graphics created with software programs often have the file extension .WMF. Other file formats include AutoCAD DXF, CBM, EPS, HGL, PIC, DRW, and WPG (White, 2002)

It is important to note that the multilayered graphic files, such as PSD or PDD, are not readable by most other programs. In order to make changes to the images at a later time, users may want to store the master copy of all of their images in draw program's proprietary format, such as Photoshop PSD format, which allows layer information to be preserved.

Another important feature available to users is a plug-in program that offers the user enhanced graphic effects. Plug-ins are third-party software products that extend the capabilities of professional grade graphic editors. There are countless plug-in programs that provide for the enhancement or change of an image beyond the already comprehensive set of tools that comes with the existing program, such as Photoshop. Special effects created by popular plug-ins include 3-D effects, drop caps, shadows, and additional text effects.

Graphics from the Web

Download from the Web

Quite often, users find graphic images from the Web that they wish to incorporate within their work. In order for the user to copy an image on a Web page, the user must follow some basic commands. On a Macintosh computer, the user should hold the mouse button down on a Web page image for a couple of seconds and a menu should appear with a command to copy the image to the clipboard in order to paste it into another document. On the other hand, a user with a Windows computer should right click the image, and from this menu copy the image to the clipboard in order to paste it in some other file. For either operating system, another option would be to save it to a disk or drive as a file and then later insert the file into the place it is needed. Please refer to Chapter 11 for further information on this topic.

Image Archives on the Web

Most popular search engine systems offer a large number of image links. A common way to find image archives on the Web is by clicking the tab or button for images, enter search key words (e.g., rain forest), then scrolling through the images that are presented in thumbnail sets (e.g., 20 at a time). The user must then click a selected thumbnail picture in order to enlarge the image and record the Web site from which the image originated. An example of a search engine system that allows the user to search by image is alltheweb.com.

From Clipart Collections

It is often necessary for students to browse images found in collections in order to use images to enhance their work. Clipart is specifically designed for this purpose. Clipart collections are groups of pictures or photographs, cartoons, icons, and buttons, all sorted into subgroups. Companies like Microsoft have collections of images on their Web sites that offer free use to teachers.

Many application programs, such as PowerPoint, contain built-in clipart collections. Programs such as *Clarisworks* and MS *Word* provide clipart collections as well. *Corel Draw* also comes with tens of thousands of images in its clipart collection. More recent versions of word processing, desktop publishing, and multimedia creation applications have clipart search functions with the availability of searching tens of thousands of images held within the image database. Moreover, numerous CDs are available for purchase that contain specific groupings of cliparts.

Many presenters and designers use clipart liberally in an effort to make a presentation colorful and engaging. Students and teachers can easily embed clipart images into their work in order to add a level of sophistication and visual enhancement.

Cameras

A digital camera differs from a standard photographic camera in that the image is stored as computer data and therefore contains no camera film. Image storage is accomplished using two methods. First, an image can be stored on removable devices. The removable devices can then be removed from the camera and inserted into a computer, which then uses an application to open and edit the file. A second method of image storage involves the use of a computer chip. The image is captured and then stored on a computer chip within the camera; a cord must then be connected from the camera to a computer in order to transfer or export the image (Milburn, 2003). The computer chip used for storing images may be internal to the camera, or may be removable. The removable chips are also known as memory cards or smart media cards. Most of the more recent digital cameras use the computer chip storage method, which uses a USB port for data transfer.

It is important to note that photographic images on digital cameras are composed of pixels in the same manner as graphic icons. Enlarging an image can be problematic in that it does not increase the details found within the image, it only makes the pixels appear larger.

Camera Features

Teachers should help students become familiar with the features of a digital camera. In general, digital cameras tend to be more complicated than analog cameras. Many of the controls are only accessible through an internal menu, rather than through external buttons or controls. Many cameras have features that can be completed either automatically or manually. Students should be familiar with all the camera's features before taking it out to shoot. It is important to read the manual in order to understand the advantages of each feature. Common features for both digital cameras and digital camcorders include (Story, 2004):

- The aperture ring is a narrow rotating ring on the barrel of the lens. It is generally located close to the body of the camera. The aperture is a measure of the width of the opening allowing light to enter a camera. Higher aperture readings will allow more light to enter a camera; hence, darker scenes can be recorded. Conversely, lower aperture readings allow less light to enter, but have the advantage of creating a large depth of field.

- The focusing ring is a wide, adjustable ring located near the front of the lens used for focusing the image.
- The shutter control is usually a small dial on the top of the camera next to the winder lever.
- Film speed dial is usually found on the left side of the top plate. Newer electronic cameras set the film speed from the film cassette itself. Some digital cameras have a manual override for this feature.
- The Auto Exposure (AE) function on most cameras will allow the user to vary the exposure system in the camera to suit a small range of environmental conditions (Story, 2004). Camera users typically find Auto Exposure functions designed for scenarios like sports, concerts, close-ups, landscapes, bright light, and low light. .The Auto Exposure (AE) feature sets the camera's exposure between standard auto mode and full manual control. Iris controls and exposure controls give the user control over the light level. When lighting is low, the iris may be opened to let in more light; conversely, when the light is bright, the iris may be adjusted to keep out the bright light. Students can be taught to preview their lighting adjustments in order to see how changes in exposure adjustments affect the image.

For either standard photographic cameras or digital cameras, the choice of lens setting can be used to enhance the image being conveyed. These lens settings have different focusing characteristics. The three most common lens settings include wide angle, telephoto, and macro.

A wide angle lens (or zoomed out):

- is best to use when shooting hand-held shots.
- will capture the maximum angle of a scene.
- will have a good depth of field.
- causes distortion problems in extreme close-ups.

A telephoto lens (or zoomed in):

- is best used for portraits.
- only captures a narrow component of a scene.

- results in a poor depth of field.
- accentuates any movement of the camera in hand held shots.

A macro mode (or very close shots):

- will focus on a very small image such as a humming bird on a flower.

The two kinds of zooms for digital cameras include the optical zoom and the digital zoom. The optical zoom is a lens with the ability to magnify a subject used with close-ups by adjusting the camera's lens assembly (thus the name "optical"). Most digital cameras include an optical zoom lens with specifications varying between 2X and 10X, 2X being less range and 10X being the most. The digital zoom is a lens with the ability to magnify an optical image digitally, using interpolation (Milburn, 2003). Digital cameras can come with quite high levels of digital zoom, but the image quality suffers noticeably as more digital zoom is applied. Although optical zoom specifications may look low compared to digital zoom specifications, it is important to note that the optical zoom does *not* result in image degradation.

Sometimes the user may wish to use a wide-angle lens. In the wide-angle lens mode, both the background and the foreground will be in focus. The viewer gets to see the whole scene. Sometimes the user may wish to use the fish-eye lens, which is an extremely wide-angle lens that encompasses as much as a 180-degree plane of vision or even greater (Story, 2004). However, it is important to note that the wider the coverage, the more distorted the image appears at the edges of the frame.

At times it may be necessary to use a telephoto lens mode. In the telephoto mode, the focus will be shallow. The background and the foreground can be out of focus with only the subject being in focus. This type of lens mode should be used when the viewer wants to emphasize the important details in a scene.

The viewfinder feature on the camera can be of great help. Each of the icons and writing within the viewfinder represents information important to the operation of the camera, telling the user, for example, that the camera has run out of space or battery, or how many pictures have been taken. Most camera viewfinders do not actually provide users with full coverage of the image area; a cut-off between 2% and 5% is common. This may mean that something placed right at the edge of the frame may not be visible in the viewfinder, or the user may have unexpected space at the edges of the negative or transparency.

Users should also be aware of the date/time imprint feature that will show the date/time imprint on images or videos. The user can turn this feature on or off.

Digital cameras also have a white balance function to compensate for different colors of light emitted by light sources (Story, 2004). The white balance feature is an electronic adjustment of light levels that helps recorded images retain their true colors. Many digital cameras offer some level of manual white balance adjustment.

Some digital cameras also contain a movie mode that allows users to record short clips of highly compressed, low-resolution video as an MPEG movie with 320 x 240 resolutions. This feature usually records audio too. Although these low-resolution movie modes cannot replace the high-quality video obtained from a digital camcorder, it is a method of capturing action events.

As with any video equipment, the rule of thumb of purchasing digital cameras is to buy the best the budget will allow. The more mega pixels (or one million pixels) a camera has, the higher its maximum resolution, and the better its picture-quality potential.

Most digital camera manufacturers comply with the pictbridge specification, which is a universal direct-print standard. This allows digital camera users to connect directly to printers that have the feature to print without the use of a computer liaison (Milburn, 2003).

In addition to the camera, an important investment should be a camera tripod. The tripod usually contains a pan head that sits on top of the tripod to support the camera. When using the tripod to shoot videos, it is important to buy a pan head designed especially for the video camera, called a "fluid head." This operates much like the shock absorbers on a car. The cushion of oil found within the fluid head allows for very smooth movement of the head as it moves to follow the action of an event (Milburn, 2003).

Shot Composition

Photographers like to create amenable compositions in their work. This can be accomplished by arranging the elements found within the composition; altering the viewpoint usually is the most effective way to control a composition.

The depth of field measures the range along a camera's line of site in which objects will be in focus (Milburn, 2003). Focus describes the sharpness of an image, or the adjustments made on a camera necessary to achieve this. The two modes of focus for a camera are auto and manual. With the manual mode, users have control of the focus. Manual focus is effective when the dominant figures are moving.

During shooting, the user should have a quick look round the edge of the frame and behind the subject before pressing that shutter release. The user should ensure that subjects fill the frames and there is no "stuff" intruding into the photo, for example,. no light pole is sticking out of someone. Photographers use the term headroom when taking portraits of people (Milburn, 2003). This refers to the space above the subject's head. On the other hand, to avoid taking pictures with huge areas of open space around the edge, make sure the subject fills the frame. This can be accomplished by moving the camera closer to the subject.

There are three basic camera shots. Wide shot is also known as the establishing shot or long shot that shows the whole scene. This is the favorite beginning shot of most video pieces because it sets the stage—the viewer gains a better understanding of this setting. These shots are also good if the scene contains movement, for example, showing a person from head to toe. A medium shot shows less of a scene than the wide shot (Milburn, 2003). The camera seems closer to the subject than the wide shot. For example, during an interview, a medium shot would show the interviewee from the waist up. The close up shot shows an even smaller part of the subject or scene. Close up shots are great for showing detail, such as a person's emotions or an insect on a leaf; this shot would show a person from the top of the chest or shoulders up. An extreme close-up shot is even closer and can reveal a person's eyes, or mouth, or images such as a bug gnawing on a leaf.

It is also important to determine the line of sight. This is the line that connects the observer's eye with the object being observed. Photographers can choose various camera angles or viewpoints to photograph a subject. One of the most commonly used shots is the eye-level shot because it is the perspective most familiar to everyone – the subject is seen from eye-level. Direct eye contact can be as engaging in a picture as it is in real life. When shooting a person, it is important to shoot the subject at their eye level. Specifically, when shooting children, this may mean stooping or bringing the camera down to their level. All by itself that eye-level angle will create a personal and inviting feeling that pulls the viewer into the picture (Milburn, 2003). In a low-angle shot, the camera looks up at the subject, making the subject seem important, powerful, or perhaps larger than it is to the viewer. For example, the image may be shot while sitting on the ground looking up at someone who is standing. With a high-angle (also called down angle) shot, the camera looks down on the subject, decreasing its importance. The subject looks smaller. This angle tends to diminish the relative stature or power of the subject. It often gives the audience a sense of power, emphasizing the subject's sense of helplessness.

Some experienced photographers train new users to move subjects away from the middle of the picture by playing tick-tack-toe with subject position. Imagine a tick-tack-toe grid in the viewfinder. Now place the important subject at one of the intersections of lines. This is the rule of thirds that also is widely applied by video photographers. Details of the rule of thirds can be found in Chapter VI.

Finally, it is important that students take control of picture taking in order to improve. Students should be allowed to become picture directors, not just passive picture takers. A picture director takes charge through picking the location, adding props, or arranging people (Story, 2004).

Scan

Scanners are very similar to copy machines. Scanners create a high-quality digital copy of an image or a relatively flat object placed on the scanner's surface. Along with the development of technology in general, the quality of scanners has improved greatly. In the past, scanners outfitted with page rollers or hand-held scanners did not produce quality images. The latest improved scanner, the flatbed scanner, dominates the current market. The flatbed scanner contains a glass plate under a lid with a moving light that scans across the image under the glass plate, creating a digital image in memory. This image is then saved and the user can save it to a file and e-mail it, or print it.

Some scanner software programs operate independently, and some have to work within a graphic program such as Photoshop. Standard scanner software is called TWAIN. This software acts to interface between the graphics program and the scanner hardware. The TWAIN driver contains the controls that allow users to operate the scanners. The controls can be adjusted, by the user, to Color, Black and White, or Line art. The resolution, the amount of area to be scanned, and the quality and balance of the image can also be adjusted using the controls. After scanning, the program then allows the user to modify the image, print it, or save it to a disk (Ashford & Odam, 2000).

Scanner modes include:

- The color mode, which creates images with the "Millions of Colors" feature. This is the best option for color photos.
- The gray scale mode, which creates images with 256 shades of gray, a very appropriate feature for scanning black and white photos, pencil drawings, and so forth.
- The line art mode, which contains only two colors, either black or white, and no gray. It is a poor choice for photographs, but works well for ink drawings and printed text.
- The halftone mode, which can be used for scanning images from magazines and newspapers.

Most scanner software offers a cropping tool, allowing the user to select the area to be scanned (Ashford & Odam, 2000). While previewing the image, most scanner software also allows the user to adjust brightness and contrast; adjust gamma correction; position the image; check for any visible dust particles on the image; and select filters, formats, or other tools before initiating the scan. The user should select a resolution that will scale the input size in inches to the desired output size in pixels (Ashford & Odam, 2000).

Once finished, users can apply various tools in image-editing software to make corrections to the image. Scanners produce bitmap images. Typically, the user should scan at the resolution required by the intended output device. If the picture is to be stored for archival purposes, the highest scan level the storage medium can process and store should be used: such is the case when schools are scanning student records in electronic formats.

In schools, the normal output device is a printer or a video monitor. If a picture is to be included in a printed report format, the resolution should match the printer and the color range in either monotone (black and white) or duotone (two-color), or matched to the printing device such as a laser printer. This is best exampled by complex school projects such as student yearbooks. If the picture is for use on a computer screen, the resolution should match the screen resolution and ability to display colors. Many experienced users suggest that images should scan at 72 dpi for the video screen. They argue that there is no advantage in wrestling with overly huge images just to discard most of the pixels when they are displayed (Ashford & Odam, 2000)

Scanner users should choose the scan resolution based on the needs of the output device that will process that image. It is important to note that lowering the scan resolution to reasonable values to fit the purpose is often the best improvement the user can make to improve the image When the scan resolution is increased, the number of pixels increases, thereby increasing the image size. However, some users are willing to trade off high resolutions with large file sizes.

In situations when teachers and students need text scanning to recover the content of texts or newspaper articles, an OCR (optical character recognition) should be used to convert the scanned image to text. Once scanned, the file can then be saved and edited (Ashford & Odam, 2000). The converted text can then be exported to a variety of file formats, including plain text, HTML, PDF, and Microsoft Word.

Professional OCR programs can also capture embedded images and maintain text columns. When scanning an image of this configuration, use line art mode with 300 dpi to copy the text to the printer, or for OCR. When scanning clean laser-printed documents, the results should be satisfactory in either mode. It is important to note that when working with magazine type print, the user should reduce the threshold into the 80-100 range. This reduction should help sustain the image quality. For detailed tips from the major scanner manufacturers, see the Web site: *10 Tips for Scanning Photos*.

Another innovative scanning device is the ICR. This device differs from the OCR scanner, which recognizes machine-made print, in that it has the capability to recognize handwriting (Ashford & Odam, 2000). The ICR or intelligent character recognition, processes hand-printed forms of writing through a scanner, and the image of the captured data is then analyzed and translated by sophisticated ICR software. The biggest drawback of using ICR for data capture is the level of accuracy achieved, due to the variable quality of handwriting.

Copyright © 2008, IGI Global. Copying or distributing in print or electronic forms without written permission of IGI Global is prohibited.

Other Graphic Sources

Numerous sources exist for obtaining images:

Capturing Images

Images can be captured so that they can be used in other computer applications. The press of the Print Screen key, on the right corner of a standard computer keyboard, will copy the image of a full screen or window to a computer clipboard, which then becomes part of the computer's active or RAM memory.

Capturing All or Part of Computer Screens

Every computer screen should be thought of as an image that can be captured in whole, or in part. The screen capture process takes a digital snapshot of the computer screen that can be pasted or cropped into other applications. Many user guides or manuals contain instructions for using this technique and describe step–by-step procedures for accomplishing this task.

Capturing Stills from Any Video Source: Videotape, Videodisc, Camcorder, or TV

A wide variety of software and hardware applications exist for capturing video from different computer platforms. However, the quality of output varies tremendously. An image can be captured from a videodisc, containing standard video, on a disc instead of a videotape. Once a videodisc player is hooked to the computer's video input device, the procedures are the same as capturing a still image from a videotape player.

Pressure Sensitive Drawing Tablets and Pens

For freehand painting, sketches, and drawing, users should consider a drawing tablet tool as an input device. Digitizing tablets use a pen-based input system, resembling a sketch pad. These systems consist of an electronic tablet and a cursor or pen. A pen (also called a stylus) resembles a simple ballpoint pen, but uses an electronic head instead of ink to pinpoint placement. The pen acts as a stylus, is pressure sensitive with buttons like a mouse, and contains an eraser at the end just like a pencil. Most digitizing tablets come with a separate pen stand and a cordless mouse. The tablet contains electronics that enable it to detect movement of the cursor or pen, and translate the movements into digital signals that are sent to the computer. It also features a transparent plastic overlay under which photos or drawings can be placed for easy tracing. The pressure of the pen on the tablet is translated as electronic dots. Each point on the tablet represents a point on the display screen in a fixed manner. This system is exampled by many delivery companies, such as UPS, that use tablet technology to record signatures upon package receipt.

With high-end digitizing tablets, some paint programs usually include the capacity for creating natural hand-drawn art using different media options. These high-end digitized tablets may also contain drawing software to draw over scanned or Internet images.

Digitizing tablets may soon take the place of overhead projectors, messy markers, and dryerase boards. Furthermore, simple drawing demonstrations given at a table to a large group may also be no longer necessary. Finally, digitized tables can incorporate computer-generated creations into other software such as Word, PowerPoint, or Front Page. A great advantage of using this system is that it allows students to incorporate images into presentations and reports that have a more creative and entertaining appeal to the audience.

Stock Photography

When students and teachers need images to enhance their projects with exact images instead of drawn images, it is often beneficial to use photographs in their projects; some of these photos are royalty free and some require a fee for use. When using photos in projects, students must learn to manipulate and edit these images.

Graphic Editing

The first edit of an image really begins with the camera or image recording device. Once an image is created or captured, it often needs to be changed. It may be that the initial image is poorly composed or it is too big to fit the image into the display space, or there is a need to remove distracting and irrelevant parts. Executing image changes commonly requires the following skills:

- Scaling or resizing occurs when the entire image is reduced to a smaller size. This generally reduces image quality, but also makes the image take up less storage space and transmit faster.

- Cropping occurs when some portion of the image is cut away. Cropping is often applied to improve the image composition, or to make an image better fit into a display space, or to make the image take up less storage space. Cutting lines, known as crop marks, may be indicated on a printout of the image or page in order to show the user where to crop the photo.
- Reformatting occurs when the user converts an image from one format to another. This is often seen when the user changes a PICT (Macintosh) or BMP (Windows) image to a Web compatible format such as JPEG, JPG, GIF, or PNG. During the process, reformatting also compresses the file size of the image.
- Reducing image resolution: Reducing resolution not only shrinks file size, but lowers the image quality.

These features can be found in common commercial graphic editing programs such as *Clarisworks*, *Appleworks*, MS *Paint*, Adobe *Photoshop*, and MS *Publisher*. There are also freeware and shareware programs that have the capacity to perform these jobs.

Graphics Formats

Often the image that is created is not in the right file format for use in another application. For example, if an image is saved, its file format may be fine for applications such as word processing, but will not work on Web pages. The user must apply a different application in order to convert the file format to something useable for the Internet. Many image applications or graphic editors have options for saving files into different formats, but when this is not available, there are applications that specialize in image conversion.

Specifically, the GIF format is used for images that are line art or images that are solid uniform colors. The JPG format is used for photographs or paintings or other images that contain subtle changes in color tone. A PNG format is also emerging as a popular standard for the Internet. GIF is used for line art and solid colors. JPG is used for photographs and other images with continuously changing shades of color.

It is important to note that at the present time, there are only 216 colors that are common to all computers and all Web browsers. Each browser sees 256 colors, but only 216 of them are common to all Web browsers. By contrast, the human eye can see approximately 12,000,000 colors. If the image contains colors that do not exist, the eyes of the computer/browser try to mix the color from the 256 colors it has available. The application tries to patch tiny dots of color together to make it look like the color it does not have in its vocabulary. This is called dithering. Pixels or picture elements are the tiny dots comprising a picture. Each pixel is simply one numeric RGB color value in the image file, as sampled by the scanner. Pixels are easily seen by taking a close look at a TV screen.

TIF or TIFF, acronym for "tagged image file format," is very commonly used in commercial printing or professional environments. Scanners produce bitmap images (.tif), as does the Windows' Paint Program (.bmp, .pcx). TIF file format is the undisputed leader when best quality is required.

Web pages require JPG or GIF or PNG image types because that is all that browsers will show. On the Web, JPG is the best choice (smallest file) for photo images.

Color depth refers to the number of possible color combinations for an image. It is a function of the bit depth, or bit resolution, of the image. 8-bit refers to images composed of 256 possible colors. 8-bit images can be handled efficiently by most computers, but are not usually photorealistic, since the human eye is able to distinguish approximately 12 million distinct colors and shades. 16-bit refers to images composed of roughly 65,000 color combinations, which, in some instances, can approach photorealistic quality. 24-bit refers to images composed of 16.7 million possible color combinations.

Animation

Animation software enables the user to transform still images smoothly from one shape to another. This is an aspect of filmmaking in which drawings or three-dimensional objects are processed in such a way as to create the illusion of motion. Animation involves sequencing consecutive images, or "frames," thus simulating motion by each image showing the next in a gradual progression of steps. The eye can be "fooled" into perceiving motion when these consecutive images are shown at a rate of 24 frames per second (FPS) or faster (Kerlow, 2003).

The cartoon is the most common form of animation, but the animation process may also include silhouettes and the animation of objects. New forms of animation include claymation, VRML, AVI animations, and *Flash* animations. 2-D (or two-dimensional) animation creates moving pictures in a two-dimensional environment, such as through "traditional" cel animation or in computerized animation software. 3-D (or three-dimensional) animation refers to having or appearing to have width, height, and depth. These techniques offer tremendous potential for artistic expression, and help foster the development of visual literacy skills.

Cel animation dominated the animation industry until the rise of computer-generated animation in the mid-1990s (Kerlow, 2003). Cel animation transposes hand-drawn pictures onto plastic sheets, each with a different element, such as a character in a specific background. The images are then layered on top of each other to create a complete scene. The composition is then photographed and incorporated in the finished film.

It is important to note that early Web animations, such as the push-pull HTML animations, are now considered very low end. Animation developed further with productions tools such as JAVA, VRML, animated GIFs, Flash, and Shockwave. Since the mid-1990s, there are a number of high-end animation software programs, such as the Complete Animator from Iota Software and Adobe AfterEffects, that allow people to create cartoons, animated GIFs, moving diagrams, and more. These software programs offer specialty animation features such as a full set of drawing and painting tools, sound capabilities, built-in compression, tweening, and ghosting functions. The output can be saved in multiple formats, including GIF89a.

Important Concepts for Animation

Modeling creates 3-D objects by modifying primitives or editing the points of polygons or splines. A model is a data file that contains the information needed to view or "render" a 3-D object. This information includes two types of information: the geometry or shape of the object, and the surface attributes of the object, data that allows the object to be properly colored so that it resembles metal, glass, wood, plastic, and so forth (Kerlow, 2003).

Frames per second is the number of still images that pass through the camera/projector per second. The user may choose how many frames per second for an animation, and determine what appears on the first frame and last frame. In 3-D animation, key frames are the pictures that define the beginning and end of an animated sequence.

Animation cameras were specifically designed for photographing frame-by-frame through stop-action lenses to allow the camera to capture fractions of movements.

Animation path is associated with any moving object. These paths are standard splines and can be saved and loaded. Occasionally, the user can edit these paths without having to reset the keyframes.

Splines are curved lines defined by mathematical functions. Splines are used by some programs to achieve smooth surfaces for 3-D objects by using polygons for animated objects to move along spline-based paths (Kerlow, 2003).

Bump mapping is a shading technique using multiple textures and lighting effects to simulate wrinkled or bumped surfaces. Bump mapping is useful because it gives a 3-D surface the appearance of roughness and other surface detail, such as dimples on a basketball, without increasing the geometric complexity. Embossed bump mapping is a common type of bump mapping (Kerlow, 2003).

Texture mapping describes the process of applying a texture to the surface of 3-D models to simulate walls, sky, and so forth. Texture mapping enables developers to add more realism to their models. Designers can use an image file, such as a bitmap or a GIF, to add complex patterns to the surfaces of objects in a 3-D scene. The term "texel" is used to describe the smallest unit of a texture map, similar to pixels being the smallest unit of a rendered image (Kerlow, 2003).

Sprite describes the texture that stays flat to the screen. This is also known as an overlay.

AVI animation is an AVI authoring tool that allows users to "import images, sort images, add sounds and logos to images, and create AVI animations and videos."

Claymation describes the animation of models constructed of clay, putty, plasticine, or other moldable materials. Simply stated, claymation involves taking photographs of clay figures postured to depict motion and verisimultaneity (Kerlow, 2003). One famous example is the movie "Chicken Run." In this animation film, objects are sculpted out of soft clay and put into motion one "frame" or movement at a time (much as in the celluloid form of animation). With the use of free-standing figures or figures on stands, the clay figures are positioned to show movement, expression, metamorphosis, character, and life-like similarities. The clay figures are not necessarily in human form, but often take-on anthropomorphic qualities.

Rendering is the process of producing bitmapped images from a view of 3-D models in a 3-D scene (Kerlow, 2003). It is, in effect, "taking a picture" of the scene. As an animation requires as many as 30 renderings for every second, rendering time is an extremely important consideration in 3-D animation. Consideration must be given to the power of the computer used, the number of polygons in the scene, the complexity of lighting, and the presence of computationally intensive elements, such as transparency and reflective surfaces, combined to affect the rendering time.

Looping refers to the number of times animation repeats itself. For example, it is common for an animation to loop 3 times, and each loop lasts less than 10 seconds. Before creating an animated GIF, the user should always ask for looping specifications.

Newer Animation Techniques

Newer methods are quickly replacing the old push and pull animation technologies. For example, JavaScript can be used to add animations to Web pages. In JavaScript the images become animated when the mouse points to them.

DHTML, a combination of HTML, style sheets, and JavaScript, can add animated effects to a Web page. The first step in creating an animated object on the Web page using JavaScript is to name the object. This helps to define the object that is to be animated for later selection by the user. This is accomplished by adding an identification (id) attribute, thereby supplying the object with a name. Designers also have to set up a style sheet to separate the Web page object from the rest of the Web page in order to ensure that the object displays independently from the rest of the page (Kerlow, 2003).

The most common form of animation today is GIF89a animation. The 89a version GIF89a graphics file is an image formatted according to graphics interchange format (GIF) Version 89a (July, 1989). The chief advantage of this format is the ability to create an animated image that can be played after transmitting to a viewer (Kerlow, 2003).

In particular, an animated GIF is a file specified as GIF89a that contains, within the single file, a set of images that are presented in a specified order. The main advantage of creating a GIF animation is that GIF is one of the most widely used formats supported by Web publishers and browsers with no additional plug-ins or controls. These animations are created by combining, together, various still images to give the illusion of motion. Typical GIF animations include a twirling icon, a banner with a hand that waves, or letters that magically get larger.

Most GIF animation software is found in freeware or shareware programs available on the Web. The user may already have software for creating animated GIFs contained within existing software programs. Many of the popular image editors and graphics suites, such as ImageReady, CorelDraw, and Paint Shop Pro, have built-in functionality for creating and assembling animations (Kerlow, 2003). In addition, other types of software, including 3-D text effect and logo programs, such as Xara 3D and Ulead's Cool 3D, can export to GIF89a. There are also add-on programs that function within other software to add animation capabilities.

Flash Animations

In addition to AVI animations and GIF animations, animations can also be created with Macromedia *Fireworks MX* and *Flash* MX. The term rich media is new media that offers an enhanced experience relative to older, mainstream formats. Standard graphic formats, such as JPEG and GIF, would not be considered rich media. Rich media is not easily defined due to the fact that new formats are regularly being introduced and old formats become part of the mainstream or disappear altogether (Kerlow, 2003). Some popular formats commonly considered rich media include Macromedia *Flash & Shockwave*, along with various audio and video formats.

A current example of rich media, *Flash MX*, creates documents by changing the contents of successive frames. Specifically, this program allows the user to move an object across the stage, increase or decrease its size, rotate, change color, fade in or out, or change shape. Changes can occur independently of, or in concert with, other changes. For example, at the beginning of a *Flash* movie, the user may want two objects on the Stage (the school logo instance and the text instance of school name) to be completely transparent. The two instances will fade in gradually and separately as the movie plays. By frame 12, the school logo instance will be completely visible. By frame 24, the text instance will be completely visible.

Two methods for creating this school logo animation sequence in Macromedia *Flash* include frame-by-frame animation, and tweened animation. With frame-by-frame animation, animation designers create the images in every frame. A keyframe is a frame on the editing timeline on which the changes are defined. When creating frame-by-frame animation, every frame is a keyframe. With tweened animation, designers create the starting and ending frames and let Macromedia *Flash* create the frames in between.

At the end, the user is then ready to publish the movie for playback. By default, the Publish command creates the Macromedia *Flash* SWF file and an HTML document with a code that inserts the Macromedia *Flash* movie in a browser window. Designers can then play the Macromedia *Flash* movie they just created by double-clicking the animation icon on the *Flash* folder of their sites.

VR Animations

The popular conception of VR (or virtual reality) involves full immersion of the user. The goal of a VR system is to place the user in a synthetically generated three-dimensional environment that can be directly manipulated. Ideally, users cease to think of themselves as interacting with a computer. He or she wears a head-mounted stereo display to provide full visual immersion, special gloves and a body-suit for movement detection and tactile feedback, and wears earphones, or uses loudspeakers, for audio immersion (Kerlow, 2003). Special input and output devices allow a user to interact with the virtual environment. When using VR, the user's motion and gestures produce the sensory feedback from the synthetic environment to the user's vision, hearing, and touch. The user's position and movement are tracked in real time, and animated perceptual feedback is experienced. The difference between VR and a motion picture is that VR technology creates a stronger illusion to the user in that it is an interactive, not a passive, experience. Although numerous examples of educational applications can be found today, its use as an instructional aid in the classroom is in the early stages.

The final step of animation is used in the rendering process, to take information from a 3-D application to displaying it as a final image. During rendering, many designers use a graphics accelerator, a graphics card, in animation production to speed up the display/preview of complicated animations (Kerlow, 2003). Graphics cards render pixels at fill rate, usually measured in millions of pixels per second (megapixels/sec). Higher fill rates can display higher resolutions and more colors at higher frame rates than other chips with lower fill rates. Memory buffers can be dedicated to a specific function or set of functions. For example, the graphics memory functions as a frame buffer, but can also be used as a video buffer.

Both FLC and FLI are animation file formats. FLC is an animation format that contains one or more frames, so the user can see animated pictures from the screen when these files are displayed. An "FLC" file has an extension ".flc." FLI files are another popular animation files. An "FLI" file has an extension .fli.

If animation is being designed for the Web, it is best to have the message come across in the first frame, because many end users will stop a Web page from loading before the entire animation has loaded, leaving only the first frame. This is especially true when the Web page being designed has a long download time. Conversely, the last frame is the final image viewed once the animation is complete and may stay on the Web page for the rest of the viewing. Consequently, the message might have more "punch" if it is on the last frame.

Rich media animations, such as the one created with *Flash*, do not always yield better results than GIF animations. Since the design costs and time for rich media animations can be prohibitive, GIF animation is often the most effective solution for schools and organizations.

Despite all of the hype surrounding rich media, critics of animation point out that some designers place too much emphasis on the "wow" factor of software or Web design rather than the message. Style and flashiness do not mask lack of substance. The purpose of an animation is to attract visitors. Animation should be subtle enough to attract attention. If an animation is too flashy or too irritating, the target audience is less likely to read the content. It is good practice to remember that the main goal should always be rich information.

Design Tips to Reduce File Sizes

When handling graphics and animations, a common question asked of designers is "How do I make image files smaller?" Graphic images should be sized down (in K) without losing the integrity of the graphic image. Remember, graphic images are primarily used to enhance a Web page's function. If graphic images considerably increase the Web pages' download time, the graphic images will have to be sized down or replaced with a smaller image, HTML default bullets, horizontal rules, or colored heading text.

A file size is very different from display size; however, both are important. File size refers to how much space an image takes up on a disk or hard drive. To determine the file size, simply look at the file size when the operating system lists the contents of a disk or folder.

On the other hand, display size refers to how many inches, centimeters, or pixels an image is tall and wide. There are commands that can make an image appear small in a Web page that do not reduce the size of the file. That is, making an image appear smaller will not speed up the display of the image and the Web page. The measurement is usually given in pixels and requires special software applications that report such information (White, 2002).

Since most Web publishers expect animated GIF banners to have a file size of less than 12K, there are a few design tips that address how to reduce the file size of the graphics and animations.

Colors

A GIF file can store from 2 to 256 different colors. Thus, when working on an animated GIF animation design, it is best to work in a 256-color palette. To help keep file size to a minimum, use only a few high contrasting and complementary colors because the more colors used in the design, the larger the file size. Utilizing the smallest color palette possible in the animated GIF will allow for more creative special effects in the animation.

Dithering

In order to display a full-color graphic image on a 256-color monitor, computers must simulate the colors it cannot display. They do this by dithering, which is combining pixels from a 256-color palette into patterns that approximate other colors. At a distance, the human eye merges the pixels into a single color. Up close, the graphic image will appear pixelated and speckled.

Using dithered images in an animated GIF banner will increase the file size. For example, photographs typically display thousands to millions of colors. If you use a photograph in a GIF banner, the resulting photo will become dithered because the GIF file format will reduce the colors in the photo to only 256 colors. Thus, if the user chooses to use photographs in an animated GIF, s/he should try and use photos that do not contain many colors in order to minimize dithering (White, 2002).

Interlacing

Interlacing involves storing partial data from a single graphic image in multiple sequences. With interlacing, equally spaced sets of lines from the original image are stored together, and these sets appear one on top of the other in sequence. The user will often see a set of horizontal lines appear first before seeing an entire graphic image: this visual effect is called interlacing.

The purpose of interlacing is to have a partial image initially appear on screen rather than having to wait for the image to download in its entirety. The main advantage of interlacing is that end users know that they are about to view a graphic image rather than viewing a blank space. However, it is important to note that interlacing adds to the download time of an animated GIF.

File Compression

Compression is a technique to make a file or a data stream smaller to allow for faster transmission or to take up less storage space. In Web design, there generally are two types of compression: lossless and lossy compression (White, 2002)

Lossless compression refers to a data compression technique where the file quality is preserved and no data is lost. Lossless compression is commonly used on GIF images, including GIF animations, but can only reduce file size to about half of its original size.

Lossy compression refers to a technique of shrinking file sizes by giving away some precision of detail. JPEG images are an example of a file that is compressed this way. By reducing the so-called quality of a picture when saved, the file size can be made smaller. Many photos can tolerate a loss of fine detail before the photo quality becomes noticeable.

For computer animations, compression is the process of reducing the size of a media file by eliminating data. Higher compression means that the compression utility (usually a software program or a combination of hardware and software) defines greater amounts of data (such as larger areas of an image) as redundant, but at certain points, the human eye will register the missing information as quality loss. For example, if a graphic is 12.2K in size and the user just cannot make it any smaller by using a small color palette and by limiting dithering and interlacing, then the latest versions of Adobe *Photoshop* and Macromedia *Fireworks* will allow the user to compress a GIF file via lossy compression.

Reducing the Number of Frames for Animations

Reducing the number of frames per second is another way of saving space for computer animations. Designers can decrease the file size of any animation by using the smallest number of frames possible.

Some special effects take longer to download than others, both in animated GIF banners and rich media banners. Glow effects and fading text effects take longer to download because (a) the animation generally requires more frames to achieve the effects, and (b) glows and fades use a larger color palette (Kerlow, 2003).

If a user wants to use glows and fading text in an animated GIF banner, it is possible to achieve a smaller file size if it compress the animation via lossy compression. The trade-off is that highly compressed images can be delivered more efficiently over a network.

Final Words

Today, multitudes of creative projects incorporate graphics and photographs. Animation software enables the user to transform still images smoothly from one shape to another. Currently, in middle schools and high schools across the country, students are expected to present complex visual ideas using a variety of multimedia applications without supportive instruction. Student ability to participate fully in public and economic life is quickly being redefined through emerging technology. Multimedia development projects involve students and faculty in the information creation cycle. Student users should then be able to move from the information consumer model to become active collaborators and cocreators of information and knowledge (*Copyright in an Electronic Environment,* 1997). Myriad multimedia techniques offer tremendous potential for artistic expression and help foster the development of visual literacy skills. As teachers and students design brochures, multimedia projects, and Web sites, it is helpful to keep in mind how the eye and the mind perceive certain colors and images, and the meanings associated with this art form.

It is important for technology teachers to become familiar with specific terms describing graphic editing. The Appendix presents a list of terms that are fundamental for working on image manipulation or enhancement (White, 2002, University of California at Santa Cruz, n.d.).

Design elements should be considered carefully in multimedia composition. Chapter VI continues with discussions of color theories, basic lighting, design and composition principles, monitor selection, and other techniques that affect media design of all formats. The audience of the multimedia projects and learners with special needs are also explored in Chapter VI.

References

10 tips for scanning photos. (2006). Retrieved June 18, 2007, from http://h50034.www5.hp.com/createuse/enhance/scanning_photos.asp

Ashford, J., & Odam, J. (2000). *Start with a scan* (2nd ed.). Berkeley, CA: Peachpit Press.

Copyright in an electronic environment: Guidelines from consortium of college & university Media Center (1997). Retrieved June 18, 2007, from http://www.dpi.state.nc.us/copyright1.html

Kerlow, I. V. (2003). *The art of 3-D computer animation and effects* (3rd ed.). Hoboken, NJ: John Wiley & Sons.

Milburn, K. (2003). *Digital photography expert techniques.* Sebastopol, CA: O'Reilly Media, Inc.

Story, D. (2004). *Digital photography hacks: 100 industrial-strength tips & tools.* Sebastopol, CA: O'Reilly Media, Inc.

University of California Santa Cruz. (n.d.). Multimedia Glossary. Retrieved June 18, 2007, from http://media.ucsc.edu/glossary.html

White, A. (2002). *The elements of graphic design: Space, unity, page architecture, and type.* New York: Allworth Press.

Sample Questions

1. A teacher can use the paint bucket of a paint program:
   a. To paint with a brush
   b. To copy color from one area or object to another
   c. To draw a curved line
   d. To fill an area or object with color

2. Which of the following tasks is the easiest for path animation to accomplish?
   a. Scrolling text
   b. Turning globe
   c. Bouncing ball
   d. Burning fire

3. A middle-school newsletter team is taking pictures of the school swimming competition. They need to turn auto-focus off when:
   a. The subject is not in the center of the frame
   b. Collecting footage in classroom
   c. The subject is in the center of the frame
   d. Collecting footage around the swimming pool

4. Which of the following statements is NOT true about the Paint Can tool of a paint program?
   a. The tool applies color (or "paint") to any area of the image.
   b. The Fill tool icon resembles a pouring can of paint.
   c. If users click in an unbounded area of the image, the color will "spill" out and fill more of the image.
   d. The tool can be used to pick up a color from an image.

5. Which of the following terms refers to cutting or trimming unneeded portions of a photographic image?
   a. Pan
   b. Crop
   c. Tilt
   d. Capture

Answers: (1) D (2) C (3) A (4) D (5) B

Appendix: Technical Lingo for Media Effects

- **Achromatic colors:** The "hueless" colors black, gray, and white; that is, the whole range of gray levels between black and white.
- **Antialiasing:** To enlarge or reduce bitmap images, the number of pixels is increased or decreased, often giving the resulting image a jagged appearance. Antialiasing can smooth out rough edges. Antialiasing is a technique for reducing the visual impace of aliasing, or the "jaggies," on a computer.
- **Brightness:** Brightness, along with saturation and hue, make up three distinct attributes of color. Brightness is the perceived intensity of light coming from the image itself.
- **Contrast:** The difference between the darkest and lightest areas in a graphic. The greater the distance the higher the contrast.
- **Dithering:** Blending colors to modify colors or produce new ones.
- **Dot pitch:** The distance between the pixels on the monitor. The smaller the distance, i.e., the denser the pixels, the clearer the picture resolution.
- **Fill:** The property of an object that determines the appearance of the body of the object. Fill may be solid, a tint or screen, a pattern, or none.
- **Highlights:** The brightest parts of a graphic.
- **Histogram:** A graphic representation of the range of tones from dark to light in a photo
- **Hue:** Hue, along with saturation and brightness, make up the three distinct attributes of color. Hue is related to wavelength for spectral colors. The terms "red" and "blue" are primarily describing hue.
- **Jaggies:** A term used to describe the stair-step effect that usually shows along curves and edges in font or bit-mapped graphics.
- **Luminance:** A color's brightness.

- **Resolution:** The clarity of the displayed/printed image. The more pixels/dots per square inch (dpi), the finer the detail (higher resolution).
- **Saturation:** Saturation, along with hue and brightness, make up the three distinct attributes of color. Saturation refers to how rich the colors are in a graphic.
- **Sharpness:** The clarity of detail in a graphic
- **Thumbnail:** The term "thumbnails" refers to images that have been reduced in size. It is a small version of a photo. Examples of thumbnails are easy to find. Image browsers commonly display thumbnails of photos several or even dozens at a time. In Windows XP's My Pictures, the user can view thumbnails of photos in both the Thumbnail and Filmstrip view modes. When the thumbnail is clicked, a much larger version of the image is displayed. Thumbnails allow a Web designer to place many small images on one page and still load or display across the Internet in a reasonable time. Cropping and scaling are used to make thumbnails.
- **Transforming color pictures to black and white:** In earlier times, pictures came in just black and white. In the last few decades, color television and color photographs and movies are ubiquitous. Taken literally, the notion of "black and white" is not exactly correct. Such photographs not only show two colors—black and white—but also lots of gray tones. When transforming a colored picture to black and white, the picture is loaded in an image editor like Paint Shop Pro. The gray-scale conversion is usually a one step process of choosing Gray Scale from the menu to complete the process.

Chapter V

Desktop Publishing for Schools

ISTE NETS_T, III. Teaching, learning, and the curriculum

Teachers implement curriculum plans that include methods and strategies for applying technology to maximize student learning.

ISTE NETS_T, V. Productivity and professional practice

Teachers use technology to enhance their productivity and professional practice.

Chapter objective: The teacher demonstrates knowledge of the principles of typography and page design, and knows how to use technology tools to create desktop publishing products.

Educational Relevance of Desktop Publishing

Almost any need to produce printed communications, from event announcements to graduation invitations, can be addressed in desktop publishing software. Desktop publishing combines text and graphics into documents by using a computer system, special software, and output devices. Examples of desktop publishing can be seen in school newsletters, flyers, brochures, books, and current event documentations.

Students and teachers alike may utilize consumer-level desktop publishing software packages designed for nondesigners, while freelance graphic designers, graphic design firms, corporations, and print shops may utilize high-end applications designed for professional and high-volume use. Despite the differences in the software, types of documents created, and where the software is used, all these uses fall under the category of desktop publishing.

Desktop publishing and graphic design can enhance a document's visual appeal. However, this type of publishing involves more than just appearance. The primary means of communication for learners is generally the written word (Lohr, 2003). Desktop publishing, used properly, enhances visual communication, and streamlines the process of disseminating information of all kinds. It provides users an opportunity to integrate patterns and designs into their work (Williams, 2003). Desktop publishing can be integrated into English language arts, social studies, science, math, music, and many other subjects.

In order for teachers to utilize desktop publishing in their classroom, they must begin by asking students to think about daily assignments in a format different from the structure of the standard essay (see Table 5.1 for a list of topics). Simple desktop publishing assignments require students to create brochures, newsletters, or even product documentation. More sophisticated projects incorporate school newspapers and yearbooks. Some school desktop publishing projects involve advanced writing

Table 5.1. A list of desktop publishing projects

Annual report	Print of fine art projects
Book or manual	Greeting card
Booklet	Invitations
Brochure	Letterhead
Forms	Magazine
Catalog	Newsletter
Certificate	Newspaper
Comic book	Presentation folder
Dictionary	Stationery
Diploma	Yearbook
Directory	

that challenges the writer's ability to summarize as well as to integrate meaningful images that support the text. The heavy use of image production tools, such as cameras and scanners, prepares the students and teachers alike for more advanced multimedia and Web projects.

A Short History of Desktop Publishing

In 1983, the first laser printers were built and marketed by Canon. This provided the first high-quality output competitive with the printing presses of the day. Hewlett-Packard produced the HP LaserJet in 1984 and in that same year, Apple Computer introduced the first Macintosh. Several other events of the mid-1980s, including the development of Aldus *PageMaker* (now Adobe *PageMaker*) and the revision of low-cost laser printers, shaped the face of desktop publishing (Williams, 2003). Aldus Corporation founder Paul Brainerd is generally credited for coining the phrase "desktop publishing." Increasingly, desktop publishing features are incorporated into standard word processors. Today, desktop publishing software is as common in schools as spreadsheet and database software.

While Macintosh is still considered by some to be the platform for professional desktop publishing, dozens of consumer desktop publishing packages were available for consumers in the 1990s. *QuarkXPress* and Adobe *PageMaker* and *InDesign* are current industry standard page layout programs. They are cross-platform software programs that allow users to combine text and graphics for desktop publishing. Their plug-ins allow for transition from printed to electronic media.

In education, most notable among these low-cost Windows desktop publishing options, Microsoft *Publisher* and Serif *PagePlus* continue to add features that make them more viable as contenders to the traditional desktop publishing applications.

Word Processing vs. Graphic Design vs. Desktop Publishing

The term desktop publishing is often confused with the concept of word processing. Desktop publishing historically means organizing images and text together for display on a piece of paper. This distinguishes such work from simple word processing, which is generally thought of as a text-only process. However, newer versions of word processors now include many features that were once reserved for desktop publishing software (Williams, 2003). Often the document is never seen on paper, just on a computer screen.

It is now a routine in some schools for even one-page assignments to contain a complex mix of main story text and sidebar text. Within this text will also be a range of artwork, photographs, and graphs and charts. Page layout and image/graphic control are the two critical features that distinguish desktop publishing software from basic-text word processors.

The page layout feature allows the user to place different fonts of text and image objects on the same page without being forced into continuous columns. The image/graphics control features of most desktop publishing software, allowing the user to resize, rotate, crop ,and otherwise shape an image, are superior to basic text word processors.

Graphic design jobs involve creating designs for concepts and ideas and then arranging the design on the page in order to visually communicate a specific message (Lupton, 2004). Graphic designers use desktop publishing software and techniques to create the print materials they envision. Desktop publishing is the process that the designer and the nondesigner use to turn their ideas for newsletters, brochures, ads, posters, greeting cards, and other projects into digital files for printing. Nondesigners also use desktop publishing software and techniques to create print projects for business or pleasure. The amount of creative design that goes into these projects varies greatly. While desktop publishing does require a certain amount of creativity, it is more production-oriented than design-oriented. In reality, the two are separate but intertwined disciplines. Not everyone who works with desktop publishing is involved with graphic design, but most graphic designers are involved in desktop publishing, the production side of design (Williams, 2003).

Choosing Desktop Publishing Software

Just as the aesthetics of a table setting makes the meal taste better, so thoughtful page design may not only make reading more pleasant, but may also effect whether the message is read or even understood. A central issue in desktop publishing can be summarized in one word: design. In word processing and desktop publishing, page layout programs enable users to format pages of text and graphics. Many word-processing systems support their own page layout functions, but professional page layout applications generally give users more control over fine points such as text flow, kerning, and positioning of graphics.

The computerized desktop publishing software aids in the creative process by allowing the designer to easily try out various page layouts, fonts, colors, and other elements. Desktop publishing is important as a tool that can enhance communication by making it possible to quickly and efficiently produce printed and electronic documents. Desktop publishing software allows the user to rearrange text and graphics on screen, change typefaces as easily as changing shoes, and quickly resize graphics, before finally committing a design to paper.

The computer and desktop publishing software, along with professionally designed templates, allow consumers to construct and print the same type of projects as graphic designers, although the overall product may not be as well thought out, carefully crafted, or polished as the work of a professional designer. In choosing desktop publishing software, one of the key considerations is determining how the material will be shared or printed. Some lower-end or consumer desktop publishing applications cannot produce the type of files needed for commercial offset printing. Even when using software capable of creating the required files, nondesigners may not understand how to properly create files for commercial offset printing.

The method of printing dictates how the desktop publishing document must be prepared. That is why answers to questions about what kind of software to use or how to set up a document begin with "how will it be printed?"

The primary considerations in choosing offset printing (also known as offset lithography) or desktop printing (such as inkjet and laser) are the colors of ink and the way the ink is placed on the paper, as well as the type of machinery used to accomplish the task (Bergsland, 2002).

Some applications provide a "fast-publish" newsletter assistant, wizard, or procedure. *Appleworks*, *Clarisworks*, and MS *Works* are the winners in ease of use and simplicity. Programs such as MS Publisher provide a basic template for further modification, and are gaining users in education. There are many more challenging and more powerful desktop programs such as *QuarkXPress* **and** Adobe *PageMaker* and *InDesign*. However, even with *Appleworks*, *Clarisworks*, MS *Works*, or MS *Publisher*, some additional skills generally have to be learned to use the template system effectively. Learning curves, software costs, compatibility issues, output file sizes, formats and quality, software features, and dissemination methods are all factors to consider while choosing desktop publishing software.

Elements of Desktop Publishing Projects

Desktop publishing products often have many visual elements: columns of text, headlines, photos, illustrations, pull-quotes, and so forth. These elements aid readers' understanding, and readers often expect to find sidebars, informational text, and other oft-repeated elements in the same place from page to page. The elements of art, words, paragraphs, and pages interact together on a well-designed page (Lupton, 2004). To make desktop publishing products easy to read, the user should consider color contrast, legible typefaces, and many other factors. (The elements of arts are discussed in Chapter IV.)

Font Selection: Typography

Typography is the study of type and typefaces; the evolution of printed letters. The choice of font, the exact size of the text, where the text breaks, and how the text reads, all are aspects of typography. A component of desktop publishing and page layout, text composition deals specifically with how fonts are arranged on the page. Some of the tasks that come into play in text composition are choosing text alignment, changing font sizes or making text bold or using italics, deciding how much space to put between lines of text or columns of text, and using typographical decorations such as drop caps (Bergsland, 2002).

To be specific, a font is a complete set of characters in a particular size and style of type. This includes the letter set, the number set, and all of the special character and diacritical marks obtained by pressing the shift, option, or command/control keys (Lupton, 2004). Font, also known as face or typeface, in common usage refers to any digital typeface that can normally be rendered in a variety of sizes. It can also refer to a related family of type, such as Helvetica or Times. A font family is a set of fonts all with the same typeface, but with different sizes, weights, and slants.

A typeface contains a series of fonts. For instance, Times Bold, Times Italic, and Times Roman are actually three fonts (even though people often refer to one entire font family as a "font.") The height of a typeface is described in points. The size of a typeface is often chosen from a series of set sizes, such as 10 point, 12 point, 14 point, 24 point, 48 point, and so on. Thanks to modern computer technology and a handy utility called Adobe Type Manager (ATM), the user can enter any point size for the typeface and have it appear smoothly on the screen and in print (Bergsland, 2002)

The three basic categories of typefaces include serif, sans serif, and decorative typefaces. Typefaces are often described as being serif or sans serif (without serifs). Serif is a line or curved extension projecting from the end of a letter form; it can be used to distinguish a class of type face, such as Times, from sans serif faces, such as Helvetica. Serif is a small decorative line added as embellishment to the basic form of a character. Serif, with little "feet," is a more traditional-looking style. Common serif typefaces include Times, Times New Roman, and Palatino. The following graphic image shows serif typefaces:

This is 16 pt bold Times New Roman.

This is 16 pt bold Palatino.

Sans serif is the class of typefaces without serifs or "feet"; it is a more contemporary looking style (Bergsland, 2002). Common sans serif typefaces include Courier, Helvetica, and Arial.

```
This is 16 pt bold Courier.
```

A decorative typeface includes script typefaces and many others.

This is 16 pt bold Italic.

The most legible typefaces are standard serif and sans-serif fonts (Bergsland, 2002). Thus, it is best to design the majority of Web sites in a serif or sans-serif typeface. According to most studies, sans serif fonts are more difficult to read. For this reason, they are used most often for short text components such as headlines or captions. Some researchers argue that, sans-serif typefaces are more legible than serif typefaces when the character size is small. Decorative or cursive fonts are much more difficult to read. If the user chooses a decorative or cursive font in the logo and wishes to use the typeface in the Web site design, it is best to use it in graphic images and to use it in a larger type size (Lupton, 2004).

Proportional Fonts vs. Fixed-Pitch Font

Another method to categorize type faces is by deciding whether the fonts are proportional or fixed-pitched. Proportional fonts are fonts in which different characters have different pitches (or widths). Proportional fonts are also called proportional-pitch fonts. In proportional-pitch fonts, different characters have different widths, depending on their size (Bergsland, 2002). For example, the letter d would be wider than the letter I. Proportional fonts, therefore, have no pitch value.

The opposite of a proportional font is a fixed-pitch font. Courier is a common fixed-pitch (monospaced) font. Most printers support the Courier font.

```
This sentence is in Courier font.
```

Truetype Fonts

TrueType is an outline font technology developed jointly by Microsoft and Apple. Because TrueType support is built into all Windows and Macintosh operating systems, anyone using these operating systems can create documents using TrueType fonts. Since being introduced in 1991, TrueType has quickly become the dominant font technology for everyday use, and is even displacing PostScript in many publishing environments

Variations of Types

There can be many variations of the same type design within a single typeface. Most typefaces have at least three variations: normal, italic (slanted), and bold. Some have other variations including condensed, expanded, light, demi, demi bold, black, heavy, or ultra, among many other possibilities (Bergsland, 2002).

Bold, or boldface, is an expression of weight, also a style of type. Italic is a general term used to describe slanted type. Italics are used to create subtle emphasis and to set apart certain names and titles. Italic fonts can also be used to add creative contrast, such as for pull-quotes or initial caps.

In general, font styles, such as italicized, oblique or condensed fonts, are more difficult to read than standard typefaces.

In order to place a typeface in the text of a product that is going to be disseminated electronically, either through CD-ROMs, Web sites, or listserv, it is best to use one of the most common typefaces already installed on computers. In order to make desktop publishing products easy to read, the user should always consider color contrast and legible typefaces.

Special Characters

Special characters can be created with proper keyboarding techniques. Most word processing and desktop publishing software have a feature called "auto-formatting," which is accessible from the Tools menu. Among the many other tasks users can define, auto-formatting replaces "straight quotes" with "smart quotes," replaces ordinals with superscript, replaces Internet and network paths with hyperlinks, and replaces hyphens (--) with dashes (–) when it thinks appropriate.

The auto-formatting feature changes some hyphens into an en dash or an em dash according to context. There are differences between the hyphen, the en dash, and the em dash (Weixel, 2003). The hyphen is the shortest of the three and is used most commonly to combine words or to separate numbers that are not inclusive. Examples, compounds such as "multiple-choice questions" and "higher-order thinking skills," phone numbers, and Social Security numbers. The en dash is the width of a typesetter's letter "N," whereas the em dash is the width of the letter "M"; thus, their names. An em dash is applied to set off parenthetical matter. For example: "Community organizations—such as YMCA—provide after-school programs." An em dash is twice as wide as an en dash. The en dash is longer than the hyphen but not as long as the em dash. According to punctuation guides, an en dash is used in a range of numbers. For example: "Unit 6 – 2." The en dash also means "through." We also use it to indicate inclusive dates and numbers: October 8–10; pp. 55–59.

Here is how to control the dash: When typing a space and one or two hyphens between text, Microsoft Word automatically inserts an en dash (–). When typing two hyphens, do not include a space before the hyphens, this results in an em dash (—).

The autoformatting feature also supports smart quotation marks, that is changes straight quotation marks (' and ") to smart quotes (For example, "This is what I want.")

Most word processing and desktop publishing software have a feature called "smart tag" that recognizes certain types of data in the documents and performs actions (Bergsland, 2002). The types of data that smart tags can be applied to include telephone numbers, time, addresses, dates, and financial symbols.

Diacriticals are the accent marks used on some characters to indicate a specific pronunciation. These diacriticals are a common occurrence in French, German, Italian, Spanish, and other languages. Some of the more commonly seen diacriticals include acute, cedilla, circumflex, grave, tilde, and umlaut. Examples: resumé (acute), façade (cedilla), château (circumflex), chère (grave), señor (tilde), naïve (umlaut) (Bergsland, 2002).

To insert a special character with auto-formatting turned off, click Insert on the menu bar and then click Symbol in the drop-down menu. In the Symbols dialog, click the Special Characters tab. Choose the special characters needed; then insert.

Another way to insert a special character is by using the numeric keypad on the keyboard to enter the ANSI code of the character. The ANSI character set includes all of the characters that you can type on your keyboard plus the accented letters used in European languages, as well as a variety of special characters.

To insert a special character by entering its ANSI code:

- **Step 1.** Turn on the Num Lock on your keyboard.
- **Step 2.** Hold down the Alt key while typing the 4-digit ANSI code using the Numeric Keypad, instead of using the number keys over the letter keys on the keyboard.
- **Step 3.** The special character will appear after typing the code, then release the Alt key.

Unique ANSI code has to be used to create a special character. For instance, the ANSI code for an en dash is 0150 and the code for an em dash is 0151. There are many tables on the Internet that show the ANSI characters and their codes.

However, when typing in a special language, most of the cumbersome steps can be prevented when using word processing and desktop publishing software created for a specific language with special language keyboards.

Other Character Attributes

Kerning, also known as letter spacing or character spacing, is the adjustment of spacing between letter pairs to achieve a more balanced appearance. Decreasing space is negative kerning. Some commonly kerned pairs include Va and To. Increasing space is positive kerning, such as the ls in "Vanilla" (Bergsland, 2002).

Tracking is the adjustment of letter spacing for words, phrases, and extended blocks of text. Tracking can be applied automatically by word processing and page layout software, or manually applied to only portions of text to enhance readability, to fit more text in a column, or for special effects.

Measurements

In terms of measurements, cpi, short for characters per inch, is a typographic measurement specifying the number of characters that can fit on a printed line one inch long (Wilde & Wilde, 2000). The measurement makes good sense only for fixed-pitch fonts, where every character has the same width. For proportionally spaced fonts, cpi represents an average number rather than an absolute number.

For fixed-pitch fonts, discussed previously, pitch refers to the number of characters printed per inch. Pitch is one characteristic of a monospaced font. Common pitch values are 10 and 12.

The point is the basic measure of type; there are 72 points to the inch, or 12 points to the pica. Therefore, point size is a measure of the size of type, in points.

In typesetting, the pica is a typographic measurement system consisting of 12 points; there are 6 picas per inch. In other words, a pica is a unit of measurement equal to 1/6 of an inch, or 12 points.

It is important to note that type sizes are not standard. Meaning, one size in a particular typeface is not necessarily the same size in dimension (length and width) (Wilde & Wilde, 2000).

Line Positioning

In terms of line attributes, some type has variations including baseline, x-heights, and so on. In typography, the baseline is the imaginary line upon which a line of text rests (Weixel, 2003). The baseline is the point from which other elements of type are measured, including x-height and leading. The baseline is also significant in the alignment of drop caps and other page elements.

An x-height is a value often expressed as a percentage that measures the height of the body of lowercase letters in a type face, or in proportion to the upper case letters (Wilde & Wilde, 2000).

Many word processors and all desktop publishing systems allow the user to specify the line spacing, which is also called line leading, a typographical term that refers to the vertical space between lines of text. The leading value also includes the size of the font. For example, 12-point text with 2 points of spacing between lines would mean a leading of 14 points.

The ruler guide is a nonprinting line that users of desktop publishing applications drag from either the vertical or horizontal rulers to help positioning elements on a page.

In page layout, rules are lines used to separate, organize, emphasize, or otherwise decorate a page. Downrules, also known as vertical rules, or column dividers, refer specifically to vertical rules placed between columns of text, used to provide greater visual separation between the columns (Wilde & Wilde, 2000).

Paragraph Designs

Users of word processing software and desktop publishing software use tabs, a nonprinting character, to change the alignment of text that follows it; the alignment may be left, right, center, or decimal. Among the many kinds of tabs, the decimal tabs are commonly used to line up the decimal points of a list of numbers.

Another common feature of desktop publishing software, text wrap, also called text flow, is the technique of flowing text around graphic elements. This feature enables teachers and students to surround a picture or diagram with text. The text wraps around the graphic.

Alignment is the placement of type relative to margins. The column setup is accessible through the format menu. Left alignment means lines share a left border, but are uneven on the right side; justified or fully justified alignment means that both the left and right sides of the text are aligned.

An in-line graphic is a graphic element embedded in a paragraph as a text character. It takes on the alignment and other characteristics of the host paragraph.

In desktop publishing, drop cap is when the first letter of a paragraph is enlarged to "drop" down two or more lines, as in the next paragraph. Drop caps are often seen at the beginning of novels or newsletters, where the top of the first letter of the first word lines up with the top of the first sentence and drops down to the fourth or fifth sentence (Wilde & Wilde, 2000). The drop cap setup is accessible through the format menus in most word processing software. Figure 5.1 is an example of a drop cap in a paragraph.

Desktop publishing designers use margins to define the area surrounding a page that separates the trim of the paper from the printing area. They also use gutter to

Figure 5.1. An example of a drop cap in a paragraph

> **D**rop cap is when the first letter of a paragraph is enlarged to "drop" down two or more lines, as in the next paragraph. Drop caps are often seen at the beginning of novels or newsletters, where the top of the first letter of the first word lines up with the top of the first sentence and drops down to the four or fifth sentence.

Figure 5.2 An example of a hanging indent

> **Hanging indent** is a paragraph format where the lines are indented a certain distance from the left margin, but the first line is indented a negative amount, so that the first line hangs over the rest of the left alignment.

define the space between pages in facing page layouts. More specifically, the space between columns in a multiple-column document is called an alley, although often both are referred to as gutters. The gutter space is that extra space allowance used to accommodate the binding process. The amount of gutter needed varies, depending on the binding method.

Indents are the additional space measured from the left and right of a text block. Indents can be left, in which all lines in the paragraph are the specified distance from the left margin. With right indents, all lines in the paragraph are the specified distance from the right margin. First indent is where the first line of the paragraph is indented an additional amount from the left margin. Note that the first indent can be a negative number up to the positive value of the left indent to form a hanging indent. Hanging indent is a paragraph format where the lines are indented a certain distance from the left margin, but the first line is indented a negative amount, so that the first line hangs over the rest of the left alignment. Figure 5.2 is an example of a hanging indent.

A pull-quote, is a small selection of text "pulled out and quoted" in a larger typeface. It is used to attract attention. A pull-quote may be framed by boxes or balloons, placed within the article, span multiple columns, or placed in an empty box near the article. A call out is a label used to identify parts of an illustration, in the same manner as a photo caption.

Page Layouts

Users of desktop publishing software are familiar with the pink and blue lines representing nonprinting guides used to align objects and control the placement and flow of text in a page layout. Nonprinting lines, often dotted, that aid in flow and alignment of text and positioning of graphics are known as guides or guidelines. Most desktop publishing software applications allow the user to drag guides onto the page or position them precisely using a dialog box (Wilde & Wilde, 2000). Guides may act differently depending on if they are placed on master template or regular pages.

The three types of nonprinting guides include margin guides, column guides, and ruler guides. A dotted or rectangular nonprinting rectangle represents the page margins of a document, margin guides are usually specified during initial page setup for the document and appear on all master and publication pages. Pages of newsletters and brochures may have as few as one column, or may contain many columns. A column is a vertical block of type, or the space used to lay out type and graphics. Column guides are nonprinting lines that define the left and right margins of columns on a page. The column setup is accessible through the format or layout menus.

Groups of guides form a grid. To position a line, a grid, another invisible structure, can be used to guide the placement of elements. This grid forms a series of guidelines that determine the margins of the piece, the space between page elements, and lets designers know where to place objects on the blank page.

In page layout, greeking (or greek, greeked text, jabberwocky text, lorem ipsum, dummy text, see Figure 5.3) is used to set up the overall layout without the actual text (Wilde & Wilde, 2000). Greeking is used as a placeholder for actual text.

Among the many ways to form bullets and lists, a lead-in list is interesting in that it repeats the same formatting to the lead-in text of the next list item when typing a bullet or number, followed by a space, some texts, followed by a colon, and then more text (see Figure 5.4).

A design that is to be visually appealing must also be comfortable to view. White space (also known as negative space) should be an integral part of page design. It is the term describing the open space between design objects to provide spatial relationships. It is an important layout technique often overlooked by the inexperienced

Figure 5.3. An example of greeking

> Lorem ipsum dolor sit amet, consectetuer adipiscing elit, sed diam nonummy nibh euismod tincidunt ut laoreet dolore magna aliquam erat volutpat. Ut wisi...

Figure 5.4. An example of lead-in text

> **Color Halftones:** Color photographs printed in magazines, newspapers, or books consist of a series of dots in cyan, magenta, yellow, and black that fool the eye into seeing millions of colors.

designer (Wilde & Wilde, 2000). While some artists concentrate on what to place on the page, they can easily overlook what to leave out. White space actually guides readers' eyes from one point to another. It can be between letters, words, or paragraphs of text; space in and outside of graphics, and between all page elements.

An adequate amount of white space makes text more readable, gains emphasis for graphics, and enhances balance between the elements on the page. White space increases the layout's appeal with less visual "noise." It is important to treat white space as more than just a background.

Other Project Components

Readers expect uniformity of layout and often expect to find page numbers in the same location on each page. They also expect to find sidebars, informational text, and other oft-repeated elements in the same place from page to page. Page elements that appear in the same position and format on every page of a multipage publication are usually referred to as standing elements (Wilde & Wilde, 2000). Standing elements are also known as repeating elements or master page elements. The standing elements provide consistency in a publication.

The banner on the front of a newsletter or other periodical that identifies the publication is its nameplate. The nameplate usually contains the name of the newsletter, possibly graphics or a logo, and perhaps a subtitle, motto, and publication information.

Often seen in newsletters and magazines, the kicker is a short phrase found above the headline. Also known as the credit line or writer's credit, the byline is a short phrase or paragraph that indicates the name of the author of an article in a magazine or other publication. The byline commonly appears between the headline and start of the article, prefaced by the word "By."

The masthead is that section of a newsletter, typically found on the second page, that lists the name of the publisher and other pertinent data such as staff names, contributors, subscription information, addresses, logo, and so on. The masthead is also an alternate name for the nameplate of a magazine or newsletter.

In word processing and desktop publishing, a style sheet is a file or form that defines the layout of a document. Parameter, such as the page size, margins, indents, rules, and typeface fonts, are specified in the style sheet. Style sheets are useful because the same style sheet can be used for many documents. For example, a teacher could define one style sheet for personal letters, another for official letters, and a third for reports. Style sheets apply to the entire document, rather than individual words, and are sometimes also called templates. In some word processing applications, template is used in place of style sheet to serve as a pattern for reference. Print tiling allows the user to print large documents in sections on small paper sizes.

The running head is a line of text, often containing the title, which is consistent across most or all the pages in a publication. The running foot is a line of text, often containing the page numbers, which is consistent across most or all the pages in a publication.

Previewing

Desktop publishing generally involves producing documents on the computer, printing drafts on a laser printer, and then offset printing the final version. The following section will discuss some of the techniques commonly used in previewing and printing school desktop publishing projects, from previewing, getting the project camera ready before printing, to offset printing, EPS, WYSIWYP, and finally to CTP during printing.

Previewing refers to displaying a document on the display screen before printing it. Previewing allows designers to see exactly how the document will appear when printed. Major word processing programs currently support the previewing step during production.

With WYSIWYG, previewing is unnecessary because the display screen always resembles the printed version. WYSIWYG is short for "what you see is what you get." A WYSIWYG application is one that enables the user to see on the display screen exactly what will appear when the document is printed. This feature is especially popular for desktop publishing.

Changing the magnification of pages in desktop publishing software is sometimes necessary, and can easily be completed using the zoom tool. The zoom tool is often represented as a magnifying glass in the toolbar. Users are able to zoom in closer for detailed work and zoom out to see the whole page.

Some WYSIWYG applications are more useful than others. Many computer systems use corresponding bit-mapped fonts to display documents on a monitor. What is shown on the display screen is not exactly what is seen when the document is printed. Second, standard laser printers have a resolution of at least 300 dpi, whereas even the best graphics monitors have resolutions of only 100 dpi. For this reason, many teachers have experienced that graphics and text always look sharper when printed than they do on the display screen, and colors often appear differently on a monitor than they do after printing.

Camera ready refers to the final state of a publication before it is printed. Historically, the term has meant that the copy is ready to be photographed and turned into plates for offset printing. Increasingly, however, it is possible to print directly from the electronic version, either by sending it to a high-resolution laser printer or to a special device that can generate plates directly from electronic elements rather than from photographs. In these cases, camera ready simply means that the document is ready to be printed.

Printing

Desktop publishing generally involves producing documents on the computer, printing drafts on a laser printer, and then offset printing the final version. Most of these steps can be accomplished in-house. However, to achieve professional quality, at a certain point, a desktop publishing project has to be sent to a service bureau to finish the final processes.

Service bureau, short for prepress service bureau, is a company that provides a variety of desktop publishing services. In particular, service bureaus have image setters that can produce high-resolution output on paper or film. This is a necessary step before printing a document with offset printing. In addition to providing high-resolution output, many service bureaus also offer scanning services, as well as general consultancy. Some service bureaus have computers equipped with desktop publishing software that can be rented by the hour.

Most service bureaus use offset printing to produce large volumes of high-quality documents. Although the equipment and the initial costs are relatively high, the subsequent printing process itself is relatively inexpensive. Offset printing is a printing technique where ink is spread on a metal plate with etched images, transferred to an intermediary surface, such as a rubber blanket, and finally applied to paper by pressing the paper against the intermediary surface.

To produce the plates used in offset printing, a service bureau requires either film or high-resolution paper output, which the printer can then photograph. Taking a PostScript file to a service bureau can achieve this purpose. EPS (acronym for encapsulated postscript) is a file format that is used for high-resolution output and special effects. This format can contain vector or bitmap art, or both. EPS can be used for commercial printing and can contain any color mode. EPS provides the most accurate color fidelity of all formats.

WYSIWYP, short for what you see is what you print, and pronounced wizzy-whip, refers to the ability of some computer systems that are able to print colors exactly as they appear on a monitor. WYSIWYP printing requires a special program, called a color management system (CMS), to calibrate the monitor and printer.

Although there are specific considerations for preparing files for offset printing, in terms of ink colors and the printing process, CMYK graphics and separations are the two main considerations as regarding choosing the right software and file preparation.

CMYK graphics: Graphics generally use either RGB (red, green, and blue) or CMYK colors. Graphics on the Web or designed for on-screen display are RGB images. Both commercial offset printing and inkjet desktop printing utilize CMYK. Dots of cyan (blue), magenta (red), yellow, and black (the K) are placed next to each other and trick the eyes into seeing millions of colors. Because offset printing utilizes CMYK inks, all full-color graphics need to be saved with CMYK colors. This simple conversion takes place within the graphics software program. Additionally, offset printing can use premixed inks in a variety of specific colors.

Separation: During the printing process, inkjet printing puts all the different ink colors on the paper in one pass through the printer. In commercial offset printing, each color of ink is applied separately. Whether printing in CMYK inks or spot colors, for offset printing, the user must supply a file that can be separated into different files for each ink color. These separations contain only the elements of the document that will print in one color of ink. The printing plates for offset printing are made from these separations. Desktop printing usually uses either inkjet or laser printers. The inkjet printer uses ink cartridges that place the ink directly on the paper. The printers with cartridges are self-contained units connected to a computer through cables. Offset lithography uses a web or sheet press that may consist of multiple units. Photographic printing plates are made of the file to be printed. The plates accept the ink, which is then transferred to the paper.

Content printing can be either in single color (e.g., black) or full color. In printing, the technique of halftone simulates shades of gray or color by varying the size of dots in a grid, or the number of pixels in a given area. Taken literally, the notion of "black-and-white," which is used to depict this type of one color printing, is actually erroneous. The printed pages not only show the two "colors" black and white, but also lots of gray tones, where the different lighter areas are shown in the finest probable detail. Another term for halftoning is dithering (Bergsland, 2002).

- **Color halftones:** Color photographs printed in magazines, newspapers, or books consist of a series of dots in cyan, magenta, yellow, and black that fools the eye into seeing millions of colors.
- **Black and white halftones:** Black and white continuous tone print outs contain millions of shades of gray. When printed, these shades of gray convert to a pattern of black dots that simulates the continuous tones of the original image. Lighter shades of gray consist of fewer or smaller black dots spaced far apart.

Recently, portable document format (or PDF) is becoming a format to present documents intended for printing and make a printable document available to a wide audience and through the Web. Adobe Acrobat Software is used to create, edit, and work with PDF files. Acrobat Reader Software is used to read PDF files created with Adobe Acrobat or other programs. An Adobe Acrobat Distiller is the software used to turn PostScript files into PDF format. Some versions of the Mac operating system include the preview function to view PDF documents. Windows users are required to install Acrobat Reader or a variety of software tools to open PDF.

Final Words

All technologies have features that can be used to extremes. Perhaps the most common critique that one can make of desktop publishing is the way that overall design fails when graphics, images, and other features effectively catch attention, yet obscure or become out of balance with the quality of the text content that they accompany. That is, design fails when more attention is given to looks than to substance.

Some researchers predict that Web pages can be a replacement for print publishing. Many of the design guidelines for merging text and images are the same for both the printed page and Web pages (Wilde & Wilde, 2000). Composers that are editing video on a computer have been stretching the term to include the publishing of digital video as desktop publishing.

There are drawbacks to desktop publishing in that it also makes it easier and less expensive to produce really bad designs. So, while desktop publishing is important, education in basic principles of desktop publishing techniques is equally important.

References

Bergsland, D. (2002). *Introduction to digital publishing.* Clifton Park, NY: OnWord.

Lohr, L. L. (2003). *Creating graphics for learning and performance: Lesson in visual literacy.* Upper Saddle River, NJ: Merrill Prentice Hall.

Lupton, E. (2004). *Thinking with type: A critical guide for designers, writers, editors, and students.* New York, NY: Princeton Arch.

North Carolina K-12 Computer/Technology Skills. (2006). Retrieved June 18, 2007, from http://www.ncpublicschools.org/

Weixel, S. (2003). *Desktop publishing BASICS.* Boston, MA: Course Technology.

White, A. W. (2002). *The elements of graphic design: Space, unity, page architecture, and type.* New York: Allworth Press.

Wilde, J., & Wilde, R. (2000). *Visual literacy: A conceptual approach to graphic problem solving.* New York: Watson-Guptill Publications.

Williams, R. (2003). *The non-designer's design book* (2nd ed.). CA: Peachpit.

Sample Questions

1. An ELA teacher is assigned to supervise a campus newsletter team. Which of the following font types is used most often for short text components such as headlines or captions?
   a. Sans serif
   b. Serif
   c. TrueType
   d. Italic

2. Which of the following word processing features allows information to be organized in rows and columns?
   a. Justification
   b. Table
   c. Word wraparound
   d. Lookup table

3. Which of the following word processing features can automatically insert a title on each page?
   a. Pagination
   b. Headers and footers
   c. Search-and-replace
   d. Lookup tables

4. Which two factors shaped the face of desktop publishing?
   a. PCs and low-cost laser printers
   b. Low-cost laser printers and developments in software applications
   c. Low-cost color toner and laser printers
   d. Developments in software applications and PCs

5. Which of the following statements does NOT apply to white space in a page?
   a. It should be an integral part of the page design.
   b. It is the term describing the open space between design objects to provide spatial relationships.
   c. It is an important layout technique not overlooked by the inexperienced designer.
   d. White space actually guides readers' eyes from one point to another.

Answers: (1) A (2) B (3) B (4) A (5) C

Chapter VI
Creating Multimedia for Special Audiences

ISTE NETS_T, V. Productivity and professional practice
Teachers use technology to enhance their productivity and professional practice.

ISTE NETS_T, VI. Social, ethical, legal, and human issues
Teachers understand the social, ethical, legal, and human issues surrounding the use of technology in PK-12 schools and apply those principles in practice.

Chapter Objective: The teacher knows how to use graphics, animation, and desktop publishing software to produce products that convey a specified message to an intended audience.

Teachers should understand basic principles of design in order to help students with multimedia composition. Chapter VI will focus on these principles along with the importance of defining an audience. This chapter will also describe color theory, basic lighting, design, and composition principles. .

Visual, Graphic, and Media Literacy in Education

Traditionally, writers have used metaphorical language to convey ideas and create images, and graphics have been used to visually reinforce writing. However, today the importance of graphics to convey meaning in texts has increased tremendously. A shift has taken place from using visuals to support text explanations to text that supports visual explanations. Kress and Van Leeuwen (1996) explain that, today, graphics hold great meaning and are central to modern texts and other meaning-making systems such as movies and Web sites. The increasing importance of visual elements in communication has also been noted by many. For example, Hammerberg (2001) explained that there has been a huge increase in the number of interactive children's books enhanced with sound or visual cues. These new books incorporate nonlinear elements similar to hypermedia. Young students today have experience with complex multimedia systems that bombard the senses and stimulate young brains.

This new type of multimedia is changing the way society communicates in the virtual and real world. As America moves to a much more visually dominated culture, students are expected to both understand and express complex messages in a variety of media; thus, the meaning of literacy has expanded beyond the ability to speak and read text. Literacy instruction has to include visual media as well as reading and writing. (Detailed discussions of multimedia and hypermedia can be found in Chapter IX.)

To be verbally literate, one must possess and be able to manipulate the basic components of written language: the letters, words, spelling, grammar, syntax, and meaning. Visual literacy is similar. To be visually literate, one must possess and be able to manipulate these basic components: dot, line shape, direction, texture, color, hue, saturation, scale, dimension, motion, and the ideas/feelings/impressions that can be communicated visually. Just as there are components and common meaning for the elements of verbal literacy, components and common meaning exist for the elements of visual literacy.

Visual literacy, graphic literacy, and media literacy are all related terms. The broad field of visual literacy is loosely defined in this chapter as the ability to communicate and understand through visual means (Lohr, 2003). It is the ability to gain meaning from and critically evaluate visual information. A visually literate person understands how visual elements contribute to the meaning of the whole.

Therefore, graphic literacy is the ability to read and understand visually expressed messages (Kress & Van Leeuwen, 1995). The skill of reading and understanding tables, diagrams, flow charts, timelines, maps, and pie charts is becoming essential in the contemporary workplace and in other roles such as voter, parent, and community member. Graphic literacy has become an important component of American education over the past 20 years. (Chapter II contains a detailed discussion of graphic literacy.) The third term, media literacy, refers to the ability to read, analyze, evaluate, and produce communication in a variety of media forms (television, video, print, radio, audio, Web, computer presentations, etc.).

In this age of multimedia, students are bombarded with messages from a variety of media. Students must learn to be critical consumers of this information, and they must be proficient in evaluating messages for meaningfulness and validity. Visual literacy instruction should work to better prepare students for the dynamic and constantly changing online world (Lohr, 2003). Advertisers have a keen understanding in how to reach youngsters. Professional visual communicators hold a vast amount of power when communicating in the modern media image-centric environment. As students learn to decode media, they also have to learn how to decode advertising. Visual literacy education should prepare students to critically evaluate the many forms of persuasion they will encounter during their lifetime, ranging from television advertising to telephone solicitations to political campaigns.

In this multimedia world, students must also learn to discern emotional appeals made through pictures, music, and video. Students have to be critical consumers of information, and they must be proficient in separating the message from the appealing media. One way to become a critical consumer of multimedia is to be a producer of multimedia. For example:

- When taking photographs, students should be taught to critically examine the images they produce in order to understand the emotional effects inherent in a photographer's choices regarding angle, focus, and other aesthetic elements.
- When using editing programs such as Adobe *PhotoShop*, students should be taught how images can be changed to create a desired impact on the viewer, even if that meaning is not inherent in the original image.
- When creating videos, students should be taught the differences between reality and fabrication, and how subtle elements like audio effects, lighting, or color moods can alter the emotional impact of a scene.

Unfortunately, there are times when students are expected to present complex visual ideas using a variety of multimedia applications without receiving adequate instruction in the process of creating visual communication. However, a student's ability to participate fully in public and economic life is quickly being shaped by the need to employ and understand the power of this technology.

Drawing upon Seymor Papert's research, scholars such as Kafai and Resnick (1996) have promoted the constructivist notion of learning by designing lessons that require students to apply "real world" constructions. Using this approach, students are allowed to work together to create multimedia projects to create messages like the professionals they are emulating. Through the construction of a multimedia project, an in-depth understanding of visual communication and visual literacy is learned along the way. By educating students to understand and communicate through visual modes, teachers empower students with the necessary tools and skills to thrive in increasingly media-varied environments. The emphasis in this approach is placed on using multimedia design to teach K-12 students to be critical consumers of information through the production of multimedia. Multimedia development projects involve students and faculty in the information creation cycle. These projects allow students to move from the information consumer role to that of an active collaborator and cocreator of information and knowledge.

When media is used effectively, it can add impact and clarity to content messages. Graphics, colors, animations, desktop publishing products, audio and visual products can emphasize, highlight, or lead end users to a take an action such as clicking on the button to a hyperlink. Media can also be used to trigger emotion because media have symbolism and color meanings that go beyond ink. When used ineffectively, they can compromise the message and confuse the target audience. The interpretation of these media depends on culture; physiology of the eye; readability; the target audience's age, profession, or industry; and personal preference (McLoughlin, 1999). As teachers and students design brochures, multimedia projects, and Web sites, it is helpful to keep in mind how the eye and the mind perceive certain colors and images, and the meanings associated with these art forms.

Composition Principles

Students must learn that each scene or graphic image composed should have a focal point, that is, a particular subject upon which the audience will focus. This could be the high school marching band, a student drama production, or a display of student science fair projects. Regardless of the particular subject, composition is important, and placement must be attained with thoughtfulness and care.

User Navigation

The Web often seems like a big tangled spider's web of information; bits of it lead to other bits and there is no "beginning" and "end." There is so much information available on the Internet that students could hardly access even a small portion. Learning in such a nonlinear environment can be uncomfortable at first, particularly if students are accustomed to learning in a context where the teacher tells them exactly what they have to learn, and how they should learn it.

With multimedia, face-to-face pedagogy or print-based education materials are not simply "replicated" in the electronic medium. The characteristics of multimedia encourage the notions of exploratory learning, which is consistent with nonlinear and "cognitive playfulness" (Simons, 1993). Linear stacks or slides communicate information in a sequential format. On the other hand, nonlinear systems are not characterized by linear or first-order equations, but are governed by any variety of complex, reciprocal relationships, or feedback loops. A nonlinear hub structure provides more choices for the user. All the components are linked to a central point on which buttons will move the user to whatever section is chosen first. The branching structure may begin at the center as a hub structure, with each choice leading to more choices or subtopics.

Nonlinear learning is perceived as more "authentic" than linear learning and more consistent with life-long learning (Brookfield, 1984). Doll and Alcazar (1998) emphasize the importance of self-directed computer learning and contrasts adopted directive-teaching approaches with naturalistic, nonlinear learning approaches.

- **Video:** Nonlinear video means the recording medium is not tape. Video in linear format is intended to be watched from beginning to end, in the order and at the pace the creator set. The audience of a video has very little choice in how to navigate. With nonlinear mode, the audience has access to the controls to rewind, skip, and replay, all at their own pace.
- **Presentation software:** When applied with electronic slideshows, this linear approach gives the creator a chance to present information in a logical, ordered way; build suspense; create a problem and then offer the solution; or start with an overall concept and then present more and more detail. A speaker will often elaborate on each point as the slide presentation is presented. However, with navigation buttons and hyperlinks, users may be able to skip ahead to another slide or go back to one they saw before. If the presentation is on a computer, the user can go back and forth between slides.
- **Other multimedia authoring tools:** Many multimedia authoring tools assist users in creating products with literally multiple layers of information that can be viewed in a nonlinear way. The creator decides where the viewer can go

by creating navigation links to other pages or resources. This format gives the creator a chance to present information in a way that builds suspense, creates a problem and then offers the solution, or starts with an overall concept and then presents more and more detail. Because it is interactive, the creator sets up the navigation options for the viewer: they control, to a degree, where the viewer will go (Brookfield, 1984). Viewers may have one option or several options to go to next, and can control how fast or slow they move through the presentation. This is good for presenting multiple levels of information, incorporating images from the Internet, CD-ROMs, video images, QuickTime movies, computer animation, and printed materials such as books or pictures. Students can also learn to design the color, page layout, and incorporate images, sound, and/or text. In some cases, each page or computer screen can be self-contained, which means that it does not require additional information or background information to be understood. However, as a whole, the whole project tells a story or delivers a complete chunk of content.

- **Web page:** Web pages are intended to be viewed and navigated on a computer screen. The content can also be printed out one page at a time. Once the creator decides where to place links to different pages, the viewer then decides where to go and at what pace (Brookfield, 1984). The creator can also link their Web pages to other pages created by other people.

Thus, the dynamic nonlinear application of technology is different from the regular class because with nonlinear programs, the students have a certain amount of control over the activity using the mouse (Doll & Alcazar, 1998). Students are not directed by the teacher as much as they would be in regular class.

Aesthetic Principles

Teachers should be aware that the technology needs and competence of children changes over time on a growth sequence. The use of an image needs just as precise a placement and a selection as the words in a sentence. A multitude of books are available on the topic of basic design principles (Lohr, 2003). Design of multimedia elements is an organization of form in cooperation with content. There are five principles designers use to give direction to their work. These five elements provide the guidelines for how to move the puzzle pieces of text, image, and white space in the frame of a printed page, computer screen, or Web page (Gage, 2000):

- **Proportion.** The consideration of the ratio of one element to another. For example, the top margin should be less than the bottom margin but the left and right margins should be the same.

- **Balance.** The optical center of a page is slightly above its mathematical center. Exact or formal symmetry, for example, would put the same size element above and below and equally distant from the center. Informal symmetry can shift the balance to be less boring and more dynamic.
- **Contrast.** Each page or frame should have one key idea. The key idea or key element should stand out from other elements by contrast. The contrast might be based on size, shading, or emotional impact.
- **Rhythm.** The repetition of elements raises interest level and draws the eye onward. The progression might be one of numbers, large to small, black to white, and unusual shape to conventional. The eye generally starts at the optical center of a page and scans right, then left and down and then right. In most cases, elements along this path get greater notice.
- **Unity** (or **harmony**). Unity is when each element of the design complements all the others and design elements of a similar purpose are grouped together. When applied to desktop publishing projects, unity is when typography is confined to a single family and white space is concentrated on the pages.

Among the five desirable characteristics of a composition, proportion refers to the ratio of one element to another. An artist creates emphasis by arranging art elements such as color, line, shape, or texture to draw the viewer's eye to a specific part of the composition.

There are many ways to show emphasis in design. Placing the focal point in the center of a composition is one way to emphasize it. A composition may have more than one area of emphasis. Variety of lines, shapes, colors, or other art elements in a composition makes it more interesting. Artists might also use variety to create emphasis and draw the eye to the focal point, which is the place the viewers' eye is drawn to.

The ancient Greeks discovered the pleasing effect of objects with a rectangular shape. This ratio of 1.61803 was named the golden ratio by the Greeks (Livio, 2002). The space between the columns found in Athens, Greece form golden rectangles. The ratio for length to width of rectangles of 1.61803 is considered very pleasing to the eye. There are golden rectangles throughout art and architect histories. Many artists have used this proportion; Leonardo Da Vinci called it the "divine proportion" and featured it in many of his paintings, including the famous "Mona Lisa" (Livio, 2002).

The Rule of Thirds is a guide for the placement of elements in an image at the intersection of thirds in the image frame and is related to the golden section or golden ratio. This is one of the most popular "rules" in photography and among artists (Gage, 2000).

Figure 6.1. With the Rule of Thirds, important elements are placed where the lines intersect

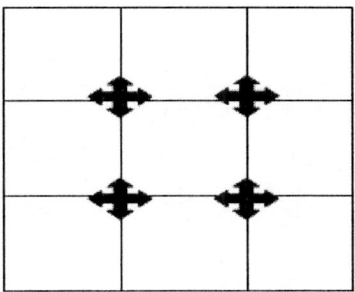

With the Rule of Thirds, imaginary lines are drawn dividing the image into thirds both horizontally and vertically. Important elements of the composition are placed where these lines intersect. (See Figure 6.1). Using the Rule of Thirds helps produce nicely balanced pictures. Using this rule helps to tighten the composition.

Balance is concerned with the distribution of visual interest, and can be described as achieving equilibrium. There are times, however, when it is desirable to deliberately throw the balance off in order to call attention to a particular aspect of an image. There are two systems for controlling balance:

- **Symmetry:** A mirror image
- **Asymmetry:** Without symmetry

Symmetry means one side is the equal or the mirror image of the other. Symmetry can occur in any orientation as long as the image is the same on either side of the central axis. This type of image has great appeal because it makes for a "good" shape relationship.

Visual information and a stimulating visual environment are also important to composition. When two items within a composition are different, they create contrast. Artists achieve contrast using different lines, shapes, colors, textures, values, and forms. This technique can draw the eye to the center of interest (Gage, 2000).

Patterns produce visual rhythm and movement that an artist can use to direct the viewer's eye around a composition.

Movement describes how elements are used to create the illusion of visual motion.

Rhythm refers to a feeling of visual movement in a composition. Artists use repeating art elements to create different types of rhythm. The way the eye moves around a work of art is often described in musical or dance terms such as flowing, staccato, quiet, or energetic (Gage, 2000). Repeated patterns also may evoke a feeling of unity. Unity or harmony can be defined as a pleasing arrangement of parts, whether it be music, poetry, or color. In visual experiences, harmony is something that is pleasing to the eye. It engages the viewer and it creates an inner sense of order, a balance in the visual experience.

Using Colors to Appeal to the Audience

Major Color Modes

Colors play an important role in visual literacy. There are a number of major color modes in use. The gray-scale mode is a file format containing up to 256 shades of gray but no color. Gray scale can be used for on-screen and commercial printing applications. The index color mode contains 256 different colors, each of which is assigned to its own numbered slot on a palette (Ames, 1996). The index color mode is the same file size as gray scale mode, but usually considered low resolution and unfit for commercial printing.

There are two other major color modes in use: additive colors and subtractive colors. Graphics generally use either RGB (or red, green, and blue) or CMYK (or cyan, magenta, yellow, and black) colors (Ames, 1996). Graphics for the Web or designed for on-screen display, such as multimedia software and electronic presentations, use RGB images. Both commercial offset printing and inkjet desktop printing utilize CMYK. Printed colors differ from monitor colors in that they are produced by overlaying ink pigments on paper (thus subtractive colors) instead of by combining different wavelengths of light (thus additive colors).

Since its inception, the RGB color system, also known as the additive colors, creates images with red, green, and blue dots of light. Red color and green color overlap to result in yellow. This is known as "additive color" and is completely different from how colors are mixed in the world of paints and pigments.

In the print industry, cyan, magenta, yellow, and black (CMYK colors) are used as the primary colors. When the user mixes all the colors, the result is gray. This is the system of subtractive colors. Dots of cyan (blue), magenta (red), yellow, and black (the K) are placed together to trick the eyes into seeing millions of colors.

Because offset printing utilizes CMYK inks, all full-color graphics need to be saved with CMYK colors (Ames, 1996).This simple conversion is done in the graphics software program. Additionally, offset printing can use premixed inks in a variety of specific colors.

Color Mixing Theories

Color theory encompasses a multitude of definitions, concepts, and design applications. Differences of opinion about the advantage of one format over another continue today. In reality, any color circle or color wheel that presents a logically arranged sequence of pure hues has merit. Hue, along with saturation and brightness, make up the three distinct attributes of color (Ames, 1996). Hue is related to wavelength for spectral colors. The terms "red" and "blue" are primarily describing hue. Saturation describes how rich the colors are in a graphic. It is related to how much white content is in the stimulus. Brightness is the perceived intensity of light coming from the image itself.

Color circle, based on red, yellow, and blue, is traditional in the field of art. Sir Isaac Newton developed the first circular diagram of colors in 1666. Since then scientists and artists have studied and designed numerous variations of this concept. It is convenient to arrange the saturated hues around a Newton Color Circle. Starting from red and proceeding clockwise around the circle to blue, the eye proceeds from long to shorter wavelengths.

Artists use a color wheel for mixing paints. A color wheel arranges colors around the edges of a circle. Primary colors are in the middle (Ames, 1996). A standard color wheel has 12 distinct hues, but does not have any visual information about saturation or value. The standard color wheel uses red, yellow, and blue as primary colors. Violet, green, and orange are secondary colors, and red-violet, blue-violet, blue-green, yellow-green, yellow-orange, and red-orange are tertiary colors.

The modern version of color palette is a collection of available color selections, ranging from 16 colors to 16.7 million. Color wheels are the colors of the visible spectrum arranged into a circle. It was invented by Johannes Itten, a Swiss color theorist, to mix pigments (Ames, 1996).

The term color scheme refers to harmonious color combinations that use any two colors opposite each other on the color wheel, any three colors equally spaced around the color wheel forming a triangle, or any four colors forming a rectangle (Ames, 1996).

Harmony can be defined as a pleasing arrangement of parts, whether it be music, poetry, or color. In visual experiences, harmony is something that is pleasing to the eye. It engages the viewer and it creates an inner sense of order, a balance in the visual experience. Color harmony delivers visual interest and a sense of order. There are a number of formulas for color harmony. The following illustrations and descriptions present some basic formulas.

There are six classic color schemes: monochromatic (uses variations in lightness and saturation of a single color), analogous (uses colors that are adjacent to each other on the color wheel), complementary (consists of two colors that are opposite each other on the color wheel), split complementary (which uses a color and the two colors adjacent to its complementary), triadic (uses three colors equally spaced around the color wheel), and tetradic (also called double complementary, uses two complementary color pairs) (Ames, 1996).

Analogous colors are any three colors that are side by side on a 12-part color wheel, such as yellow-green, yellow, and yellow-orange. Complementary colors are any two colors that are directly opposite each other, such as red and green and red-purple and yellow-green. These opposing colors create maximum contrast and maximum stability.

Harmony is a dynamic equilibrium. However, nature provides a perfect departure point for color harmony (Gage, 2000). For example, red, yellow, and green create a harmonious design of a flower with its leaves, regardless of whether this combination fits into a technical formula for color harmony. When something is not harmonious, it is either boring or chaotic. At one extreme is a visual experience that is so bland that the viewer is not engaged. The human brain will reject understimulating information. At the other extreme is a visual experience that is so overdone, so chaotic that the viewer does not want to continue looking at it.

Color Meanings

Colors do not have only sensorial but also psychological effects and special meanings. Warm hues are stimulating, while cool hues are relaxing (Gage, 2000). These effects are taken into account when designing multimedia products or decorating the interior of buildings.

- Red is the color of fire and blood. It is associated with energy, war, danger, strength, power, determination, as well as passion, desire, and love.
- Gold evokes the feeling of prestige. The meaning of gold is illumination, wisdom, and wealth. Gold often symbolizes high quality
- Yellow produces a warming effect, arouses cheerfulness, stimulates mental activity, and generates muscle energy.
- Light yellow is associated with intellect, freshness, and joy.
- Green is the color of nature. It symbolizes growth, harmony, freshness, and fertility.
- White is associated with light, goodness, innocence, purity, and virginity. It is considered to be the color of perfection.
- Black is associated with power, elegance, formality, death, evil, and mystery.

Color Psychology or the Moods of Products

The relationship of values, saturations, and the warmth or coolness of respective hues can cause noticeable differences in one's perception of color. Color space is a scientific model for understanding color and color combinations (Gage, 2000). There are four different groups of colors:

Warm Colors: Red, Pink, Yellow, Gold, Orange
Cool Colors: Blue, Turquoise, Silver
Mixed Cool/Warm Colors: Purple, Lavender, Green
Neutral Colors: Brown, Beige, Ivory, Gray, Black, White

The type of project will influence what colors are selected for school graphic projects. For example, red has very high visibility, which is why red is widely used to indicate danger (high voltage signs, traffic lights). Red is also used to indicate courage. It is a color found in many national flags. This color is also commonly associated with energy, so a designer might wish to use it when promoting energy drinks, games, cars, and items related to sports and high physical activity (Gage, 2000). On the other hand, in the finance industry, the color red signifies financial loss; and in the health care industry, the color red is associated with danger or an emergency.

Graphic Colors and Target Audience Cultures

Selecting colors for graphic projects is not as simple as using colors based on personal preference. Culture, readability, the psychological factors are all considerations in graphic design. Color packs a lot of nonverbal communication. The addition of a color can subtly change the meaning of a design element and how it is perceived.

Sometimes colors create a cultural reaction. When designing a graphic, care should be taken in the selection of colors when targeting a specific country, global audience, or culture. For example, though the color purple is also associated with royalty in European countries, the color orange is associated with royalty in the Netherlands. The color white is associated with death in China and India, whereas white is associated with purity in Western cultures. Moreover, white carnations signify death in Japan and green hats mean a man's wife is cheating on him in China. In India, red signifies life and creativity while in China, it signifies happiness, joy, and festivity. Thus, it is important to remember that colors are full of symbolism and that they follow trends as well.

Colors and Legibility

How the human eye processes color is also a consideration for selecting graphic colors. In order to make the text on a background legible, it is very important to use colors that provide a high contrast. Black and white are the two colors that provide the highest color contrast. Yellow is the first color the eye processes. So, when trying to call attention to some text on a dark-colored background, yellow can be an excellent color choice. However, yellow may not work as a background color of a banner. It is important to note that purple is one of the hardest colors for the eye to discern, so it might not be a good overall color choice.

Color Context

How color behaves in relation to other colors and shapes is a complex area of color theory called color context. The relationship of values, saturations, and the warmth or coolness of respective hues can cause noticeable differences in the viewer's perception of color (Gage, 2000). Observing the effects colors have on each other is the starting point for understanding the relativity of color.

Red appears more brilliant against a black background and somewhat duller against the white background. In contrast with orange, the red appears lifeless; in contrast with blue-green, it exhibits brilliance. Light yellow tends to disappear into white, so it usually needs a dark color to highlight it. Black contrasts well with bright colors. Combined with red or orange, other very powerful colors, black gives a very aggressive color scheme.

Clashing or contrasting colors are directly opposite each other on the color wheel. Despite the name, colors that clash are not always a bad combination if used carefully. These paired colors may provide great contrast and high visibility (Ames, 1996).

Using Lighting to Convey Meanings

Effective lighting helps the viewer better understand photographs and videos. When shooting at the beach, the user might consider a filter to cut through some of the haze. At a dark auditorium, the user might need an on-camera light to brighten the area.

If, for example, a high school team is requested, by the manager of a small coastal town, to interview an elderly fisherman for the oral history of the town, what would they need to consider for correct lighting?

Figure 6.2. A scene that uses a combination of the three kinds of lighting

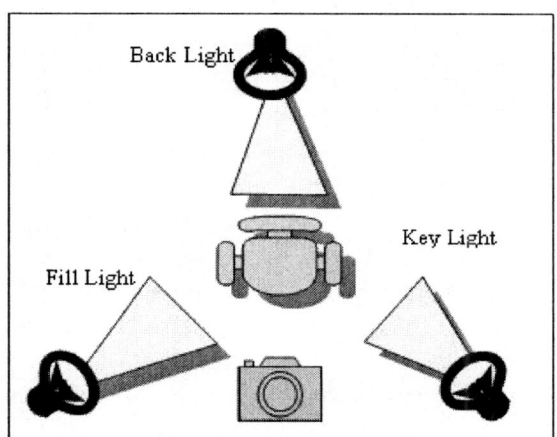

First, the students would need to set up the camera or camcorder and see how the subject looks without any special light. Chances are there will not be enough light for good video. Good lighting consists of three elements: key light, fill light, and back light.

We are used to seeing objects in nature illuminated by the sun, or by strong artificial light from a direction. Strong directional light creates a highlighted side and a shadow. When lighting artificially, the key light tries to replace the sun (Long, 2004).

If we used the key light alone, the opposite side of the face would be in deep shadow. In this case, we use the fill light to soften the deep shadows created by the key light (Long, 2004). The fill light reduces contrasts in the dark areas of the composition, helping the still picture or video camera to produce a better image.

Backlight is used to create visual separation of the subject from the background. It creates a halo of light around the subject.

The standard way to light a scene is to use a combination of these three kinds of lighting (see Figure 6.2). Use the main light as the key light. It will determine the mood of the scene as it is the most powerful. Typically, the key light will light the subject from above, slightly to the front, and off to one side. This provides a natural and interesting shadow pattern (Long, 2004). Soft key lights are flattering on the face. The fill light is usually soft and removes some of the shadows from the key light. The backlight separates the subjects from the background and defines the outline of the subject. It will also help create a three-dimensional feel.

Finally, the base light is the overall light level necessary for the video camera to produce a usable signal. This minimum is usually stated in *lux*, a measure of light. The lower the *lux* rating for a camera, the more sensitive the camera will be.

Lighting a Location

In order to achieve the basic setup when lighting a location, place a floor lamp with a 100-watt bulb to the right of the camera. This will be the key light. Place another lamp on the left, with a lower wattage bulb in it. This is the fill light. Then, use a small directional lamp, such as a gooseneck lamp or desk lamp, as the back light for the subject. Aim the small lamp so that it falls on the subject's hair and shoulders.

Make sure the key light, fill light, and backlight are not in the shot. Look at the monitor or in the viewfinder of the camera or camcorder. If more fill is needed, if the shadow side is too dark, try either increasing the wattage from the fill light or using a reflector to bounce light from the key light back onto the subject's face from the left. A reflector can be as simple as a sheet of shiny poster board or as sophisticated as special material made for studio use. A reflector is especially useful outdoors, where electrical power and supplemental lighting are not available. When shooting outdoors, consider purchasing a 5.5-inch LCD monitor that will mount right on the camera.

Move the lights closer or further away to increase or decrease the amount of light falling on the subject. When satisfied, white balance the camera (Long, 2004). If the camera is not white balanced, all of the footage will have a yellow cast.

Mood

Lighting helps to establish the mood of a video story. The height of the key light can play a critical role in determining the mood of the final product. Natural light typically reaches us from about 45° above. The key light should usually be located about 45° to the right or left of the camera, while the fill light is commonly located 30° to 45° from the camera, opposite the key light, yet at the same height. Like the key and fill lights, backlight should be about 45° above the subject, and should be on as close to a direct line with the camera as is practical (Long, 2004).

Light from directly in front, at eye level, washes out all these shadows, and makes the face seem very flat. This type of lighting is often used in movies when the intention is to make the actor look stressed and pale, while light from below creates a tension and distress effect.

Light Color

Different light sources create different color characteristics. The human eye naturally compensates for this, recognizing colors regardless of which type of lighting from which they are viewed. However, the video camera is much more discriminating.

The color most affected by this phenomenon is white. Sunlight, incandescent light, or fluorescent tubes create different color characteristics. Find a location lit by a standard light bulb and look at a white object through your camera's viewfinder. You will see that it has a yellow tint. Then view the same object under fluorescent lights (Long, 2004). It will have a blue tint. Viewed in natural daylight, it will look even bluer. Changing the angle, intensity, and color of lighting can dramatically alter the mood of a scene. For a romantic look, try softening the shadows and changing the color of the lights to a warm gold or a light pink. For a bold high contrast feel, use more intense light and deep shadows.

Light colors can also be changed by the use of "gels," colored sheets of plastic. Moreover, a diffuser is a thin material placed in front of lighting units to soften and disperse light. Diffusion material is also used to alter the quality of light (Long, 2004). Diffusion material often has a cloudy look, and light passing through it is softened and flattened.

Changing light color and diffusion can also be achieved with some pretty low-tech solutions. Hanging a sheet over a window to diffuse the light coming through it or experimenting with various light sources when shooting indoors can soften and diffuse light. Many times, simply turning off one offending light will correct a difficult color balance problem.

Finally, it is important to note that lights generate a great deal of heat, and it is very easy to start a fire with a cloth sheet or paper diffusion medium placed too close to a light. Fortunately, commercial video gel and diffusion media are usually flame proofed.

How Much is Enough?

Good video images require adequate illumination. A safe generalization about light is that the more light that is available, the clearer the picture and the more saturated the colors will be. However, too much light is almost as bad as too little. Remember to allow the story or message to determine the role that light plays in the productions. One of the best rules for the beginner trying to light a subject is to keep it simple.

Bright sunny days are especially difficult for videographers. The bright sunlight may wash out the shadows that help define objects. Conversely, bright sunlight may cause dark shadows. Whenever possible, avoid shooting in harsh sunlight. Consider purchasing a polarizing or daylight filter for the camera if filming outdoor scenes (Long, 2004).

It is important to try to avoid red eye. Red eye occurs as a result of flash reflection. The flash of light reflects off the blood vessels behind the retina in the eye. The effect is most common when light levels are low, outdoor at nights, or indoor in a dimly lit room.

For professional results, give the lighting the same careful consideration that should be given in selecting the performers, music, and script. Creative lighting can reinforce the story. Lack of attention to the lighting can destroy a scene (Long, 2004). When shooting indoors, boost the level of the ambient light, irrespective of the use of key-, fill-, or backlighting.

Final Words About Lighting

It is important to have lighting that fits with the project's purposes. Ideally, the light should come from where the camera is set up; this will prevent shadows on objects or people's faces. It is good for the light source to come in front or above the subject. In general, the source of light should not come from behind the subject. If a light source is behind an object, it will seem dark and the viewer may not be able to see the details of the object (Long, 2004).

Final Words

Effective technology users can tell a story through any electronic medium. Like any good storyteller, the student should begin by asking "Who is my audience? How can I construct the graphic, animation, or video to interest and entertain this audience?" Good multimedia projects are those that provide interest and lead the users along with the action.

Multimedia, or new media, is changing the way society communicates in the virtual and real world. As we move to an increasingly visually dominated culture, students are expected to code and decode complex messages in a variety of media, and literacy instruction has started to include visual media.

In general, multimedia products attract more "wows" from the audience or users than other text-based computer programs. Despite all of the hype surrounding rich media, critics point out that some designers place too much emphasis on the "wow" factor of software or Web design rather than the message. Style and flashiness do not mask lack of substance. It is a good practice for teachers to emphasize content over pizzazz; the main goal should always be intellectually challenging and correct information.

References

Ames, J. (1996). *Color theory made easy: A new approach to color theory and how to apply it to mixing paints.* New York: Watson-Guptill.

Brookfield, S. (1984). Self-directed adult learning: A critical paradigm. *Adult Education Quarterly, 35*(2), 59-71.

Chen, L. I, Nath, L. J., & Parker, E. M. (2005). Using technology in the middle school and high school classroom. In J. Nath & M. Cohen (Eds.), *Becoming a middle school or high school teacher in Texas* (pp. 309-350). Belmont, CA: Wadsworth/Thomson Learning.

Clements, D. H., & Nastasi, B. K. (1992). Computers and early childhood education. In M. Gettinger, S. N. Elliott, & T. R. Kratochwill (Eds.), *Advances in school psychology: Preschool and early childhood treatment directions* (pp. 187-246). Hillsdale, NJ: Lawrence Erlbaum Associates.

Doll, W. E., & Alcazar, A. (1998). Curriculum and concepts of control. In W. F. Pinar (Ed.), *Curriculum: toward new identities* (pp. 295-323). New York: Garland.

Gage, J. (2000). *Color and meaning: Art, science, and symbolism.* Berkeley: University of California Press.

Hammerberg, D. (2001, January). Reading and writing "hypertextually": Children's literature, technology, and early writing instruction. *Language Arts, 78*(3), 207-16.

Kafai, Y., & Resnick, M. (1996). *Constructionism in practice: Designing, thinking, and learning in a digital world.* Mahwah, NJ.

Kress, G., & Van Leeuwen, T. (1995). *Reading images: The grammar of visual design.* New York: Hyperion Books.

Livio, M. (2002). *The golden ratio: The story of PHI, the world's most astonishing number.* New York: Broadway Books.

Lohr, L. L. (2003). *Creating graphics for learning and performance: Lesson in visual literacy.* Upper Saddle River, NJ: Merrill Prentice Hall.

Long, B. (2004). *Complete digital photography.* Boston: Charles River Media.

McLoughlin, C. (1999). The implications of the research literature on learning styles for the design of instructional material. *Australian Journal of Educational Technology, 15*(3), 222-241.

Simons, P. R. (1993). Constructive learning: The role of the learner. In T. Duffy, J. Laowyck, & D. H. Jonassen (Eds.), *Designing environments for constructive learning.* New York: Springer Verlag.

Sample Questions

1. What is the purpose of anti-aliasing for computer monitors?
   a. To load images faster
   b. To create transparent effect
   c. To increase resolution
   d. To smooth jagged images

2. An elementary teacher is preparing an electronic slideshow for her English Language Learners students in order to introduce folktales to her students. Which of the following techniques would be most useful when preparing this slide show?
   a. Design a slideshow with graphic
   b. Design a slideshow with oral explanation
   c. Integrate the Internet with the slideshow
   d. Use effective slide transition

3. Which is the most desirable feature of instructional materials using hypermedia?
   a. Using plenty of sounds and graphics
   b. Engaging
   c. Easy navigation
   d. Trying out the most features the hypermedia can offer

4. A middle school newsletter team plans to design a poster to convey the feeling of happiness and celebration. Which of the following is the best background color for this purpose?
   a. Blue
   b. Yellow
   c. Purple
   d. Green

5. Strong directional light creates a highlighted side and a shadow. When lighting artificially, we use which of the following lights to replace the sun?
   a. Fill light
   b. Key light
   c. Base light
   d. Back light

Answers: (1) D (2) A (3) B (4) B (5) B

Section III

Video Technology and Multimedia

Chapter VII

School Multimedia Design Teams and Projects

ISTE NETS_T, I. Technology operations and concepts
Teachers demonstrate a sound understanding of technology operations and concepts.

ISTE NETS_T, V. Productivity and professional practice
Teachers use technology to enhance their productivity and professional practice.

Chapter objective: The teacher knows general design guidelines and the different roles and responsibilities involved in developing a multimedia project.

The chapter introduces the major instructional design models in education. The chapter also identifies the different roles and responsibilities involved in developing a typical title. A detailed scenario of the design and development process for multimedia projects is also included.

Instructional Design Models

Instructional design models aid teachers in the creation of instructional materials. Often they include visualized representations of the design process. The visualization will generally display the main phases and their relationships of a task. In traditional instructional design (ID) models, each of the steps has an outcome that feeds the subsequent phase (Reiser & Dempsey, 2002). These are generally called "linear" models because step 1 is followed by step 2, and so on, until the entire process is completed.

There are many types of ID models, including some relatively new ones that are nonlinear. However, the term ISD or "instructional systems design" is the general term used to designate the most popular and traditional type of ID model used today. This ID model was developed by Walter Dick and Lou Carey (1978, 1990). Dick and Carey are widely viewed as the torchbearers of the ISD approach, and their authoritative book, *The Systematic Design of Instruction* (1990), is widely used as a text in instructional design courses.

Previously, during the 1960s, Robert Gagné's text, *The Conditions of Learning* (1965), was a milestone text that related different classes of learning objectives to appropriate instructional designs. His work contributed greatly to the field of instructional technology with regard to instructional design. Gagné (1965) proposed a systems-approach model of designing instruction that could be utilized to help learners understand the process. Gagné introduced the idea of task analysis to instructional design. That is, an instructional task could be broken down into sequential steps: a hierarchical relationship of tasks and subtasks.

Currently, there are more than 100 different ISD models; however, the version of the systems approach, a process comprised of a series of phases, is referred to as the ADDIE model. This systems approach of instructional design contains the following major phases: analysis, design, development, implementation, and evaluation (Reiser & Dempsey, 2002):

- Analysis
    - Determine the instructional goal.
    - Analyze the instructional goal.
    - Analyze the learners and context of learning.

- Design
  - Write performance objectives.
- Development
  - Develop instructional strategies.
  - Develop and select instruction.
  - Develop assessment instruments.
- Implementation
  - Implement the system.
  - Revise the instruction, if necessary.
- Evaluation
  - Design and conduct the formative evaluation of instruction.
  - Conduct summative evaluation.

Each step in the ADDIE model receives input from the previous step and provides output for the next step; thus, each component is carefully linked. This interactive model of instruction can be viewed as a systematic process in which every component is crucial to achieve the goal of successful learning. These components include the learner, instructor, instructional materials, and the learning environment. The many components of the system interact to enhance learning. The model focuses on what the learner will be able to know when the instruction is concluded. Currently, almost all ISD models in use today are based on the generic ADDIE model and its components.

Managing Multimedia Projects for Education

Educational multimedia projects present the same kind of management issues that other types of complex educational projects face. The teacher needs to consider variables that range from how the project would look onscreen to what the students, equipment, budget, schedule, and resources allow (Lee & Owens, 2000). In order for teachers to understand project management, they must have a clear understanding of the steps involved in the process. The main steps in the development process include plan, prototype, develop, author, test, and project dissemination (Ivers & Barron, 2005):

Step 1: Plan

Teachers must tell students that before they begin the project, they must think through the following aspects of the project: audience, concept, purpose, schedule, personnel, budget, and equipment for the project. It is suggested that the student draw a storyboard that sketches out the content, screen by screen, and identifies the multimedia effects the student may want to use in the project.

Simple projects, such as a short presentation, may only need a brief, 1- or 2-page outline. Larger projects require more planning. Sometimes project planning entails a more complex format involving a project specification form.

Step 2: Prototype

To ensure the quality of the project, a prototype may be developed in order to test the design ideas for usability before proceeding.

Creating a storyboard (see Figure 7.1) is the process of sketching the contents of a project on planning worksheets or with development software. Similar to the flowchart for computer programmers, the storyboard does not have to be a work of art. Graphics can be hand drawn. The idea of storyboarding is to give the project team enough information so each member can take the storyboard and begin to develop his/her portion of the final product. The team members will work together in creating the storyboard.

Based on the input from the team members after reading the storyboard, a prototype will be created to demonstrate how the learner will move through and interact with the content, and how the program will look. Most project prototypes contain at least the project's entry page, sometimes also called the front screen, and main menu page for the proposed project (Lee & Owens, 2000). A design prototype should also specify the fonts and colors to use, how different design and media effects interact, and how

Figure 7.1. A storyboard template

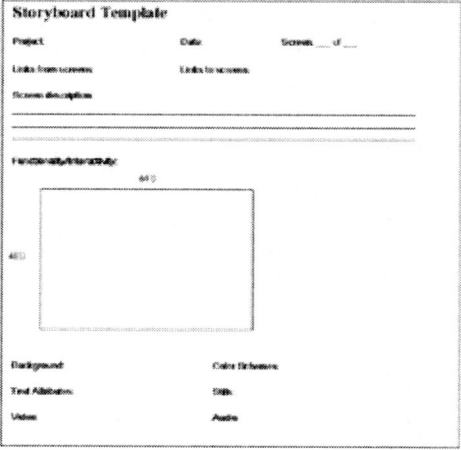

the navigation system works and looks. This gives the design team members an early "head's up" to the final project, and helps to identify any unexpected issues. After seeing the design, project team members may return to the storyboard to reshape their ideas.

Step 3: Develop

Using the design plans, the storyboard, as well as the prototype as blueprints, the team can develop the content and media effects. The team needs to establish standards for the consistency of media development, such as what level of quality needed for the sound or video clips, or the color system that can be applied to graphics and video. During this phase, the tester or someone acting in that role reviews the content and media to see whether they work well together.

Step 4: Author

During the authoring phase, the design team integrates the content and media into its final form. Depending on the software product used to create the project, this step may involve using a programming language, or it may be a matter of importing the design into multimedia authoring software.

Step 5: Test

Testing involves three things: proofreading the content on screen for errors such as spelling, checking the title's technical performance for problems such as the synchronization of media effects, and verifying that the title works on different hardware configurations. Projects often demand making tradeoffs in schedule and budget.

Step 6: Project Dissemination

The final step in the production phase is to build a master copy of the project. The master serves the purpose of organizing all the files in the project to make it easier to locate and retrieve files as needed.

The next phase depends on the plan for distribution of the project. The equipment involved in replicating a title on CD-ROM, DVD, or other newer media is getting cheaper; yet the process to duplicate a large quantity may be time consuming (Simkins, Cole, Tavalin, & Means, 2002). It is important to test the master copy for content and virus before it is handed off to make sure it performs the way the final project should perform.

Phases three and four often overlap each other: For example, the content has to be ready before the developers can integrate it into the final project. However, writers need to integrate the materials and review it on screen to edit the content well. Most projects involve several cycles of media development, authoring, review, and revision (Lee & Owens, 2000).

Multimedia Project Life Cycle

Every project is different, but most follow basic project implementation steps. Other professionals prefer to describe the multimedia project life cycle as follows (Ivers & Barron, 2005):

1. **Determine project scope:** Consider the audience, purpose, content, budget, schedule, resources, equipment, and the distribution.
2. **Letter of understanding:** Upon completion of the previous phase, a letter of understanding will be submitted describing the project and its specifications.
3. **Contractual agreement:** Upon approval of the letter of understanding, a contract will be written for the project.
4. **Storyboard:** Storyboarding is a convenient tool for visual communication. This important step in courseware development takes time to develop, but can save enormous time later during authoring.
5. **Prototype:** As explained in the previous section, a prototype is a working model of the final product. It is intended to demonstrate the visual design and functionality to project managers and clients. A prototype is created to demonstrate how the user will navigate through the program and interact with the content, and how the program will look (Cope, 2003).
6. **Script development:** Working with the subject-matter expert, writing a script of the narrative and presentation.
7. **Media development:** After a detailed list of the graphical and audio items to be used in the project, the developers and other designers set forth to create media elements including sound effects, voice-over narration, animations, digital photography, illustrations, video, and so forth.
8. **Authoring:** Authoring is the process of placing all the design and media elements into a complete software package. The authoring software is used to create content navigation and presentation along with interactive exercises, student tracking, and record keeping.

9. **Alpha testing:** Alpha testing is an early testing phase of the project. This early review allows the client to evaluate the project, even though the full functionality of the program may not yet be implemented.
10. **Beta testing:** The beta version is a full-functioning version of the product with all known problems resolved. Both the client and the design team will review the beta version to search for any remaining problems (Dancyger, 2002). At this final stage of development, the project should require very few changes or modifications.
11. **Project delivery:** Before master copies are released, any final changes requested by the client are made to the project. The program is prepared for delivery. Packaging is designed as required, and for CD or DVD delivery, disk duplication is scheduled (Cope, 2003).

Several of these steps can overlap each other. Most projects involve several cycles of media development, authoring, review, and revision. In fact, the project is likely to evolve as the resources change (Ivers & Barron, 2005). For example, the content has to be ready before the developers can integrate it into the final project. However, writers need to integrate the content and review on screen to edit the content well.

Multimedia Design Team or Production Crew

The Education Arena

As for educational multimedia design, developing a multimedia project also involves skill sets ranging from project management and interface design to sound preparation and programming. Sometimes, budgets and schedules require multimedia developers to juggle more than one role (Lee & Owens, 2000). Although multimedia tools make it possible for one person to perform every task, few technology application teachers or students have the combination of technical, artistic, and management skills necessary to fill every role. As a rule, multimedia projects are best developed by teams with a range of expertise. The more students understand each production crew's role and responsibilities, the better they will perform in these functions (Simkins et al., 2002):

- Roles and responsibilities of project manager
    - Report to the supervisors.
    - Organize the team members.
    - Provide project management leadership for the overall project.

- Track and monitor project budgets, deliverables, and milestones.
- Schedule meetings to review status of work.
• Roles and responsibilities of instructional designers
  - Research K-12 educator user requirements for portal development, multimedia tools, and video-mediated learning.
  - Determine screen layout.
  - Create flowcharts.
  - Specify the project design in the storyboards.
• Roles and responsibilities of content experts/writers/script writer
  - Content experts are also called subject matter experts (SMEs). For many multimedia projects in education, SME and writers are the same individuals.
  - Research the content.
  - Help storyboard.
  - Write all of the text.
  - If the content experts and the writers are different people, the content experts work with the writers to help communicate the right information.
• Roles and responsibilities of developers /program authors/lead programmer
  - Evaluate existing off-the-shelf software.
  - Digitize existing material for use on professional development program.
  - Design and develop prototype applications and multimedia learning objects.
  - Troubleshoot problems found in product prototype.
  - Write the code that integrates all of the media effects into a working program.
• Roles and responsibilities of video specialists/camera operator
  - Prepare the video, which may involve shooting the original videotape.
  - Convert the data on the tape into a digital format for the computer.
• Roles and responsibilities of audio/video specialists/sound engineer/audio technician
  - Prepare the voice narration, sound effects, and music.
  - Convert traditionally recorded sounds to a digital format that a computer can handle.
• Roles and responsibilities of graphic artists/art director
  - Create the graphical parts, such as the screen elements and buttons.
  - Prepare the drawings, scanned photographs, and animations that are specified in the storyboard.

- Roles and responsibilities of testers
    - Verify that every aspect of the title works correctly.
    - Check every word, screen, and media effect to ensure their quality.
    - Run the title on different hardware configurations.

The entire multimedia production team together has to establish a consistent design for the title by specifying what the navigation system looks like, where information and media appear on screen, and what fonts, colors, and graphical design elements to use. Keep the multimedia design projects simple at first. Then tackle more complex multimedia effects and title design as student expertise grows.

The Commercial Sector

It is also important to know the major roles of a commercial team, because school multimedia teams sometimes will be working side by side with a commercial team. In commercial film production, an "executive producer" is someone who is either financing a film or is representing the group who finances a film. The responsibility of an executive producer is to make sure that everyone else is doing his/her job; that the project is on schedule and is not over budget. The executive producer will work closely with the director if any concerns arise, to make sure that the film is being made as planned.

In commercial film production, a director is responsible for overseeing the creative aspect of a project from start to finish (Simkins et al., 2002). When a director reads a script, his or her vision will be responsible for presenting it with specific shots, lighting, mood, nuance, and emotion. The director works closely with the writer for improving the script. He or she is responsible for approving every camera angle, lens effect, lighting setting, and set design. The director also works closely with the cast, meeting before each scene to do a run through. He or she will also listen to each suggestion of the actors. At the end of the day, the director, producer, and key crew members will screen that day's footage (called dailies) in deciding if scenes will need to be reshot (Simkins et al., 2002). The director will also be involved in postproduction when the film is edited into its final form. He will also listen to the suggestions of crew members. Utilizing each person's talent is what makes a director, and the film, a success.

Media Acquisition

A multimedia project unavoidably has to use a number of logos, audio/video clips, graphics, animations, texts, quotes, Web sites, backgrounds, photographs, cartoons, newspaper articles, screen captures, references, and other media clips. There are several ways for school multimedia design teams to acquire media (Simkins et al., 2002).

First, students may need to consider developing their own effects. With a creative idea, the team can create original multimedia effects for the project. Creating their own effects offers two advantages: the control over the concept and quality of the effects, and the ownership of copyright.

The next choice for a school multimedia design team is to convert existing material into useful formats (Simkins et al., 2002). Many multimedia titles are rooted in existing printed, taped, or recorded materials that can be digitized to use on a computer. For example, students can use a scanner or video frame grabber to convert existing artwork to computer-ready graphics. However, make sure students have written permission when dealing with copyrighted material. A school multimedia design team may also acquire effects from professional services that sell or license books, music, sound effects, voice narration, film clips, and other effects to use in the project.

Another alternative, not commonly used in schools, is to hire professionals to prepare the multimedia effects. Hiring professionals can be expensive, but it provides some advantages such as quality, control, copyright ownership, and compatibility. This option makes good sense when students are preparing sound or video effects because expertise and a controlled working environment make a significant difference in quality.

The final resort is to locate materials in the public domain. For example, many of the materials that the United States government produces are available for teachers and students to use.

However, teachers should pay close attention to copyrights. Using copyrighted materials without permission may have costly consequences, even when students use the materials in a limited way and have no commercial plans. If students want to use someone's work, first find out if it is copyrighted. If it is, arrangements must be made for written permission to use it.

Maintenance of Media

Multimedia projects often include hundreds of media effects. To work efficiently, students and technology application teachers have to work out a system for tracking and managing them. Teachers can approach tracking and storing multimedia effects in a number of ways. One of the ways to track multimedia effects is to set up a database with the following information (Simkins et al., 2002):

- File names
- File type
- Usage

- Artist or developer who created the effect
- Legal & copyright status, fees/royalties
- Version number
- Archive location

Students and teachers alike in the school multimedia design team face the demands for large amounts of space needed to store multimedia effects (Simkins et al., 2002). They have to consider effective ways to transfer media so that team members can collaborate effectively, backup project files for the short-term, and archive multimedia effects for the long run.

Final Words

Multimedia design projects are complex programs, requiring proper planning to develop and deliver projects. For example, a high school multimedia design team is asked by a local business to develop a new employee orientation video. Identifying the client's special needs can be tricky, but it is critical for a successful multimedia project. Here are some questions and information that must be gathered by the school design team as the team shapes the content of their multimedia project for a new employee orientation video (Simkins et al., 2002).

Audience

Always tailor the quantity and style of the multimedia effects to be used to the audience. In this example, the school team is presenting a new employee orientation video to a local business. Students will want to avoid cute animations and sounds, and stick to effects that accurately convey the substance of the information. On the other hand, a multimedia presentation usually demands many fancy effects (Lee & Owens, 2000). The audience will also decide the final dissemination of the project. If, for example, students are preparing a project for a small group to use, they may simply copy it onto CDs and DVDs and distribute the project this way. If, on the other hand, students are preparing for a larger audience, they may consider moving the project to the Web platform.

Purpose

Multimedia effects need to speak to a particular audience. Before choosing the media, consult with the client and be clear about the response needed from an audience.

Decide the purpose, whether to educate, entertain, inform, or persuade the audience, or some mixture of these goals. Keep these goals in mind when preparing effects. In our new employee orientation project example, the purpose is to educate and, inform, and at the same time motivate the audience.

Content

Use the content to drive the effects to be used. Some content lends itself to multimedia effects. For example, some pictures lead to a vignette of video clips and key words that instantly reveal a process. Other content may work better with illustrations in person. In this case, video designers have to make arrangements to video record (Lee & Owens, 2000).

Budget

If students are working with a limited budget, keep the project simple. Be realistic about what the budget supports and achieve the quality desired within the budget.

Schedule

Preparing and testing multimedia takes time, depending on the complexity of what students are doing. Producing elaborate multimedia effects can be time consuming. If time is an issue, opt for creating simple effects.

Resources

The resources needed depend entirely on the kind of project created. Developing a more complex project often works better with a team of people, each trained in specific areas. Effective communication with at least one contact person within the local business which requests for the new employee orientation project is important for the team to get the resources needed. For example, the contact person may show students a printed copy of the new employee orientation manuals the company used in the past. He/she may let students use the audio/video clips previously developed for other occasions. He/she may wish to have students contact the human resources director of the business who eventually is going to train new employees using this multimedia project.

Equipment

The team needs to assess both their school equipment and the minimum configuration expected for their audience use. Multimedia effects demand significant computer power for preparation and play. Furthermore, preparing certain media requires special equipment for achievement of desired quality.

Distribution

Multimedia titles often take a lot of storage space, so it is important to know how students plan to distribute the project before development. If, for example, they plan to run the project over the Internet, they should work with simpler effects to minimize file size. If students plan to use a DVD, local area network, or intranet to distribute the work, they will have fewer storage constraints (Dancyger, 2002).

References

Cope, P. (2003). *Teach yourself digital video and PC editing*. New York: McGraw-Hill.

Dancyger, K. (2002). *The technique of film and video editing: History, theory, and practice* (3rd ed.). Burlington, MA: Focal Press.

Dick, W., & Carey, L. (1978). *The systematic design of instruction*. New York: Harper Collins.

Dick, W., & Cary, L. (1990). *The systematic design of instruction* (3rd ed.). New York: Harper Collins.

Gagné, R. (1965). *The conditions of learning*. New York: Holt, Rinehart & Winston.

Ivers, K. S., & Barron, A. E. (2005). *Multimedia projects in education: Designing, producing, and assessing* (3rd ed). Westport, CT: Libraries Unlimited.

Lee, W. W., & Owens, D. L. (2000). *Multimedia-based instructional design: Computer-based training, Web-based training, and distance learning*. San Francisco: Pfeiffer.

Reiser, R. A., & Dempsey, J. V. (2002). *Trends and issues in instructional design and technology*. Upper Saddle River, NJ: Merrill Prentice Hall.

Simkins, M., Cole, K., Tavalin, F., & Means, B. (2002). *Increasing student learning through multimedia projects*. Alexandria, VA: Association for Supervision & Curriculum Development (ASCD).

Sample Questions

1. A high school student team is invited by a local TV station to participate in the creation of infomercials. The first task for the team to complete is:
   a. Storyboarding
   b. Casting
   c. Finding financial support
   d. Investigating the daily routine of a news anchor

2. What are the major job responsibilities for an executive producer of a multimedia project?
   a. Finding good scripts
   b. Hiring and financing
   c. Story boarding
   d. Creating the prototype

3. Which of the following descriptions about multimedia project is NOT true?
   a. Most projects involve several cycles of media development, authoring, review, and revision.
   b. The project is likely to evolve as the resources change.
   c. At the end, packaging is designed as required, and for CD or DVD delivery, disk duplication is scheduled.
   d. The steps in the cycles of media development, authoring, review, and revision cannot overlap each other.

4. Which of the following description about prototype is NOT true?
   a. A prototype will show how the program will look in detail.
   b. A prototype is a working model of the final product.
   c. A prototype is intended to demonstrate visual design and functionality to project managers and clients.
   d. A prototype is created to demonstrate how the user will navigate through the program and interact with the content.

5. Which of the following early testing phases allows the client to evaluate the project, even though the full functionality of the program may not yet be implemented?
   a. Alpha testing
   b. Development
   c. Authoring
   d. Project delivery

Answers: (1) A (2) B (3) D (4) A (5) A

Chapter VIII

Video and Sound in Education

ISTE NETS_T, I. Technology operations and concepts
Teachers demonstrate a sound understanding of technology operations and concepts.

ISTE NETS_T, V. Productivity and professional practice
Teachers use technology to enhance their productivity and professional practice.

Chapter objective: The teacher demonstrates knowledge of strategies and techniques used in the preproduction, production, and postproduction of video products.

Educational Relevance of Audio and Visual Productions

Two decades ago, computerized word processors transformed the world of the writer. No more cutting and pasting pages with a pair of scissors. The user could get everything "just right" on the computer screen before it was printed. A similar technology breakthrough has occurred in audio and video production. Not long ago, schools spent over $100,000 for the cameras and computers. Now, technology application teachers can have a "movie studio" for students for under $5,000 with a digital camcorder, a computer, and necessary software.

The new digital, nonlinear, video editing makes it possible for anyone to be a producer. Instead of shuffling words on computerized word processors, students are juggling video clips with computerized video editing software. When footage from the camera is recorded onto the computer hard drive, the computer can manipulate the audio clips and digital images in many ways. In today's classroom, students may have a postproduction facility sitting right on their desktops. When students make copies of their work in the digital format, they do not lose picture quality as they did in the past with the analog format. Today, student musical creations or student selected music resources from CDs, Internet files, instruments or tapes are critical components in multimedia production. Also, lyrics and other art work produced by students can add the power of an affective element to their work.

To aid students with audio-video productions, it is important that teachers learn the nuts and bolts of incorporating various multimedia elements into video and multimedia projects. For instance, technology application teachers must become knowledgeable of downloading music from the Web and become familiar with software that allows for cut and paste music editing, and programs that allow for the instant creation of royalty-free music in custom lengths.

For many technology application teachers, audio and visual technology is a brand new territory. Not only are audio and video media different from other productivity tools, but the procedures, hardware, software, and the technical language used differ as well. Furthermore, many schools currently do not have the purchasing power to obtain editing decks for students and teachers to explore this new area of technology.

Audio Use and Equipment

When using audio in multimedia production, it is important for students and teachers to have a general understanding of the technological aspects of audio production. In general, sound produced by the computer is either synthesized or digitized for playback. When incorporating audio into multimedia projects, teachers learn to record and edit audio for stand-alone use or for inclusion in student multimedia projects. Students can obtain audio clips from CDs or audio cassette recordings. Clips can then be edited and exported to CDs, DVDs, memory sticks, or saved as files in a variety of formats.

Hardware considerations for an audio editing workstation require built-in digital audio circuitry or an additional audio adapter card. A speaker converts electrical signals to sound. On the contrary, microphones (mic) convert sound into electrical impulses, usually for recording or amplification.

When audio sounds are captured, the equipment converts the analog signal to digital. Conversely, when audio sounds are played back, audio sounds are converted from a digital form back to an analog form that can drive a speaker. Disk space requirements depend on both sampling method and time length (Eargle, 2001).

Specifications of Microphones

Many people have the misconception that microphones only pick up sound from sources that are nearby. However, some microphones are designed to receive sound sources from different angles. There are a wide variety of microphones; the most important factor in choosing a microphone is by the pickup patterns of microphones:

- **Omni:** This simple microphone design will pick up all sound, regardless of its point of origin, and is thus known as an omnidirectional microphone. It generally has good to outstanding frequency response.
- **Bidirectional:** This type of microphone accepts sound striking the front or rear of the diaphragm, but does not respond to sound from the sides. Most often it is placed above an instrument.
- **Cardioid:** is a "Heart" shaped pattern, exhibited by some microphones, that reduces pickup from the sides and back. This pattern is popular for sound reinforcement or recording concerts where audience noise is a possible problem. The major drawback is that sounds from the back are not completely rejected, but merely reduced (Eargle, 2001). The second problem is that the actual

shape of the pickup pattern varies with frequency. Furthermore, the frequency response for signals arriving from the back and sides will be uneven.

- **The hypercardioid:** has a narrower heart-shaped pickup pattern than that of cardioid microphones. This pattern gives a better overall rejection and flatter frequency response than the cardioid pattern at the cost of a small back pickup lobe. The hypercardioid pattern is often seen as a good compromise between the cardioid and bidirectional patterns.
- **Shotguns:** These types of microphones are almost always built with a long tube protruding from the front. However, this tube has a series of holes or slots along the side that act as a phase canceling device for sounds coming from the rear of the microphone. These properties make them ideal for pinpointing and capturing the audio of something from far away without capturing as much of the surrounding sound. Shotgun microphones are sometimes called line microphones and are used to record dialogue for film and video.

Getting Good Audio Effects

Ideally, when recording interviews, one staff will run the camera, another staff member will ask the questions, and one staff will hold the microphone. Usually the person asking the questions can also hold the microphone.

Pay special attention to the distance from the source audio to the mic and the background noise. If possible, use a clip-on lavaliere mic that clips on to the person's clothing or a hand held microphone for interviews. The rule of thumb is, the closer the microphone is to the source of sound, the better. If a lavaliere mic is used, be aware of things around the mic that may rub against it and interfere with the audio recording.

Audio Editing

Music, audio books, recorded speeches, sounds, and sound effects can all be found in digital audio formats including RealAudio, WAV, and MP3. Digital audio describes sound recording and reproduction systems that work by using a digital representation of the audio waveform. The advantages of digital audio include (Eargle, 2001):

- Enables individuals to easily record and edit or erase.
- Large numbers of copies can be produced at low cost.
- Provides fast, random access to different segments

Special purpose digital audio editing software is used to edit, mix, or analyze audio. Typical features of audio editing software include the ability to (Alldrin, Petersen, & Molendra, 1998):

- Record audio from cassettes, vinyl records, the radio, through a computers' microphone, or line-in connector
- Record a speaker's dictation through a microphone
- Record and edit audio for broadcasting
- Apply special effects, such as fade, echo, reverse, and more
- Digitally remaster and restore old recordings with noise reduction and save them in the latest digital formats
- Edit music for dance programs, student plays, gymnastics, or other school performances
- Analyze human speech, bird song, music instruments, and so on

Audio can normally be digitized through standard sound cards; these cards come with most computers. A sound card is an add-in circuit board that enables the computer to accept audio input from a microphone to edit, trim, or mix recordings; to play sound files stored on disks or CD-ROMs; and to produce audio output through speakers or earphones. For output, sound cards can create or synthesize sounds, like a keyboard/synthesizer, and play previously recorded sounds, like a tape recorder/player.

Figure 8.1. The audio editing interface acts as a visual communicator and allows users to drag-and-drop and manipulate sound clips. Audacity is a cross-platform application that supports Windows and Linux as well as Mac. The graphic is used with permission from Audacity, Inc. at homepage: http://audacity.sourceforge.net/.

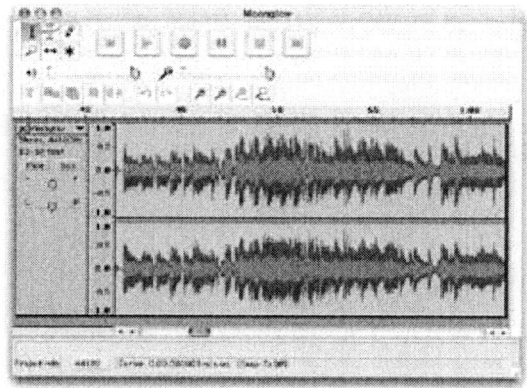

Editing sound on a computer usually involves cutting, pasting, and moving files. Sound designers have to zoom in to get a better view of the sound wave pictures or play back multiple times during the process. The software editing interface acts as a visual communicator and allows users to drag-and-drop and manipulate sound clips (see Figure 8.1).

One of audio's effective uses occurs when sounds are mixed with a sound mixer for multimedia projects. In live recording, through mixing, sounds are combined from different microphones, such as narration and ambient sound. The sound technician responsible for mixing often uses a device called a "mixer," that allows for the adjustment of the balance and levels of sound from these different sources. In editing, this also refers to combining more than one recorded soundtrack in the finished product. Through audio mixers, audio can be a blend of student narration, sound effects such as door bells, creaking chairs, or recorded music. To accomplish this, first plug the computer, microphone, and DVD or CD player or other sound source into the mixer, and then the mixer's output can be connected to a VCR or another computer.

Synthesized sounds are sounds created by computer circuitry. MIDI, or musical instrument digital interface, is a type of emerging synthesized format. Rather than recording sounds, MIDI instruments and software record finger actions, such as what note is being played, when, and for how long. MIDI files contain both musical information and performance data. To playback MIDI files, users need a sound card that can interpret the MIDI note data (Alldrin et al., 1998).

Sound Effects

It is worth mentioning that music and special sound effects can be very effective as a transitional accent for multimedia projects. For example, in a HyperStudio stack on "How Does the Jury System Function?" a middle school student can choose a dramatic orchestral accent between cards, implying serious work. Sound effects can be added to the buttons on the cards to provide feedback to the users that a button is clicked.

Nonmusical elements on a soundtrack other than dialogue are called sound effects. Appropriate sound effects can enhance the impact of movement, provide feedback to user interaction, and build atmosphere. All sorts of sound effects may be created in the studio and added to a multimedia production later.

In music and film/television production, typical sound effects, such as echoes, reverb, and flanging, are used in recording and amplified performances. With echoes, one or several delayed signals are added to the original signal. The remainder of sound that exists in a room after the source of the sound has stopped is called reverberation. We have all heard reverberation when doing something like bouncing a basketball in a large enclosed school gym. Even though we may not always notice it, all rooms have some reverberation. The characteristics of the reverberation are a big part of the subjective quality of the sound of any room in which we are located.

Popular sound effects also include car starts, door bells, door openings, creaks, church bells, telephone ringing, thunder, animal sounds, and water running. There are inexpensive transitional sound effects resources through CD-ROMs and online stores of multimedia companies. With some editing skills, teachers and students can also lay another effect, or part of an effect or music, over the first. For example, have a dog barking over a fountain, or have a dialog going on at the beach.

Usually no formal instruction is really necessary to turn teachers and students into sound effect artists for school-related projects. A few good examples will do it. Users can also download from online libraries royalty free sounds, public domain sound effects, and a wide collection of archives of general sound effects.

Audio Players and Formats

Just as a VCR is needed to play a videotape, the right kind of player has to be used to see or hear digital recordings. A digital audio player (DAP) is a device that stores, organizes, and plays digital music files, while a digital-to-analog converter (DAC) is the sound card component that plays sounds stored in a file. Digital audio comes in many different formats, and multiple formats will be a fact of life for the foreseeable future. There are three main types of digital audio players (Katz, 2002):

- MP3-based players
- Flash-based players - These are devices that hold digital audio files on internal or external media, such as memory cards.
- Hard drive-based players or digital jukeboxes - These are devices that read digital audio files from a computer hard drive. The Apple iPod is an example of popular digital jukeboxes.

There are three major categories of audio file formats:

- Uncompressed formats, such as WAV, AIFF, and AU.
- Formats with lossless compression, such as lossless Windows Media Audio (WMA).
- Formats with lossy compression, such as MP3.

These three formats are compatible with both Windows and Macintosh. Microsoft's WAV file or WaveForm format is the most commonly supported audio file format for computers. It is the default format for digital audio on Windows PCs. The WAV format can also be downloaded to a computer and stored. This format can be played without being connected to the Internet. The WAV format can also be downloaded to a computer and stored. Most Web browsers can play these files without special software. Although they take longer to download than RealAudio files, they are convenient because they can be inserted into PowerPoint presentations. However, as file sharing over the Internet has become popular, the WAV format has declined in popularity due to its file size. AIFF is the default audio format for the Macintosh, and AU is the default format for SUN systems. The RealAudio Player is used to play sound recordings using "streaming" technology. It is real-time, live audio on the Web.

Standard formats make it easier to produce products that are less costly and more compatible with each other. The compatibility provided by standard formats helps assure consumers that their music will not become obsolete. There are also proprietary audio formats. If a format does become obsolete, plenty of tools are available for converting digital audio to newer formats. Cassette tapes, compact discs, and PCM are examples of standard audio formats that benefit both consumers and manufacturers.

For audio, the 8-bit format is highly compressed and is usually contrasted to 16-bit, the sampling rate for most CD-quality sound. Much of the digital audio and video found on the Web can be seen or heard in a standard Web browser. However, sometimes specialized tools or viewers are needed.

CODEC or Encoder/Decoder

Technology application teachers also need to distinguish between a file format and a CODEC. CODEC is an abbreviation for "encoder-decoder," which describes a device or program capable of performing data compression to make sending and receiving more efficient. CODECs are often used in videoconferencing and streaming media solutions. There is more software that enables teachers and students to create their own music and passages for different desired lengths from seconds to long minutes, and in different forms from musical scores to speeches. These programs can be used to create royalty-free music for student projects, allowing Web posting or videotape production. Music for multimedia can also be handled as a pictureless *QuickTime* movie. *QuickTime Pro* is very good at converting sound files into *QuickTime* files. The program can also edit, clip, compress, and scale the tracks.

Video

It is now possible for technology application teachers to have a "movie studio" for students for under $5,000 with a digital camera, a computer, a tripod, editing and authoring software, and some cables. Students and teachers can now make short digital movies with software that often comes with the computer. Video projects can be valuable serving as a model for coming technologies by requiring teamwork, communication, and planning. Video is also an unbeatably engaging medium for students (Cope, 2003).

For example, a high school team is requested by the manager of a small coastal town to interview a fisherman for the history of the town. After shooting, the high school team has two half-hour tapes that they want to combine into a single 15-minute tape by cutting pieces out of each of the long tapes. Team members have to go through each tape with the editor, select and record the pieces for use, add titles and music, review the finished piece, and make any changes necessary. This project will take even more time if they have numerous short clips that have to be trimmed or if they have transitions to insert.

Video production is generally divided into three stages (Cope, 2003):

- Preproduction (Pre) Scouting locations, constructing sets, arranging for lighting, planning special effects, editing the script—all the arrangements that precede filming a production.
- Production The process of filming all of the essential material for a production.
- Postproduction (Post) The work performed on a movie after the end of principal photography, such as editing and digital compositing.

Preproduction

Production Crew

The structure of the video production team is not much different from the multimedia production crew that is discussed in Chapter VII, with its project manager, scriptwriter, artist, tester, and so on. However, a special term, "camera crew," is used to describe the group of crew members who set up, load, operate, assist, focus, and move the camera.

The director is the principal creative artist on a movie set. The director communicates to actors the way that he/she would like a particular scene played. Typically, a director has complete artistic control over all aspects of the movie, including casting, script editing, shot selection, shot composition, and editing (Vaughan, 2003). The producer is the manager of all business and financial aspects involved in making a film. The cinematographer, the director of photography or DP, first cameraman, or lighting cameraman, is the artist or technician in charge of photography. His or her expertise with lights, lenses, cameras, film stock, and processing establishes the "look" and "mood" of a film. The cinematographer typically works in close consultation with the director.

The camera operator is the person who operates the camera, works closely with the director, and sometimes is the director himself. A production assistant (set production assistant, PA, gopher, personal assistant, assistant to producer) is a person responsible for odd jobs on the set, either for the production as a whole or for individual actors or film makers (The University of North Carolina, 2003).

In addition to the camera crew, a casting director is the staff member who auditions and helps to select all of the speaking role actors. The background artist is the person responsible for designing or constructing the art placed at the rear of a set. The set designer is the person under the art director responsible for creating the movie's physical environments. A presenter is the person who introduces a production on screen or via voice-over. The prompter is the person who supplies actors with their lines if they forget. In addition to the major camera crew, sometimes a second unit is formed to be responsible for filming shots of less importance, such as inserts, crowds, scenery, and so forth.

Scripting

Like any good storyteller, good videos are those that provide interest and lead the viewer along with the action. Scripting is a general term for a written work detailing story, setting, and dialogue.

The assembly process is for assembling of the scenes and sequences of a film into approximately the order they appear in the script. There are several ways to make a rough or general representation of the production. The purpose of doing this is to help scriptwriters or directors plan what they need to gather to create the production. There are three types of planning tool: storyboard, shot list, and script (University of North Carolina, 2003).

The storyboard refers to a series of drawings depicting what is planned to do. Typically, a storyboard is series of drawings that approximate a sequence of moving images. It can depict different types of shots, shot transition and length, and use of soundtrack. It can help to conceptualize a shooting script, which is a written list of described shots itemizing camera position, shot length and transition, and soundtrack.

Through the script-editing process, a script is reviewed and changed based on input from sources such as the director or producer. To communicate, a story board can be used for a given story line to bring those new plot elements to life. Scriptwriters use scenes to indicate a continuous block of storytelling either set in a single location or following a particular character. The end of a scene is typically marked by a change in location, style, or time. The script from which a movie is made usually contains numbered scenes and technical notes. For continuity, a staff member will be assigned to track which parts have been filmed and how the filmed scenes deviated from the script; the staff member will make continuity notes, creating a lined script.

Scriptwriters try to tell a story with a camera, with an opening to set the stage, and build up to a climax or high point at the end. They know the tricks of avoiding abrupt cuts between scenes. Instead, they work for smooth transitions from one idea to another. Planning ahead keeps things clear of confusion and chance.

Every event has a beginning, a middle, and an end. Scriptwriters have to tell a story. The project should begin with information that establishes the "who, what, why, where, and when" of the event. The middle of the story should be captured through story events with the camera and video. At the end, the scenes should follow the events as they unfold. It is important to remember the story plan and try to follow it. With the beginning, the middle, and the end in mind, even if students do not edit this footage, they will have a well-developed narrative document of the event.

Video records a sequence of activity to form a miniature story. A scene is a continuous block of storytelling either set in a single location or following a particular character. The end of a scene is typically marked by a change in location, style, or time.

Terms commonly used by scriptwriters include the following:

- **Cut:** A clean break between consecutive shots. This is the instantaneous, direct switch from one picture to another.
- **Sequence:** This term is often synonymous with "scene." This is a group of related shots showing a single piece of action. This is a term used in gathering video and editing. For example, a sequence could be a wide shot of the beach, followed by a medium shot of a few wind surfers, followed by a single wind surfer zipping through the water.
- **Shot:** The basic unit of meaning in a moving-image text. It can be described according to its length, or duration, the way it is framed, and the arrangement of elements within it.
- **Shot transition:** The transition of one shot to another, which can be achieved by a cut, a dissolve, a wipe and so forth.

A video that does not have a story line can be a documentary video, which intends to describe and explain the subjects, and to inform the audiences. But even documentary videos require commentaries or narrations written by scriptwriters. Documentaries explore subjects in a way the public expects to be factual and accurate. They may be balanced by including various viewpoints, or they may be subjective, offering the viewpoint and impressions of one producer. Voice-over is an off-camera narrator who puts their voice over the video. The purpose of the voice-over is to describe what is happening on the video or provide information.

Title is written material which appears on a film and is not a part of an original scene. Subtitles appear in the main body of a film, generally placed near the bottom of the frame, to present the dialogue or commentary, or most commonly to translate dialogue from a foreign language into the language of the audience. Close-captioned (CC) is a system that displays the current dialog on screen for deaf or hard-of-hearing viewers. Through the dubbing technique, dialog is replaced with another language. Head titles or credits are titles at the beginning of a film that usually include the main title, the title carrying the name of the film itself. Sometimes called roll-ups, credit rolls, creepers, or scrolls, crawls creep slowly and horizontally in front of the camera. Credits are used to designate the actors in a film and the technicians who made it.

Production

Shooting

In telling a story with video, each event must be analyzed as to how it will be approached by the camera. Before beginning, make sure the camera is eye level with the speaker. Begin the sequence of shooting with a wide shot, also called an establishing or master shot. This gives the wide shot of the entire setting and lets the viewer know where the action is taking place. It is advised to take this shot just before the presentation begins, as the speaker is getting set up, or just as the speaker begins. Follow it with a medium shot and conclude with close-ups. It might show just the speaker from the waist up. Students may want to use this shot for the majority of the presentation. Smoothly zoom to get detail with a close-up shot. For example, if the speaker refers to a poster, zoom in to see the detail of what is on the poster. Students may want to use this shot periodically, then go back to a medium shot. When the presentation is over, students may want to end with a wide shot. This will show all the action as the presentation ends, and the person goes back to their seat or "off stage."

Zooming may be necessary to make a transition between shots. However, it is important that students learn to use the camera's zoom feature sparingly. Since the human eyes do not zoom, it is often disconcerting to watch footage with lots of zooming. It is important to note that even small movements can look like earthquakes in the footage. If students must zoom, they need to zoom slowly and use a tripod for the telephoto feature.

Photographers use the line of action, an imaginary line, to help stage camera positions for shooting action. It is typically "drawn" along the line of sight between two characters in a scene, or following the movement of characters, cars, and so forth. Photographers also use the line of sight, to connect the observer's eye with the objects the observer is looking at. Ideally, all shots of the action are taken from one side only of the line, to maintain consistent screen orientation and direction of movement.

There are two sources of movement when shooting video: the subject, and the camera itself.

It is important to keep the camera steady and allow the subjects to move, such as when videotaping a play actor. First, frame up the subject, then let the actor perform on the stage.

A common camera move is a "pan," in which the camera is traversed from left to right. The cameraman can let the camera follow the motion of the subject in a "pan." Suppose the subject walks down the hallway. The cameraman could keep the camera steady and let him walk into the frame, cross the frame, and exit the frame, or let the subject walk into the frame from the left, follow him with the camera as he walks past, and then allow him to disappear from the frame. This would be "panning." To do a pan smoothly, the cameraman has to use a tripod. With slow motion, an action of a shot is slowed down relative to the film's contextual pace.

Remember to leave enough room in front of the subject so that the audience gets a sense of where the subject is going. Otherwise, the subject will appear to be running into the edge of the frame. Specifically, if the frame were divided into thirds, and the subject was walking from frame left to frame right, try to keep the subject in the left-hand third of the frame when following the action with the camera. Then, stop moving the camera and allow the subject to walk out of the right side of the frame, leaving only the empty frame behind.

If the camera or editing system can measure frames, use this as a counter to log the videotape. Photographers use time code, the number of seconds or frames, to determine where scenes are located on a videotape. Time codes can be found when looking through the viewfinder when logging and editing tape. This is essential during editing and other postproduction work.

Also remember to leave at least 10 seconds of blank tape at the beginning of each cassette of tape. If recording someone who is speaking, be sure the camera is recording 5-10 seconds before the action begins. For example, when recording an interview with a client who is going to give a brief introduction of a product, start the camera, and tell the client to count silently to five and then begin speaking. This will give the client a few seconds to focus on what to say, and will also guarantee that the beginning of the introduction is captured. Video shoot the scene for at least 5 to 10 seconds before going on to the next shot. Also, at the completion of the zoom, remain stationary on the new scene for at least 5 seconds.

Copyright © 2008, IGI Global. Copying or distributing in print or electronic forms without written permission of IGI Global is prohibited.

Postproduction

Analog and Digital Videos

Analog videos employ linear editing techniques. Linear video editing is the process of selecting and modifying the images and sound recorded on videotape. Analog video can be edited with special adapter hardware using a computer screen to display analog videos. With analog videos, it is good to place shots in the desired order. It is more difficult to change shots later, although it can be done.

Digital videos employ nonlinear editing techniques. Perhaps the biggest difference between analog and digital editing is that the user can easily move the shots around and reorder them. It is important to think of digital editing as word processing for the video. The user is able to edit on the computer, change the order, erase clips, add clips, and so forth. With nonlinear editing, the computer assists editing of video without the need to assemble it in linear sequence (Goodman & McGrath, 2002). To digitize is to convert wave-based analog media into digital format so that it can be understood by computers. Digitizing is also known as "capturing," and sometimes "encoding."

When it is time to print a finished product, with analog editing, students and teachers can create a master as they work. With digital editing, students finish the product then "print" it out onto a tape or disk. Only digital video enables students to create their own video and have quick access to different segments on a disk. Analog videotapes do not provide random access. Laser discs do provide random access, but cannot be economically created.

Video Editing

Modern camcorders are mini-studios with features most users overlook. In-camera editing, macro lenses, music tracks, animation, and simple special effects are possible with any off-the-shelf camcorders, including the older models still found in many schools (Goodman & McGrath, 2002).

To perform digital compositing by combining separately filmed or digitally generated components through editing, special purpose software is required. Professional video-editing software, such as Adobe *Premiere* and *Final Cut Pro,* can be used to edit video clips. For schools and classrooms, editing software, such as Windows *Movie Maker* and *iMovie,* are available. Adobe *AfterEffects* can be used to create visual effects. A typical multitrack digital audio and video mixing program can be used to (Alldrin et al., 1998):

- Mix a number of sound tracks into a single stereo file.
- Create presentations with background music and video.
- Edit school and home produced videos and add text captions and compositing effects.
- Record and edit songs with separate instrument and vocal tracks.
- Capture video from a video recorder or other video source.
- Combine multiple layers of video into one AVI, QuickTime Movie, or Windows Media Video file.
- Support WAV, MP3, AIFF, OGG, WMA, and other digital audio formats as well as AVI, MOV, WMV, MPG, and other video formats.

The GUI interface of the audio and video software performs editing instantly, which means users can drag-and-drop, trim, copy, paste, and split files with almost no processing time. Many real-time effects can also be applied to files. Although most of these programs have some point-and-click features to simplify development, some require some knowledge of programming language.

Other terms and concepts related to digital editing with professional grade software include:

- **In point** or **inset point:** The place on the tape to start the edit.
- **Out point** or **outset point:** The place on the tape to finish the edit.
- **Preroll:** The amount of time that it takes for the camera to start rolling before actually recording or editing. This allows the tape to come up to speed before the edit is made.
- **Master:** The original version of the raw footage.
- **Dub:** To copy, "dub," or "double" a project. In general, to get the highest quality copies, try to make all of the copies from the master.

Video editing also involves the complicated and recursive processes of choosing the clips, capturing video, creating contents, using templates and background, adding transitions, adding titles, and applying audio effects. Sometimes professionals use an edit decision list to keep track of all of the necessary video objects including texts, images, videos, audios, and animations.

- **Choosing the clips:** Before assembling the clips, the teachers and students will want to select clips that fit in with their purposes. They have to be familiar with the video log (or shot list) to know the shots they have. They should also refer to their storyboard to see how the clips they have fit in with what they originally conceived. It is also a good practice to number the clips in the order that they will appear on the finished product (Goodman & McGrath, 2002). Choosing and numbering their clips will make the editing process go smoother because there are fewer decisions to make while actually using the editing equipment.

- **Capturing video:** Capture and playback of digital video is a challenge for mid-1990s computer hardware. Nowadays, digitization of video is usually accomplished with add-on devices for computers known as "video capture cards," although firewire ports, which are increasingly becoming a standard on out-of-the-box systems for both Macs and PCs, can also perform this function (Vaughan, 2003). Video capture cards record/digitize pictures for use with a computer. The software should be also compatible with virtually any standard Webcam or camcorder. The pictures may be still images or movies.

Creating content Most audio and video editing software has an editing timeline interface that acts as a visual communicator and allows users to drag-and-drop any picture, title, graphic, video, or audio file. Most professional level editing software accepts many file types:

Graphics: BMP, JPEG, GIF, PNG

Sound: WAV, MP3, WMA

Video: MPG, AVI, WMV, ASF

Figure 8.2. A screen capture of Video Magic Edit ™ with timeline interface (the graphic is used with permission from Deskshare Inc. homepage at http://www.deskshare.com/)

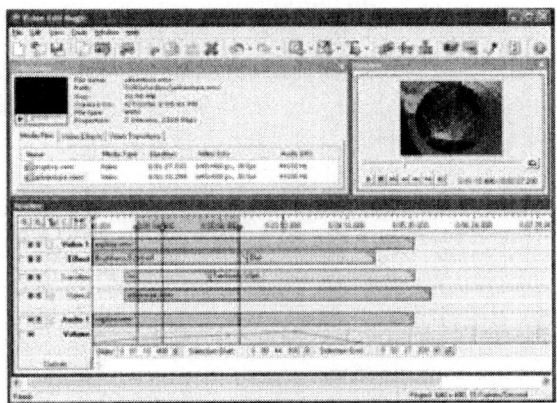

Digital editing, using the timeline interface, makes it possible to edit a portion of a movie by digitizing one or more frames and altering them electronically or combining them with other digitized images, and then outputting the modified frame. This allows the user to create overlays that are keyed insertions of one image into another. In video, the overlay procedure requires synchronized sources for proper operation. See Figure 8.2 for a screen capture of Video Magic Edit ™ with timeline interface.

- **Using templates and background:** The virtual backgrounds and templates that come with editing software give professional TV "looks" created by broadcast designers, much like the MS PowerPoint templates . Each includes fonts, backgrounds, effects, music, and more in a matched style and color scheme. The professional background replacement feature places the included green backdrop behind presenters to digitally replace the background with any image, graphic, or video clip. This is an easy way to put the presenters in front of a TV-style animation, an exotic location, or in front of a school's logo.
- **Adding transitions:** Professional level video-editing software usually includes a professional library of ready-to-use 3-D video effects exactly like those used on prime-time TV. There are over 100 transitions from smooth page peels to dramatic shattering effects. Dissolve is an editing transition in which one shot fades out as the next fades in, so that both are briefly superimposed.
- **Adding titles:** The software also can add titles and captions that time the content and match what is being discussed in the presentation. Then they will appear on-screen automatically at that point in the presentation.
- **Applying audio effects:** If planning to use music, be aware of the impact of music and sound effects on the piece. Choose them carefully to reflect the feeling and pace of the shot. Through mixing, sounds are combined from different microphones, such as narration and ambient sound (Alldrin et al., 1998). In editing, this also refers to combining more than one recorded soundtrack in the finished product. Through audio mixers, audio can be a blend of student narration, sound effects, or recorded music. One way to try experimenting with adding music and sound effects after the shoot is to use the "audio dub" feature on the camera. This feature allows the user to record audio over the video captured just by pressing down the button while playing the video in the camera. However, bear in mind, if this feature is used, it will erase all other audio on that part of the tape.
- **Sharing your movie:** When ready to produce the final presentation, press Record. Sharing the results can be accomplished by pressing Publish and selecting the type of file, including the popular Windows Media Player® and RealPlayer® formats, or save directly to a Web site. Here are a few output approaches:

- Attach to an e-mail
- Create streaming video
- Burn a DVD or CD
- Add to a PowerPoint show
- Place on a Web site
- Save to videotape (DV)

- **Media library** Includes a large royalty-free media library with everything needed to go from start to finish quickly, including quick-start templates, transitions, titles, graphics, music tracks, animated backgrounds, virtual sets, and even entire prebuilt shows for common topics. The directory includes individual tabs for fast and easy access to the library as well as any file on the PC or network.

Video Players and Formats

Video clips can be imported from tapes, both miniDV and VHS, digital camera via direct connection, analog video camera, via a connection through the VCR, and removable media, including USB and firewire hard drives. With these video-editing features, students and teachers can make movies or other video from a wide variety of video and audio sources, create and edit video projects using either consumer- or professional-level software, and save finished products to a variety of digital and waveform media. When the editing is finished, video clips can be exported by recording to DVD, to the tapes, or both miniDV and VHS. Digital video is available in a variety of file formats including Real Media, QuickTime, and MPG (Dancyger, 2002). Files can also be saved in a variety of file formats, including streaming media formats for use on the Internet.

NTSC, PAL, and SECAM are the three major video standards worldwide. NTSC is the standard for video signals in the US, Japan, and Canada. NTSC uses 30 fps. According to the NTSC standard, full-motion videos are digital video running at 30 fps. A full-motion video does not necessarily fill the screen. Instead, full-screen videos are digital videos that fill the entire screen using 640 x 480 pixels for typical graphic. PAL is the video format used in Australia and Western Europe. SECAM or sequential color with memory is the video format used mostly in France. PAL and SECAM both use 25 fps. In other words, when watching video footage, a sequence of 25 still pictures is displayed each second, which is different from the US standard NTSC. Digital video can be converted from analog formats such as videocam, VCR, laser disc, and TV.

Just as the user needs a VCR to play a videotape, a player is needed to see or hear digital recordings from computers. Much of the digital audio and video found on the Web can be seen or heard in a standard Web browser. However, sometimes, specialized tools or viewers are needed. These are software drivers, plug-ins, and other multimedia support tools.

Platform Default Formats

AVI or audio video interleaved is a Microsoft format for digital audio and video playback from Windows 3.1. It is the default Windows format for saving video with sound. Lately, it has been replaced by the ASF format, but is still used by some multimedia developers. AVI is fully compatible with MS PowerPoint, which makes it widely used in school settings. This format can also be played on the Windows Media Player.

The *QuickTime* MOV format is the Macintosh counterpart of AVI. QuickTime (.MOV) is a cross-platform real-time video and multimedia data format developed by Apple Computer. QuickTime files can include text, sound, and video. The *QuickTime* format can be displayed within a Web browser or in a separate window. The *QuickTime Player* is available for both Windows and for Macs.

The MPEG or moving picture experts group format has evolved and now includes MP1, MP2, MP3, and MP4 compression systems. This format is downloadable to a computer.

Macromedia *Flash* is a plug-in for animation and interactivity. It is used for visual effects, games, and animations. The plug-in software, Macromedia *Flash Player,* can be downloaded form the Macromedia Web site.

For digital stills and video, the 8-bit format is a measure of color depth and refers to images composed of 256 possible colors. An 8-bit video display setting on a monitor is often referred to as VGA. A 16-bit video display setting on a monitor is often referred to as "high color." A 24-bit video display setting on a monitor is often referred to as "truecolor."

Streaming Formats

To have the Internet-transmitted video displayed on a computer screen faster, the technology of streaming audio/video is used to begin playing media on the client side *before* it is fully downloaded from the server side, that is, begins playing as it is coming in, in real time. The major players of the streaming audio/video technology are RealNetworks *RealVideo,* Microsoft *Netshow,* and Apple "streaming" *QuickTime.*

ASF (active streaming format) is a Microsoft file format for digital video playback over the Internet, or on a standalone computer. It acts as a "wrapper" around any of a number of compression types, including MPEG. This "wrapper" supports many standard formats and compression types.

RealVideo delivers broadcast-quality video over the Internet in real time over modems operating at 28.8 kbps and up. The RealMedia (.RAM or .RM) files are streamed and play as they download. As a result, they start playing quickly before the entire video is downloaded. On slow connections, they may pause occasionally as the stream catches up, so they do not have the smooth flow of some videos. These files are only temporarily stored on the computer, so an Internet connection is needed for viewing.

Final Words About Video Production

Each project is different and the complexity of each project differs, too. Nevertheless, all video footage can be improved by editing. Editing lets the user tell a video story in a particular way, and gives the user the flexibility to combine shots from different angles.

Most of the editing is now digital based (Chaptman & Chaptman, 2004). Included in the planning should be a consideration of how to handle the relationship between pictures and music, and between pictures and narration if incorporating either into the finished tape.

For instance, a middle school class wants to make a photo montage together—a presentation of still photos of a field trip to the state capital with titles and some captions, the whole set to music. About 35 pictures an hour can be captured to tape. Each photo will stay on screen 5 seconds, so, each finished minute of tape will use about 12 pictures. A 10-minute photo montage will use about 120 pictures that, at 35 per hour, will take about 3 1/2 hours to capture. Adding a title will take another few minutes, adding captions to specific pictures can add a couple of minutes per caption. Adding music will take a half hour to an hour. Pretty soon, the middle school class' 10-minute photo montage will probably take 6 hours from start to finish, and could take considerably longer if they make lots of changes in picture sequence or add lots of complex transitions between pictures.

Each project is different: each client's degree of preparedness is different, and the complexity of each project differs, too. There really is not any way to predict the quality and the cost accurately, and projects almost always take longer than you think they will.

Technical Lingo

Audio/video production is a brand new area for new technology applications teachers to explore. Not only are the media different, but also the procedures, hardware, software, and the technical language used. Students and teachers who are involved with video production have to learn the professional lingo for clear communications among the crew members and with the clients. Commonly used technical jargon includes the following list of terms:

The rate at which the graphics processor renders new frames or full screens of pixels is called "frames per second" (FPS). Frames are single pictures in a computerized "movie"= or digital video. Thirty fps is considered full-motion, television-quality video. Film usually runs at 24 fps, video at 25 fps.

Key frame is a complete video frame that contains all the image details, not just the changes from the previous frame. The number of images per second displayed in a stream of video is called frame rate. The frame-grabber feature of video capture cards can capture a single frame from a video stream and store it as a still image.

When converting video or audio waves to digital format, the sampling feature of digitizing software picks out points along the wave and records these points. These snapshots can then be replayed in much the same way that motion pictures are recreated from the single frames. The higher the sampling rate, the more accurate the computer's representation of the wave because there are more snapshots or points per unit time (Cope, 2003). In digital video, when the computer cannot keep pace with the displayed images, it drops frames in an attempt to catch up. See Table 8.1 for a list of technical lingo used by video professionals.

Table 8.1. A list of technical lingo used by video professionals

- **Back Projection:** A technique in which action is projected on a screen behind live actors. A popular early use of back projection was to simulate car rides.
- **Call Sheet:** A listing of which actors will be required for which scenes, and when they will be required
- **Casting:** The process of hiring actors to play the characters in a script, typically done by a casting director with input from a director, or producer.
- **Clip:** A media segment such as an audio or video file incorporated within a larger context
- **Cross-cutting:** Refers to parallel action that is edited together to represent action happening simultaneously in different places.
- **Cut:** A stop in the action. In editing, it means the place where one shot moves to another.
- **Dissolve:** An editing transition in which one shot fades out as the next fades in, so that both are briefly superimposed.
- **Dolly Shot:** A shot taken by a camera mounted on a mobile dolly. The camera may dolly in for a close-up or dolly out by rolling away from the subject.

Continued on next page

Table 8.1. continued

- **Editing:** The selecting and combining of shots in the way they will appear on the movie screen. The work progresses from assembly to rough cut, then fine cut, at which point the sound editor is usally brought in.
- **Establishing Shot:** A full shot used to open a new scene. It shows significant details and characters, so that viewers can get their bearings before the camera focuses more tightly.
- **Fade:** A smooth, gradual transition from a normal image to complete blackness(also called "fade out"), or from a complete blackness to a normal image (also called "fade in").
- **Fast Motion:** A shot in which time appears to move faster than normal, usually achieved by skipping frames.
- **Feature film:** A move that lasts 60 minutes or longer and is intended for release.
- **Footage:** Any length of film. It is important to note that the footage shot for a particular effect, moment, scene, and film. Footage can also refer to a particular sequence of events depicted in a motion picture, or, a particular portion of the film.
- **Full Shot:** A shot that encompasses the action taking place before the camera in its entirety.
- **Full Motion:** Refers to NTSC-quality video—a video signal that is 30 fps and at least 640×480 pixels in size.
- **Insert:** Refers to a shot that will be edited into the final version of the movie, which are often closeup or extreme closeups that serves to explain or illustrate. An example could be a close-up of a projected slide that an actor refers to.
- **Jump Cut:** Used to refer to a deliberately abrupt transition between scenes or shots, which disrupts the continuity of time and space.
- **Lock it Down:** A direction given by the director or assistant director for everyone on the set to be quiet
- **Long Shot:** A shot in which the object of the actor or actress is distant from the camera, often used to place a person within his or her environment.
- **Low-Angle Shot** or **Up Angle:** A shot in which the subject is viewed from below, usally emphasizing or enhancing the importance of the subject.
- **Macro Lenses:** These lenses are essential for shooting close-ups of flowers, insects and other small items at life-size magnification or larger. They require optical characteristics, sharp definition, and true color fidelity.
- **Medium Shot:** A shot that is tighter than a long shot and wider than a closeup.
- **Mix:** The process of assembling and balancing the elements of dialogue, music, and effects electronically, thereby creating the final soundtrack.
- **Montage:** The term refers to a series of brief scenes used to quickly establish a mood or dramatic setting.
- **Morphing:** Changing one image into another by moving corresponding elements rather than by cross-fading.
- **Pan:** A shot taken by a camera moving horizontally. Whip pan (also known as swish pan) is an extremely fast pan, resulting in motion blur.
- **Pan and Scan:** A process by which an action on film is determined on a shot-by-shot basis. With pan and scan, less significant parts are eliminated. This is away of compensating for television's narrow aspect ratio when transferring film to video.
- **Point of View** (POV, POV Shot, or First-Person Camera): A camera angle which represents the view of a character in the film to show what that character sees. For example that point of view might be a neutral observer who records events without taking sides or the narration could be omniscient to show all points of view.

Continued on next page

Table 8.1. continued

- **Props:** short for "properties". The furnishings used to create a set or prepare a locations for shooting.
- **Retake:** The re-shooting of a scene.
- **Rough Cut:** A draft of a folm that follows assembly but precedes final cut.
- **Shot or Take:** In filming, this includes everything from when the camera starts to when it stops. After editing, a shot refers to the footage left in that strip of film, which is then put together with other shots to make a scene.
- **Shutter speed:** Refers to the length of time ni which light is collected for each frame in the video footage.
- **Stock Footage:** Refers to the shots in a film that duplicate from other films or a film library.
- **Tilt:** Refers to camera movement in a vertical plane. If the cameraman wants to show a tall building but can't get it all in the shot, he might start at the bottom of the building and go up to the top.
- **Traveling Matte Shot:** A shot in which forground action is superimposed on the background.
- **Special Effects:** Refers to artificial effects created on the set, as opposed to the visual effect that is created in post production.
- **Vignette:** Refers to a well-constructed scene in such an highly artistic fashion that this segment of a motion picture could stand on its own.
- **Visual Effects:** Modifications to a film during post-production.
- **Zoom:** The zoom lens of a video camera enables users to go from a wide-angle view to a close up at the push of a toggle.

An Interview Scenario

Here is a project scenario that integrates audio, video, and lighting techniques:

Before the Interview

Decide on clearly defined production roles ahead of time. Schedule the interview so that all needed people and equipment are available. Decide on a location for shooting. Keep in mind the visual background and potential background noise. Consider whether to shoot both the interviewer and the interviewee, or just the interviewee. If it is appropriate, ask the person to be interviewed to wear camera friendly clothing. That is, ask them to avoid wearing tight patterns because they look like they are moving through the camera. Frequently, white does not work well either because it is very bright.

During the Interview

To put interviewees at ease, give the person a general idea of the questions to be asked. When asking questions, try to be clear and to the point. Ask follow-up questions when appropriate.

If the interviewee wears glasses, adjust the angle of the glasses or the light so the viewer cannot see the lights reflected off the glasses. Get shots of items the interviewer talks about. These could be documents, a special poster, a building, and so forth.

Designers use the term "talking head" to refer to a full screen shot of a person talking. The phrase "just a bunch of talking heads" has a derogatory meaning that it is very interesting visually. For interviews or presentations, the source of light should not come from behind the person giving the presentation.

Headroom, talking room, and walking room leave space in the shot for the action, whether it be words or movement. When conducting shots of people, photographers use the term headroom to refer to the space above the subject's head. Different amounts of headroom are needed depending on the intent of the creator of the video. In general, when standing right in front of someone, there will be space all around them; they are not cut off by a frame. Leaving headroom, or space beside them, imitates real life. When interviewing someone talking, generally do not have the camera looking directly at the subject. Generally, the person should be looking off to the left or right of the camera a bit. Frame the shot so that there is sufficient talking room. That is, leave some extra space in front of the subject's face. If the person is talking to another person, this shows space between them. If the person is in motion, walking room gives them space to walk to (Dancyger, 2002).

Over the shoulder or a cutaway is usually a shot of the interviewer, who can be listening, nodding, or responding to the guest. This is frequently used in interviews to show the person asking the questions (University of North Carolina, 2003). It is usually referred to as "over the shoulder" because the photographer is literally shooting video of the interviewer over the shoulder of the interviewee. These are very useful when editing because it provides an easy way to transition.

Also, be careful when setting up an interview to make sure that there is nothing in the background that might look odd. For example, if there is a tree in the background, be sure that it does not look like it is growing out of the subject's head. If videotaping for a class or placing material on the Internet, an interviewee's agreement is needed. Make sure the person signs a release form. This form is written authorization signed by the person allowing for the video to be shown or aired.

After the Interview

When the crew returns to the school, view the tape and discuss what went well during the interview process and what could have gone better. Another critical question to discuss is how useful the interview was to the project?

The Production Sequence

To debrief the chapter, let us use the same example of a high school team requested by the manager of a small coastal town to interview an elderly fisherman for the oral history of the town. The following includes the 12 production steps involved in a video production.

- **Step 1. Identify the purpose of the production:** If there is no clear agreement on the goal or purpose of a production, it will be impossible to evaluate success. Is the purpose to instruct, inform, entertain, or to generate feelings? Or, is the real purpose to raise the audience's desire to take some action? Some productions even have more than one goal.
- **Step 2. Analyze the target audience:** Based on such things as age, sex, socioeconomic status, educational level, and so forth., program content preferences will differ. These preferences are also different for different parts of the United States. Audience characteristics are referred to as demographics. These regional demographic variations can, in part, be seen by differences in the local programming broadcast in different parts of the country, and sometimes by the films and network programming that some local stations decide not to air. Chief among the content issues are sex and violence, both of which have a positive relationship to ratings. Compared to standard broadcast television, educational video has different needs and expectations. But, here, too, demographic characteristics, such as age, sex, and education, also influence a production. Both producer and scriptwriter also have to be fully aware of the audience's experience, education, needs, and expectations.
- **Step 3. Develop a production proposal:** Summarize the plan and put it down on paper. After the program proposal or treatment is reviewed and approved by the teacher, a full script is developed.

    The first version of the script is generally followed by numerous revisions. A storyboard may be developed. A storyboard consists of drawings of key scenes with notes on dialogue, sound effects, music, and so forth. Throughout the rewriting process, a number of story conferences or script conferences typically take place. It will be at this point that any remaining research on the content will be conducted. During these sessions, such things as audience appeal, pace, problems with special interest groups, and so forth, are discussed and alternative ideas are considered. Today, larger video productions create detailed storyboards with computer software (Chaptman & Chaptman, 2004).
- **Step 4. Develop a production schedule:** Next, create a tentative schedule. Generally, broadcast or distribution deadlines will decide the production schedule. Not planning the steps carefully might cause a missed deadline, which could render the production worthless.

- **Step 5. Select key production personnel:** In addition to the producer and writer, select the production manager and director, the key creative team members, and the technical staff.
- **Step 6. Decide on locations:** Next, if the production is not done in the school, decide on key locations. It has been shown that audiences like the authenticity of "real" locations, especially in dramatic productions. In some cases, sets may have to be repainted or redecorated, signs changed, and so forth.
- **Step 7. Decide on talent, costume, and sets:** Depending upon the type of production, auditions may take place at this point as part of the casting process to selecting the actors for various roles. Once the talent or actors are decided on, the selection of costumes can start. These decisions ultimately have to be approved by the director. Even though sets may not be finished, rehearsals can get underway.
- **Step 8. Decide on the remaining production personnel:** Make decisions on remaining staff and production needs. At this point arrangements can be made for key technical personnel, equipment, and facilities.
- **Step 9. Obtain permits, insurance and clearances:** At many semipublic interior locations, such as shopping malls, and public locations, such as schools, it is not possible to just go to the location of your choice and start filming. Exterior production is sometimes limited to certain areas and to specific hours.
- **Step 10. Select video inserts, still photos, and graphics:** At this point decisions can be made for shooting or acquiring any video clips, still photos, and graphics that might be needed.
- **Step 11. Moving to rehearsals and shooting:** Depending on the type of production, rehearsal may take place either minutes or days before the actual shooting. Productions shot live-on-tape, which are without stopping except for major problems, must have early walk-through rehearsals, camera rehearsals, and dress rehearsals. Productions shot single-camera, film-style, are taped one scene at a time. Rehearsals can take place right before each scene is recorded.
- **Step 12. The editing phase:** After shooting is completed, the producer, director, and video recording editor review the footage and editing decisions are made. Using this edited tape and an EDL (edit decision list) as a guide, the production then moves to online editing, where much more sophisticated equipment was used to create the master copy, the final edited version of the tape. During this final editing phase, all necessary sound enhancing and special effects are added.

As nonlinear, digital editing becomes popular, the need for an off-line editing phase may be eliminated, or at least made optional. Editing is important to the creative process.

References

Alldrin, L., Petersen, G., & Molendra, M. (1998). *The home studio guide to microphones.* Swanton, VT: Artistpro.

Chapman, N., & Chapman, J. (2004). *Digital multimedia.* Hoboken, NJ: John Wiley & Sons.

Cope, P. (2003). *Teach yourself digital video and PC editing.* New York: McGraw-Hill.

Dancyger, K. (2002). *The technique of film and video editing: History, theory, and practice* (3rd ed.). Burlington, MA: Focal Press.

Eargle, J. (2001). *The microphone book.* Burlington, MA: Focal Press.

Goodman, R. M., & McGrath, P. (2002). *Editing digital video: The complete creative and technical guide.* New York: McGraw-Hill/TAB Electronics.

Katz, B. (2002). *Mastering audio: The art and the science.* Burlington, MA: Focal Press.

Simkins, M., Cole, K. Tavalin, F., & Means, B. (2002). *Increasing student learning through multimedia projects.* Alexandria, VA: Association for Supervision & Curriculum Development (ASCD).

University of North Carolina. (2003). Retrieved May 9, 2006, from http://www.unc.edu/cit/guides/irg-14.html#c

Vaughan, T. (2003). *Multimedia: Making it work* (6th ed.). Columbus, OH: McGraw-Hill Osborne Media.

Sample Questions

1. One important feature of nonlinear video editing is:
   a. It allows you to reorganize clips or make changes to sections
   b. Any unwanted electrical signal unrelated to the original signal can be automatically deleted.
   c. Keyed insertion of one image into another.
   d. The picture is reduced to a small number of colors or luminance

2. A teacher needs to transfer audio and video from VCR or camcorder to a computer. The teachers should use a:
   a. Digital video
   b. Video capture card
   c. Record device
   d. DVD

3. For a video project, a student plans to start from a close-up on the top portion of a building and gradually move down. This is a feature of:
   a. Tilt
   b. Pan
   c. Establishing shot
   d. Dolly shot

4. A school media specialist needs to achieve the effect of changing a truck into an elephant in an animation application. This effect is known as:
   a. Cartoon
   b. Skin
   c. Morphing
   d. Cast shadow

5. A school media specialist needs to coordinate animation clips for a project. Which of the following features from video editing software best supports her need?

   a. Timeliner
   b. Preview
   c. Layers
   d. Stage

Answers: (1) C (2) B (3) A (4) C (5) A

Chapter IX

Design, Produce, and Distribute Educational Multimedia Products

ISTE NETS_T, I. Technology operations and concepts

Teachers demonstrate a sound understanding of technology operations and concepts.

ISTE NETS_T, IV. Assessment and evaluation

Teachers apply technology to facilitate a variety of effective assessment and evaluation strategies.

ISTE NETS_T, V. Productivity and professional practice

Teachers use technology to enhance their productivity and professional practice.

Chapter objective: The teacher knows how to design, produce, and distribute multimedia products.

In 1945, Vannevar Bush proposed a "memex" machine that would let people quickly access items of information whose meanings were connected. The term hypermedia now refers to linked media or interactive media. In 1960, Ted Nelson coined the term hypertext to describe a database he developed called Xanadu, based on Bush's earlier concept of hypermedia. In the system, items of information from all over the world were logically connected with hypertext links. Over the years, hypermedia has been redefined as "hypertext" with links not only to text, but also to other forms of media: sounds, graphics, movies/video, animation. The term hypertext is now commonly used to refer to HTML-coded references that point to other Web pages.

Today, the term multimedia can refer to a combination of different media types including text, pictures, sounds, video clips, and animation. Multimedia clips pulled into *HyperStudio*, *PowerPoint,* or *AppleWorks* can have an amazing impact when combined with music. Students will discover the power of mixing music and audio files with still or video images as they create multimedia projects for history, language arts, or science classes. The current trend in most software packages is to include all the features of multimedia. The widespread uses of multimedia systems in education suggest an even stronger reliance on these products in the classroom of the future.

It is important for technology application teachers to have a broad understanding of multimedia authoring programs, including specific knowledge of input/output devices, project dissemination, viewers or plug-in software for multimedia projects, general design principles, and evaluations of multimedia projects.

Multimedia Authoring Programs

Experts recognize presentation of information within a multimedia format as effective and desirable (Howard & Taylor, 2005). Therefore, teachers should have specific knowledge of multimedia presentations so they can help students with multimedia presentations.

The term authoring suggests writing. Companies design multimedia authoring programs so teachers and students can produce courseware and programs. These authoring programs help the user develop computer programs in computer languages that can be otherwise quite difficult to learn (Howard & Taylor, 2005). With the help of some authoring software, students can combine writing activities with color illustrations and sounds. Other authoring systems produce attractive multimedia projects, electronic presentations, banners, and posters. Most multimedia authoring programs contain tools for the creation, recording, editing, and transfer of multimedia. The products of the authoring software range from simulations to tutorials. Although most of these programs have point-and-click features to simplify development, some require knowledge of programming-language concepts.

At the "lower" end of multimedia authoring programs, presentation software, such as Microsoft *PowerPoint,* provides simple ways to place multimedia into electronic presentations (Howard & Taylor, 2005). HyperStudio, which sits somewhere in the middle, provides more interactive capabilities than presentation software, but cannot achieve all that a professional authoring package can offer. At the "higher" end of multimedia authoring programs, authoring software, such as Macromedia *Authoware* and *Director,* allow multimedia professionals the flexibility to create movies and nonlinear courseware with audio, video, and animation support that could be output to the Web through plug-in or to the MP3 device.

The term rich media refers to new media that offers an enhanced experience compared to older, mainstream formats. Standard graphic format, such as JPEG and GIF, would not be considered rich media. Rich media are not easily defined by its members, due to the fact that new formats are regularly being introduced, and old formats become part of the mainstream or disappear altogether. This chapter will focus on three major categories of multimedia:

- Presentation software such as Microsoft *PowerPoint*
- Card-based systems such as *HyperStudio*
- High-end multimedia authoring software such as Adobe *Director*

Presentation Software

Presentation software comes in a package, such as Microsoft *PowerPoint,* that allows users to create "electronic overhead transparencies" or "electronic presentations." Typically, these programs are easy to use. Presentation software does have multimedia capabilities as extensive as authoring software.

Some presentation software is built around a slide metaphor. The audience sees each single unit as a slide. Electronic presentations can be created using a variety of slide layouts, some with text and object placeholders.

The common steps used in conducting a presentation with the support of an electronic presentation tool are as follows:

- Choose appropriate software to create an electronic slide presentation.
- Use or edit templates that are consistent in layout.
- Use outlining tools to create simple presentation templates.
- Use principles of design (proportion, balance, contrast, rhythm, emphasis, unity).

- Add multimedia to slides (e.g., illustrations, charts, sounds).
- Present slide show using a projection system (e.g., data display projector, LCD panel, TV monitor).
- Demonstrate appropriate presentation skills, focusing on pace and image/message transitions.

Many beginners of electronic presentation software start by using a template. The term template refers to the background, font selection, color settings, and overall look of an electronic slide in a slide show. A selected template can be used as background from slide to slide (*Microsoft PowerPoint Glossary,* 2006). The presentation package offers a selection of templates, but users can also create templates. It is important to note that there is now a complete industry of designers creating more and more *PowerPoint* templates.

To be truly unique, users can create their own templates with logos, contact information, and other special features. To start customizing a template, the user should click on View→Master→Slide Master to access the Slide Master, which controls the look of the slides (*Microsoft PowerPoint Glossary,* 2006). The user should apply designs in order to create the desired look. When the user develops the template, he/she should save it as a template by clicking on File→Save As and selecting the Template file format. The user can then access this template from within the electronic presentation program.

Placeholders are predefined areas on Master slides or AutoLayouts that designate where specific objects or text should be placed. Objects within a presentation product may include a picture (photograph or sketch); a shape (square, rectangle, line, etc.), a text box, a rectangle filled with a heading or a paragraph, other multimedia clips, and so forth. Figure 9.1 provides an example of a title place holder and a subtitle place holder.

Figure 9.1. An example of a title place holder and a subtitle place holder

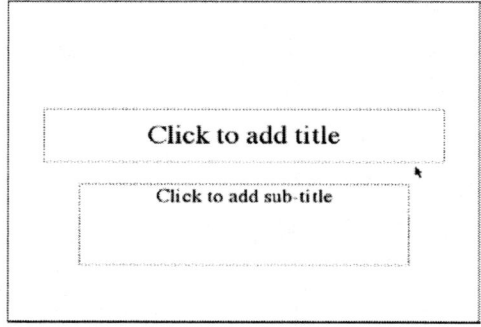

Presentations can be quickly produced from an existing electronic document (e.g., a report or paper already on file). Often, the user can simply copy and paste the document into the presentation tool. After copying, users must remember to convert each major heading in the document to a slide title, convert minor headings to bullet points, delete extra text from the slide, and add graphics when appropriate. To complete the transformation, they should add a reference or a hyperlink to the source document. For further enhancement, multimedia components, such as audio files, video clips, graphics, charts, photographs, and cliparts, can also be added to the slide presentation.

Adding Audio

Music and sound effects can be very effective as a transitional accent for multimedia branching. For example, in a slide show on "How Laws are Made," a middle school student can choose a dramatic orchestral accent between slides. Sounds effects can then be added to the buttons on the slides to provide feedback to the users that a navigation button has been clicked.

Students can also add sound files to their presentations from a variety of sources. For example, they can download files from the Internet or transfer them from special sound effects CDs. However, presentation programs do not recognize all sound file types: WAV and MIDI are two of the types of files not usually recognized.

When adding sounds from a file, recording sound files, and adding music from CDs, students should follow the following steps.

Adding Sound From a File

If the students desire to use a new sound, they should make sure the file is downloaded and saved, preferably in the same folder as the presentation. They click on **Insert menu >Movies and Sounds >Sound from File.** In the **Look In** drop-down menu, they specify the drive and folder where the sound file is located. In the file list, they click the desired sound file then click OK. The program may then ask whether the user wants the sound to play automatically or on mouse click. If a student chooses mouse click, it is necessary to click the icon during the presentation to start playing the sound.

To record sound files, they plug a microphone into the **mic** jack on the computer's sound card. To record a narration for a slide, in Normal View or Slide View, they click on the desired slide to add the recording. Then from the menu, click the **Insert>Movies and Sounds >Record Sound**. When the Record Sound dialog box appears, they type a file name for the recording in the Name box. They use the Play, Stop, and Record buttons to record the narration. If it becomes necessary to change the recording, they delete the file and start over. When satisfied with the recording, they click OK. The Record Sound dialog box will close, and a speaker icon will appear in the middle of the slide.

If a CD-ROM drive is installed on the computer then CD music tracks can be added to slide presentations. However, music tracks can only be added to slides; the track will not attach to objects, animations, or transitions.

Adding Video

Before placing a video file in presentation software, it must be digitally encoded using a CODEC, as explained in Chapter 6. The CODEC to use for Microsoft *PowerPoint* will be **Apple Cinepack** or just **cinepack**. After encoding the video, the user must make sure the file has a suffix name of **.mov** or **.qt** for Windows. When saving the files, the user should create a new folder for storing all of the encoded media files that will be incorporated in the presentation. He/she should save the slide show file to the same folder. When using another computer, the user should be sure to transfer the entire folder, **not just** the slide show file alone, or else the video cannot be found. After that, the user must i**nsert the video into the slide show file following** steps that are very similar to those for inserting sound: Select **Insert Menu > Movies and Sounds > Movie from File. Finally, f**ind the movie file in the folder and double click on it to trouble shoot.

Adding Transitions

The slide-to-slide transition effects for electronic presentations will not only add pizzazz but will also help maintain viewer interest in the presentations. For example, with the proper set up for slide transition, a slide may appear from a certain direction or may have an auditory prompt. To create transitions, open the electronic presentation and then select the desired slide on which to add the transition effect. Then go to the Slide Show menu. Select Slide Transition. Customize the speed and movement from this slide to the next in the presentation by selecting either "On mouse click" or "Automatically after x seconds," where "x" is a number the user must enter. Click Apply to apply these changes to one slide or click Apply to All to apply these changes to the entire presentation. From the same starting point, users can also customize the transition from one object to another.

Adding Hyperlinks

Hyperlinks cause the selection of an object to link to different slides in the current presentation, a different presentation altogether, a non-*PowerPoint* document, or an Internet Web page. They can also run a program, start a macro, or play a sound.

To create a hyperlink based on an object or text on a slide, right-click on the object and select **Action Settings** (*Microsoft PowerPoint Glossary,* 2006). In the Action Settings dialog box, choose either Mouse Click or Mouse Over. Select the button "Hyperlink to" and then select the destination or action.

Adding Action Buttons

Navigation buttons can greatly enhance the user interface of an electronic presentation. To add navigation buttons, go to **Slide Show/Action Buttons** and select the navigation button icon. Mark the navigation button on the slide and s**ave** the work, if prompted. Select the "**Hyperlink to**" setting to associate with the button.

It is important to note that any object can be turned into a hyperlink. Also, the user can create an object to be used specifically as an action button. *PowerPoint* provides a selection of built-in shapes that can be used for this purpose.

Adding Animations

In order to animate slides, select Custom Animation. A dialogue box will then pop up with a large number of animation types. To start, open up a new presentation with a blank slide. Insert an object or sound icon from the file into this slide. For example, the user may now have a picture and a speaker icon in the middle of the slide. The user can then move the icon to another part of the screen. Since the picture and the sound are going to be controlled through a mouse click, the user may want to make the sound icon invisible. Perhaps the biggest problem about using animation is that the Windows program defaults to animate on mouse click. This default may cause speakers to get out of track with the sequence. The solution to this is to change "Start Animation" to "Automatically one second after the previous event." To prevent problems, try to view the animation with Preview. After troubleshooting, go to Slide Show and the slide will automatically build as the speaker speaks. If this is completed for every animation object, the user will have better control over the order and timing of effects.

Among the various views for different needs, the Normal View provides a comprehensive view for each slide with notes and outline. Slide Sorter View displays multiple slides and lets the user quickly change the order of the presentation. The Slide Show view is also called preview. It is used to present the formal presentation. This is also the view that shows all animations, transitions, and multimedia clips in action.

Printing a Presentation

PowerPoint allows the user to print the presentation as slides, notes, handouts, transparency, or even outlines. Choose File > Print from the menu bar. This will bring up the "Print" dialog box. Select File menu > Print. This will bring up the "Print" dialog box. If "print handouts" is selected, the user has the option to choose the number of slides to print on each page. For instance, the "3 slides per page" option is useful because it displays small versions of the slides on the left half of the page, and leaves space for students to write notes on the right side of the page. If "print outline view" is selected, only the text of the slides (none of the graphics or animation) will print.

Final Suggestions

It is important to note that *PowerPoint* offers many features and options beyond those covered here. Electronic presentations can greatly enhance understanding and improve retention of information, but they are not without potential pitfalls. Transition, navigation buttons, and animation effects can be distracting. These features and effects should be used sparingly and adjusted for speed so that they do not distract viewers. Sheppard and Pavlik (n.d.) offer the following tips for electronic posters and oral presentations:

- **Understand the medium:** Well-designed presentations use appropriate, pleasing formats, colors, templates, and contrast combinations. Poorly designed presentations distract from the message.
- **Slide content:** Keep content simple and short. Do not put too much information on one slide.
- **Select appropriate fonts:** Fonts should enhance the presentation without distracting the viewer. Fonts should be legible and of a size that is large enough to be read at a distance. Limit font styles, font sizes, and weights to two or three selections and retain these throughout the presentation. Use standard upper and lower case letters for best readability:
    - **Headings:** Differentiate headings from the main body by using larger type, or a different font, or color.
    - **Main text body:** maximize font size and minimize words per slide.

- **Test font sizes:** Make sure people in the back or sides of the room can easily read your text.
- **Illustrations:** Keep drawings simple and lines bold. Illustrations with solid colors or text should be made into graphic GIF or JPEG file formats. Then use the "insert picture from file" command to guarantee that *PowerPoint* does not change the graphs unexpectedly. Use a universal color palette to ensure image colors remain consistent when transferred across computers.

To avoid problems with the presentation computers and digital projectors in the presentation room, leave at least a 10% blank margin of "safe area" around the text and pictures. Besides, electronic presentations packed with fancy transitions require more processing power and may slow the pace of the presentation. Keep transitions between slides smooth. Some transitions may not be compatible with the operating system or software version available at the meeting site.

Card-Based Systems

Before the advent of presentation software applications such as MS *PowerPoint*, Apple's *HyperCard* was often used as a general-purpose presentation program. *HyperCard* was originally released in 1987, and was finally withdrawn from sale in 2004. Even in the late 1990s, *HyperCard* authors began moving to systems such as *SuperCard*, *HyperStudio*, *MetaCard*, *Digital Chisel*, and *Authorware*. It is one of the first products that made use of and popularized the hypertext concept to a large popular base of users. See Table 9.1 for a list of basic features of multimedia authoring systems following the *HyperCard* model.

The *HyperCard* program defined a whole category of software. *HyperCard* is based on the concept of a "stack" of virtual "cards," and has been used for all sorts of hypertext and artistic purposes. Cards hold data, just as they would in a rolodex. In

Table 9.1 A list of basic features of multimedia authoring systems

Creating a new stack	Adding a text object
Drawing, Navigation	Moving between cards
Creating a border	Editing an object
Adding sounds	Adding a graphic object
Using the Paint tools	Adding an animation
Adding an action button	Adding QuickTime video and QuickTime VR video
Adding a blank card	
Importing a card background	Adding auto-play
Moving a graphic	

addition to the virtual cards, *HyperCard* uses HyperTalk, a programming language, to manipulate data and give opportunities for users to interface. *HyperCard* users often utilized HyperTalk as a programming system for rapid application development.

HyperStudio was patterned after the *HyperCard* model. Like *HyperCard*, *HyperStudio* is based on the card paradigm, but it adds rich interface tools. *HyperStudio* programs consist of stacks that, in turn, consist of groups of cards. The user can visualize this by thinking of the *HyperStudio* stack as a literal "stack of cards." Each card has information on it. Once the background has been established for a card, other objects, such as text, graphics, and buttons, can be placed on top of it. When users cycle through the cards, they can see the information.

HyperStudio targets younger audiences. To support its educational market, *HyperStudio* requires less programming than *HyperCard*. New beginners can choose to use the GUI interface for initial development. Only when this fails to meet needs does a developer need to go to *HyperLogo*, *HyperStudio*' programming language. An English-based scripting language, HyperLogo allows users to choose commands from menus instead of typing them in, which makes it easier for beginners and occasional users.

Like other *HyperCard* spin-offs, *HyperStudio* has evolved into a more mature and versatile package containing the following features:

- **Compatibility with different types of multimedia elements:** Users can include audio, video clips, and movies. It is impossible to place a movie on an index card, but placing one on a *HyperStudio* card requires only a few clicks of the mouse. *HyperStudio* has the ability to add videos in *QuickTime* and Windows "AVI" video file formats, and virtual reality clips to stacks. Adding video can dramatically improve the user's stacks by adding real images and sounds.
- **Compatibility with dynamic hyperlinking:** Developers may link one card to several others, allowing users to view the cards in a variety of ways. Navigation from one card to another is supported through default and customized buttons and several other alternatives, including invisible buttons (buttons that are triggered not by selecting a button icon, but by selecting a predefined area of the screen. This area can be a clip-art graphic, a piece of text, or just part of the background. They allow the user to hide buttons or associate actions with large graphics or text).

High-End Multimedia Authoring Software

The two previous types of software are based on the slide-show and cue-card analogies, and are commonly used to create software demonstrations, simple front ends to command-based tools, interactive presentations, and so forth (Howard & Taylor,

2005). Card-based and slide-based systems provide for fixed-size, full-screen nodes. All of the text in the node must fit on the electronic cards or slides. One criticism is that it forces writers to chunk text into nodes, which may be unnaturally small for the given document. When sophisticated content is required, high-end multimedia authoring software is needed. Authoring software can be used to create more complicated multimedia productions. Macromedia builds the industry-standard tools such as Director for producing multimedia, both stand-alone and Web based. There are also special tools, such as *Flash,* for online multimedia.

This category of multimedia software is by far the most versatile. It can be used to create multimedia projects from simple slide shows to full-blown games and interactive applications such as computer-based training, online surveys, interactive quizzes and tests, electronic encyclopedias, computer-based games, interactive kiosks, interactive presentations, screen savers, CD-ROM/DVD content creation, and advertisements and more. There are literally thousands of uses for this type of software.

Some products allow users to author in a WYSIWYG environment (*what you see is what you get*), while others use a timeline-based environment. Although most of these programs have some point-and-click features to simplify development, most require some knowledge of programming language. Many of the programs involve learning advanced programming and scripting languages to utilize their full capabilities.

The content created on high-end multimedia authoring software is definitely intended for distribution and the software generally has some means of exporting projects to self-running, self-installing files. There may be add-ons available for exporting presentations to self-running files for distribution purposes. Users of high-end authoring software are likely to find support for a wide variety of multimedia file formats including images, video, animations, and sound. High-end products in this category also offer database support for data-driven content. Completed presentations are frequently published in multiple formats, which may include print, the Web, or electronic files. This type of software now has the ability to export to HTML for posting presentations on the Web.

Hardware and Software Requirements of Recording Studios

Early recording studios often lacked isolation booths and sound baffles. In the 1960s, recordings were analog recordings on ¼-inch or ½-inch eight-track magnetic tape. In the early 1970s, recordings progressed to using 1-inch or 2-inch 16- or 32-track equipment. The first modern project studios came into being during the late 1980s, with the advent of affordable multitrack recorders, synthesizers, and microphones.

The phenomenon has flourished with falling prices, MIDI equipment, and inexpensive digital hard-disk recording solutions (Chaptman & Chaptman, 2004). These types of inexpensive technologies can be used effectively with young children and adolescents in today's classroom.

Tape recorders support early literacy experiences. They allow children to listen to recorded stories or songs, or to follow along in a book as they hear it being read on tape. These activities integrate all aspects of literacy: speaking, listening, reading, and writing. They help children develop their storytelling ability and understand how sound translates to print.

Cameras record students at work, as well as performances and special events. Students can tell a story with pictures.

TV/VCRs play back videos of class activities and recordings of students. Students and families have a chance to see the results of their projects and learn from watching their own performances.

Portable keyboards can be used in many different situations: in the classroom, out in the schoolyard, at home, or on field trips. They allow children to type, edit, and electronically store text. The text can be transferred to a computer for formatting and graphics if desired, or sent directly to a printer.

The mixing console/desk in contemporary recording studios employs a signal-management device that receives, combines, and balances signals; provides control of volume and tone; and allows routing of signals to selected destinations.

Distribution boxes provide management and distribution of signals for cable TV, antenna on coaxial cable throughout the building. Now everyone can watch student broadcasts from the TV in the school administration office, or classrooms, or enjoy a DVD from the library. It is like putting a home theater system in every classroom in the building.

Recently, general purpose computers are assuming a larger role in the recording process, being able to replace the mixing consoles, recorders, synthesizers, samplers, and sound effects devices. A computer thus outfitted is called a digital audio workstation (or DAWS). Professional audio editing software packages are created for this type of computer-based recording studio. Apple Macintosh hardware tends to be favored in the recording industry, though much software is also available for other platforms. In order for the personal computer to become a multitrack audio recorder/editor/effects-processor/mixer, the right kind of software applications have to be purchased.

A small, personal recording studio is sometimes called a project studio. Such studios often cater to specific needs of an individual artist, or are used as a noncommercial hobby. For example, a middle school or high school that offers multimedia courses may be equipped with a project studio.

The built-in audio inputs and outputs on a computer are acceptable for basic multimedia editing work, but an external interface will give the user more control and better media quality. USB2 or firewire is needed for multitrack. It is also advised to have a second drive to record audio onto. To ensure fast data transfer, the user should have an efficient computer processor, a firewire, or USB2 connection.

When compared with USB, firewire, also known as IEEE1394, is a more common method of capturing audio and video onto a computer. Firewire transfer rates are many times faster than standard USB and offer a more robust and reliable connection.

When creating multimedia projects, one must fit quality and time to available disk space. How much room required depends on specific aspects of the project (Chaptman & Chaptman, 2004).

MP3 is a compression standard that produces compressed, high-quality audio files. To create an MP3 file, the user needs a program that copies a song from a CD or download from the Internet to the hard drive, and an encoder to convert the file to the MP3 format. The user must also have MP3 player hardware or software for the computer in order to play the music.

A major challenge is that multimedia increases the need for access to powerful computers and the latest technologies with video and sound production capabilities (Li & Drew, 2003). Another challenge facing technology teachers involves the connection problems associated with importing and exporting multimedia projects. Students frequently import video media clips into computer workstations. However, because these decks usually serve four to eight multiple computers via firewire, connection problems are frequently encountered. The same problem occurs when using digital video cameras: the connection fails after frequent use. Moreover, uploading and downloading Web-based multimedia projects demands fast transmissions and large bandwidth. High-quality project presentation and media storage presents yet another challenge for schools and districts as they strive to support the technology needs of students and teachers on campus.

Obviously, more funding is needed to provide students and teachers access to state-of-the-art computers and related multimedia technologies including video-editing software, digital image editor, audio authoring, DVD production, dual decks (DV/VCR), visual editor, and so forth. This technology is needed to provide students with a studio environment where they can work on high-end multimedia projects in a quiet atmosphere. The multimedia studio environment is also very conducive to group work and discussion (Vaughan, 2003). If there is one rule to follow in the realm of audio it is this: always buy the best equipment the district can afford.

It is also important to note that many external audio interfaces provide good mic preamps, digital inputs, metering and headphone monitoring, and it is worth the extra expense and bulk to improve the quality and control of the audio input. When working with audio, remember the old adage, KISS — Keep It Splendidly Simple — is the rule. It seems Murphy's Law dominates all aspects of audio production: anything that can go wrong probably will. The more microphones, wires, and connectors that are used, the more buzz, hum, and equipment failure is likely to occur.

The future will undoubtedly bring technical improvements that will allow for high-quality media content. Teachers should look for computers with larger disk storage capacity and sophisticated hardware audio compression techniques that will enable these improvements

Advice on Equipment Care

If users take good care of the equipment, it will last longer, and they will have more time to use it for completing creative projects. The following tips are offered for the care of multimedia equipment. It is common sense not to store equipment where it may be stolen, where it is very hot, where it will receive direct sunlight, or where there is moisture. Also, users should always remove the tape and battery from a camera after using it, and avoid using a camera in hot, wet, or windy conditions.

Help Your Students Create Projects

Secondary students are quite capable of preparing multimedia or digital stories. This introduction to communication and presentation is easily learned when the teacher provides a model.

Teacher or student projects that incorporate Web pages, digital still images, video, and sounds are becoming very common in the content areas. Teachers are now using video and digital images as resources for analyzing, planning, and developing new models of educational practice. Digital portfolios and digital storytelling projects are also incorporated into the higher grades.

Some ways that teachers can increase the level of expectation for a *PowerPoint* project is by increasing the number of slides required or by adding a research requirement for other graphics sources. Project expectations can be communicated clearly to the students if the teacher uses an evaluation rubric.

Whole class presentations are an exciting way to demonstrate what students have learned, and an ideal format for cooperative learning and sharing. Encourage students to begin with short presentations that contain only a few slides. Remind students to keep the text and graphic images simple. It is also important for students to begin their project by creating a project plan.

Evaluating Multimedia Projects

When creating electronic presentations, access to various computer tools opens up a multitude of creative avenues for both students and teachers. The convergence of digital video and computers has opened up an exciting new world of curriculum-based projects for students.

Jonassen (1999) described the attributes of a well-designed multimedia product with the following terms:

- **Essential:** The task fits into the curriculum.
- **Authentic:** The task uses processes appropriate to the discipline. Students value the task.
- **Rich, not superficial:** The task leads the students to think critically. The content is rich and provides the depth and broadness.
- **Engaging:** The task is thought provoking. Students interact with the content and/or other students.
- **Active:** Students are constructing meaning and deepening understanding.
- **Feasible:** The task can be completed within reasonable time. It is developmentally appropriate and safe for students
- **Equitable:** The task develops thinking in a variety of styles, and also contributes to positive attitudes.
- **Open:** The task has multiple avenues of approach, making it accessible to all students.

Middle and high school teachers may also evaluate students' multimedia products and projects using established criteria related to design, content delivery, audience, and relevance to assignment (Chen, Nath, & Parker, 2005).

The ISTE and many states prescribe skills and technology knowledge that must be assessed by current and beginning teachers (ISTE). When evaluating student's projects, teachers mainly use observation, but they may also employ interviews, computer tests, projects, and so forth.

Of course, when creating a rubric to evaluate students' technology projects, teachers may consider many factors including students' ages and experience with technology and the type of technology use demanded (Chen, Nath, & Parker, 2005). If a teacher is working with word processing only, an assessment instrument or rubric would look very different indeed. In general, there are four areas that teachers should note when evaluating student products: criteria related to design, content delivery, audience, and relevance to assignment.

In a multimedia project scoring rubric, the content refers to the topics, ideas, concepts, knowledge, and opinions that constitute the substance of the presentation; multimedia refers to the integration of media objects such as text, graphics, video, animation, and sound to represent and convey information; and collaboration refers to working together jointly to accomplish a common purpose.

Whether teachers are selecting a culminating project or designing supportive learning activities, these characteristics provide a yardstick for measuring the product. Teachers should keep these in mind as they explain project criteria or make decisions about evaluation.

Multimedia Dissemination Formats

Teachers also must understand how to disseminate information, particularly publishing information. When choosing an effective dissemination method, most educators and multimedia professionals will consider methods that are inexpensive, fast, convenient, and compact.

Instructional multimedia projects can be disseminated from a computer, over the Web, on optical discs, or by using several other new mediums. CD-ROMs or DVDs have become two of the most popular ways to store and share information. Most of the newer computers have the capacity to store or "burn" information onto CD-ROMs or DVDs, as they do with floppy disks. Blu-ray, also known as Blu-ray disk (BD), is the next generation optical disc format, which will hold up to 50 gigabytes. More recently, the Web is quickly replacing optical disks as a popular dissemination method for information. Information can be conveniently provided by teachers through a Web page that can be accessed by others on the Internet.

Some electronic presentation software comes with a "pack and go" feature to make the dissemination of its products easier, especially presentations with special sound effects. Most pack and go features "wrap up" the presentation and all of its elements, along with the optional program Viewer, into an executable file so users can load and view it on any machine. More advanced electronic presentation software contains a "package wizard," which is a series of dialog boxes that walks users through packaging a presentation so they can play it on other computers.

Copies of student presentations can be produced as hard copy print out, transparencies, or slides. If they are to be printed in black and white (also known as monochrome), teachers need to ensure that the graphics are clear and do not obscure the text. Before printing a slide presentation, decide whether to print in color or black and white, and ensure that the slide size and orientation is correct. Change these settings using the Page Setup and Print commands on the File menu. Use the "Print

What" drop-down list to select whether you want to print just the slides, notes, or handouts with multiple slides per page. The "handouts with multiple slides per page" feature allows users to choose a number of slide miniatures to be printed on one page to be distributed to a conference audience.

At the end, the electronic presentation should be saved onto a storage device. When using MS *PowerPoint*, a presentation is normally saved as a "ppt"file format or extension. *PowerPoint* Show, with the extension of "name.pps," is also a useful file type so that the file is able to run regardless of OS. The user can also create a template and save it with "pot" extension.

Live Presentation

Monitor displays help teachers provide information to others through live presentation or electronic posters and kiosks. Teachers always want to use high-quality monitors for video. Computer monitors can also be used to show teacher-made or packaged slide shows, such as *PowerPoint*, to view information from the Internet, or to run a CD-ROM or DVD program.

A presenter conducting a live presentation usually uses a data projector, an LCD display device, to project computer images onto a screen. The data projector connects to laptop and desktop computers using a VGA connector. A teacher may also use document cameras during a live presentation; this is a digital device that allows a two- or three-dimensional objects to be projected on a screen. For example, a teacher may project a page from a textbook on the screen using a document camera in order to direct student attention to specific information.

Usually the presentation has to be transported from the system on which it was composed to the system needed for printing or display. The teacher should ensure that the presentation file is not too large for conversion to another medium.

If the presentation uses sound effects, teachers want to ensure that the target system has the proper audio device. Also, teachers need to check the screen to determine if the color range and resolution are suitable, especially if video clips are important in the multimedia project. When using videos, the target system should be checked to ensure that it has enough memory and the proper processor capacity to run the video. Many presentations have been delayed as the presenter tried to get the content or special effects to display correctly on unfamiliar meeting room equipment.

Using VCR, and Other Optical Disc Formats to Publish Projects

Fortunately, for classroom use, VCR hardware equipment has become quite inexpensive. Projects published on videotape tend to be easier to disseminate to parents, circulate to other classes, or broadcast on local cable or district closed-circuit systems. Once multimedia projects are created at the workstation, the data can always be output onto a Zip cartridge, CD-ROM, VCR tape, and so forth, or incorporated into student projects with *HyperStudio*, *PowerPoint*, *KidPix*, or the Web.

Pulling video in and outputting video to tapes requires video cards. Multimedia projects authored by teachers and students can remain as computer-based works or be "published" on videotape using an inexpensive video output card or scan converter. These cards snap onto boards on desktops, slide into PCMCIA slots on laptops, and are increasingly built into multimedia computers. A camcorder connected to a video card can also be used as a scanner to grab stills. It can also be used with programs such as *HyperStudio* to digitize videos of students' drama productions or lab demonstrations. These multimedia projects can be saved as *QuickTime* files and output onto the tapes or cassettes. "Printing" to a VCR solves RAM and hard drive problems, and lets students build large multimedia projects without bringing down the school server. Tapes or cassettes, with a wealth of images from a period, event, or demonstrations, become very rich resources.

Helping students package the finished project serves two purposes: it protects the products, and it provides an opportunity to display the student's creativity even before the production has been viewed (Simkins, Cole, Tavalin, & Means, 2002). Users should protect the VHS video cassettes by enclosing them in cardboard boxes or plastic cases and storing them in a cool, dry place. Storage in a protective sleeve safeguards the cassette and prevents dust and dirt damage to the tape.

Output to the Web

File size, transmission speed, and software compatibility are major concerns when multimedia instructional projects are distributed through the Internet. If the correct procedures are not followed, then publishing large multimedia projects to the Web instead of to a VCR or CD may have the unexpected consequence of disabling the school or district server. Most projects with videos, images, and audio are very large.

Multimedia projects such as district board meetings or student drama performances can also be placed on an intranet Web server or on the Internet for downloading. This can be accomplished before or after a live presentation, or as a supplement to another dissemination approach. It is a good practice for educators to require students to cite all resources for follow-up research. It is also important to check the school district's rules before posting material online.

Files for the Web are typically placed on the server or downloaded from the server through a process known as FTP (File Transfer Protocol). Binary is the preferred transfer format to upload Real Audio. It is important to note that the size of the file is the amount of disk storage space taken up by a file, which is measured in bytes. Generally speaking, smaller files will load faster on the Web. It is to a developers' advantage to make files as small as possible. However, even with the modern video-streaming technology, file size is still a major concern for distributing multimedia projects over the Net. *56.6 kbps* is the most widely accessible bandwidth. At the lower kbps, music will become noticeably garbled and unwanted artifacts may be heard. In all cases, educators should try to encode the project files for transmission through standard 28.8 and 56k modem users (Simkins et al., 2002).

Compression is the process to reduce file size; this is often called "zipping" or "archiving." The compressed or zipped file can be from a large file, or can contain several files that have been squeezed into a single file. MP3 is a typical compression standard that produces compressed, high-quality audio files. To create an MP3 file, the user should have a program that copies a song from a CD or from the Internet to the hard drive, and an encoder to convert the file to the MP3 format.

A user who accesses the Internet using a 56k modem and attempts to view a streaming video clip that has been prepared for transmission through higher speed transmission, will get very choppy video that plays for a second or two and then pauses for several seconds until more video data is transferred to their computers. Or even worse, this scenario may cause a computer to freeze up.

A number of plug-ins, also known as viewers or players, have been created and distributed to the end-users in response to software compatibility problems for multimedia projects (Li & Drew, 2003). A plug-in is a type of program that integrates with a software application to extend its capability.

In addition to the concerns about file sizes, transmission speed, and software compatibility, it is important that teachers always check the school district's rules before uploading multimedia projects to the Web and publishing material online.

Kiosk and Digital Signage Projects

A kiosk is an electronic "news stand" or booth, or a small physical structure that displays information for people walking by. A sophisticated kiosk system lets users interact and may include touch screens, sound, and motion video.

The kiosk multimedia project can be created using HTML pages or presentation software such as *PowerPoint*, setting the typeface large enough to attract people from a short distance, and removing the Web browser's tool bar so that the display screen is effectively in "kiosk mode." The kiosk browser easily allows an administrator to configure restricted access to folders and Web sites, limit or disallow file downloads, as well as other additional features.

The content of the project can be a school map that allows visitors to pinpoint the location of a classroom by interacting through a touch screen monitor. It can also display the times and locations of major events going on in an organization. Touch screens enable a user to enter and display information without the need for a mouse or keyboard. The presentation can be designed to simply loop through a series of pages, or to allow user interaction and exploration. Alternative input methods must be considered, however, for those who cannot use touch screens, such as people with physical disabilities.

Concerns when Seeking Media Clips

While electronic resources make the job of finding images easier, educators still have to be vigilant about the copyrights and permissions of graphics they use on Web pages, especially photographs.

The Internet is a great resource for those who do not have graphics of their own. There are resources that have online graphics or graphics on other electronic devices free-for-the-taking by simply downloading the selected graphics.

Because of the requirements for applying educator's Fair Use principle to limited audiences, Google's image collection works well when communicating within a local community, including word processing, newsletters, and slideshows, as long as these images will not be placed on the Web.

In addition to the free-for-the-taking sources, images copied or captured from any electronic device or Web pages will raise numerous copyright issues. When seeking images that will be placed on a Web page, or if needing to work with images that can be legally kept for longer than 2 years for educational purposes, it is important to locate Web sites that provide images for free without violating copyright policy. For example, the American Memory Project of the Library of Congress provides over seven million media files, the majority of which are still images.

By whatever means an image is acquired, they must be properly labeled with the source, the date retrieved, and creator and Web page address or software titles. Furthermore, if the Web page from which the image is taken does not give specific permission to use its images, it is best to cite the source and not violate copyright law.

When permission is explicitly given on a Web page, carefully read and follow the instructions for that permission. If possible, ask for written permission from the original sources. Educators have to be familiar with the laws and updates and have to remind students when teaching relevant skills. U.S. Copyright Office published *Frequently Asked Questions about Copyright* (2006) to the general public. For educators and students, Copyright in an Electronic Environment (1997), hosted by North Carolina Department of Public Instruction, is a good resource.

Final Words

Hypertext and hypermedia add depth, elaboration, and interactivity to content through associative, audio, dynamic visuals, and video texts that can potentially affect the nature of learning across the curriculum (Lee & Owens, 2000). Interactivity of computers allows for adapting content to meet individual student needs.

The setting, purpose, and the developmental stages of the children will help users decide the best options for a particular project or program selection. Drawing programs and music-making programs are examples of multimedia programs that may have these characteristics. Students can create pictures and music that reflect a variety of abilities and interests.

Most importantly, the selection of the medium used is strongly influenced by the project's purpose. Effective multimedia projects will enhance the use of technology in education as students and teachers learn to use innovative tools and resources for teaching and learning.

References

American Memory Project (n.d.). Retrieved June 18, 2007, from http://memory.loc.gov/

Chapman, N., & Chapman, J. (2004). *Digital multimedia*. Hoboken, NJ: John Wiley & Sons.

Chen, L. I, Nath, L. J., & Parker, E. M. (2005). Using technology in the middle school and high school classroom. In J. Nath & M. Cohen (Eds.), Becoming a middle school or high school teacher in Texas (pp. 309-350). Belmont: CA: Wadsworth/Thomson Learning.

Fewell, P. J., & Gibbs, W. J. (2006). *Microsoft Office® for teachers* (2nd ed.). Upper Saddle River, NJ: Merrill Prentice Hall.

Howard, S., & Taylor, L. (2005). *The implementation guide to student learning supports in the classroom and school wide: New directions for addressing barriers to learning*. Thousand Oaks, CA: Corwin Press.

International Society for Technology in Education (n.d.). NETS_T: Educational technology standards and performance indicators for all teachers. Retrieved February 11, 2006, from http://cnets.iste.org/teachers/index.shtml

Jonassen, D. (2005). *Modeling with technology: Mind tools for conceptual change.* Upper Saddle River, NJ: Merrill, Prentice Hall.

Lee, W., & Owens, D. L. (2000). *Multimedia-based instructional design: Computer-based training, Web-based training, and distance learning.* San Francisco: Pfeiffer.

Li, Z., & Drew, M. (2003). *Fundamentals of multimedia.* Upper Saddle River, NJ: Prentice Hall.

Microsoft PowerPoint glossary. (2006). Retrieved June 18, 2007, from http://www.intelligentedu.com/microsoft_powerpoint_glossary.html

Mills, S. C., & Roblyer, M. D. (2006). *Technology tools for teachers: A Microsoft Office® tutorial* (2nd ed.). Upper Saddle River, NJ: Pearson Merrill Prentice Hall.

North Carolina Department of Public Instruction. (1997). *Copyright in an electronic environment: Guidelines from consortium of college & university media centers.* Retrieved June 18, 2007, from http://www.dpi.state.nc.us/copyright1.html

Sheppard & Pavlik (n.d.). Tips for a successful electronic presentation for electronic posters and oral presentations. Retrieved June 18, 2007, from http://www.conferences.uiuc.edu/vodafone/images/StepsToBetterVisuals.pdf

Simkins, M., Cole, K., Tavalin, F., & Means, B. (2002). *Increasing student learning through multimedia projects.* Alexandria, VA: Association for Supervision & Curriculum Development (ASCD).

U.S. Copyright Office. (2006). *Frequently asked questions about copyright.* Retrieved June 18, 2007, from http://www.copyright.gov/faq.html

Chapman, N., & Chapman, J. (2004). *Digital multimedia.* Hoboken, NJ: John Wiley & Sons.

Vaughan, T. (2003). *Multimedia: Making it work* (6th ed.) Columbus, OH: McGraw-Hill Osborne Media.

Sample Questions

1. A high school student team is designing an interactive CD. Which of the following is an important feature to provide on the CD?
    a. Integrate graphics
    b. Provide tool bars
    c. Sitemap
    d. Audio features

2. Which of the following is a good classroom use of multimedia projects?
    a. Special education reports
    b. Learning tutorials
    c. Keeping classroom inventories
    d. Student research presentations

3. Which of the following is a common practice for the first slide of a slideshow used for professional meeting?
    a. An animation to engage the audience
    b. An introduction page with organization logo and presentation title
    c. A first page to start introducing the content
    d. A reference page with cited work and bibliography

4. Hypertext or hypermedia format means:
    a. Using many kinds of media.
    b. Moving quickly from screen to screen.
    c. Allowing the user to jump from one related idea to another.
    d. Using animation.

5. Which of the following is the most desirable feature of instructional materials using hypermedia?
    a. Using plenty of sounds and graphics.
    b. Engaging.
    c. Easy navigation.
    d. Trying out the most features the hypermedia can offer.

Answers: (1) C (2) D (3) B (4) B (5) B

Section IV

Webmastering

Chapter X

Administration of Educational Web Sites

ISTE NETS_T, I. Technology operations and concepts

Teachers demonstrate a sound understanding of technology operations and concepts.

ISTE NETS_T, V. Productivity and professional practice

Teachers use technology to enhance their productivity and professional practice.

ISTE NETS_T, VI. Social, ethical, legal, and human issues

Teachers understand the social, ethical, legal, and human issues surrounding the use of technology in PK-12 schools and apply those principles in practice.

Chapter objective: The teacher demonstrates knowledge of strategies and techniques for Web site administration.

District Technology Infrastructure

Technology infrastructure is the system of cabling, phone lines, hubs, repeaters, switches, routers, and related devices that connects computers throughout an organization. In a school district, a wide area network (or WAN) is the "backbone" that connects all local area networks (or LANs) and computers across the various sites and campuses. Good telecommunications infrastructures allow users to access information and connect with other people throughout the organization, and via the Internet to the world. Without a complete infrastructure, such capabilities are available only on a limited basis (Kurose & Ross, 2004).

A WAN generally provides its users with the capability to use e-mail, connect to the Internet, and interface with other, external computer systems. WANs usually are "closed" systems, configured to prevent persons outside the WAN from accessing information housed within it. The WAN connects LANs together throughout the system; LANs in turn connect the computers and printers within a single building, such as a school or central office building. LANs connected to a WAN can offer their users the Internet and the other capabilities mentioned. It is not uncommon to see some school district stretched across hundreds of square miles using several telephone companies. Districts have to negotiate with phone companies to agree on the lines used by district WANs; sometimes it could be as complex as ISDN in one area, T1 in the second, and fractional T1 and 56 kb/s in the third (Lucas, 1997). In some cases, bridges are used to create links between the various telephone lines; then, adapters and modems are used to complete the network solution, allowing

Figure 10.1. A sample District Technology Plan (Elkhart Community Schools, 2005)

Current infrastructure and infrastructure plans:

Currently, the Elkhart Community Schools' WAN (wide-area network) is composed of an amalgamation of ISDN, ADSL, and T1 lines in a "double star" topology. Several buildings connect via 768K ADSL lines to the primary star; others connect via 128K ISDN lines to the secondary star at Central High School, which is connected to the primary star via a shared T1 line. The WAN is connected to the Internet via three IHETS T1 lines. The district is currently investigating various wireless and fiber-optic scenarios to determine the most cost-effective manner in which to create a more robust WAN, and it is anticipated that a project to create this high-bandwidth infrastructure will be completed within the next 3 years.

Among its functions, the WAN provides Internet access; content filtering; client and Web-based e-mail service; SPAM filtering; gateway-level antivirus protection; intrusion detection; a firewall; and secured access to district-based student, personnel, and financial management systems. As connections to district schools are made more robust, other services that are currently duplicated and distributed at each building will be consolidated in the district's data center.

Each building in the district has a local area network (LAN) that provides functions such as user authentication; file services for administrators, teachers, and students; student records management; library automation; and access to the WAN. Most buildings are 100MB switched network environments, although some offer only 10/100MB shared connections. Because the district's LAN equipment is upgraded at a rate of two to three buildings in each year, all buildings should offer a minimum of switched 100MB capacity within the next few years.

Copyright © 2008, IGI Global. Copying or distributing in print or electronic forms without written permission of IGI Global is prohibited.

the WAN to tie together all the buildings in the district even across phone company boundaries.

Most school districts have developed a formal long-range technology plan. Moreover, the plan usually includes specific implementation time frames for the ongoing technology development process. For example, Figure 10.1 displays a sample District Technology Plan (Elkhart Community Schools, 2005).

At minimum, all district locations have at least one computer connected to the WAN. Many facilities, such as high schools, middle schools, or administrative offices, have dozens of computers connected to the WAN. Most schools and other sites have a local area network with at least one computer that helps manage e-mail, printers, and shared files using the network operating system. Some sites have as many as five or six file servers on their LAN, depending upon individual needs. Districts' phone systems may also operate on the same network or on a separate network. In addition, most district technology staff technicians can provide telephone and on-site support in a variety of ways, including:

- Provide system access information for a new staff member or teacher, or for staff with new job responsibilities.
- Troubleshoot access problems.
- Refer staff member or teacher to appropriate training.
- Refer staff member or teacher to second-level assistance, if needed.
- District's technology department staff determines campus wiring based on a variety of factors, with the department director conveying these decisions verbally to the superintendent. Common priorities used by district technology departments are for selecting networks favored by high schools first, then middle schools, then elementary schools.

WAN

District LANs are linked together into a WAN to allow campuses and buildings at different locations to communicate with one another. Schools may also have special WAN needs related to specific instructional objectives. In some cases, district WANs are supported by outside vendors.

WANs may also connect extremely large geographic areas, such as an entire state, or the United States, or the world. Dedicated transoceanic cabling or telephone lines, radio waves, satellites, or infrared light beams are used to connect this type of huge network (Kurose & Ross, 2004).

While using a WAN, schools can communicate with places like Washington, DC in a matter of minutes without paying enormous phone bills. It is important to note that a WAN is very complicated. It uses multiplexers to connect local and metropolitan networks to global communications networks like the Internet. To users, however, a WAN will not appear to be much different than a LAN. Most school district WANs perform the following functions (Elkhart Community Schools, 2005):

- Provide for Internet access;
- Allow students and faculty at any campus to access the district's library system;
- Allow users of older Apple products to access the WAN with an appropriate interface;
- Connect to the district's financial, personnel, and student software applications;
- Provide Microsoft Exchange e-mail system connectivity for use of e-mail;
- Manage TCP/IP addresses allowing for monitoring, administration, and control of these addresses on the district's WAN;
- Provide access to the Internet via remote sites;
- Provide Internet support services such as proxy, firewall, and filtering services.

LANs

LANs are the basic means by which districts and schools provide access to a variety of information resources. LANs are usually limited to a specific geographic location, such as a site or a building. Rarely are LAN computers more than a mile apart. District LAN staff usually support standard, district-wide information systems and provide second-level support for network growth and problem resolution (Elkhart Community Schools, 2005).

In a typical LAN configuration, one computer is designated as the file server, which stores all of the software that controls the network, as well as the software that can be shared by the computers attached to the network. Computers connected to the file server are called workstations or clients. The workstations are usually less powerful than the server, and they may have additional software on their hard drives. On most LANs, cables are used to connect the network interface cards in each computer. The physical topology of a network refers to the configuration of cables, computers, and other peripherals, and may be configured in one of several shapes. For more explanations on LANs, refer to *An Educator's Guide to School Network* (Winkelman, 2005). Important considerations when choosing a topology include:

- **Cost:** A linear bus network may be the least expensive way to install a network; there is no need to purchase concentrators.
- **Length of cable needed:** The linear bus network uses shorter lengths of cable.
- **Growth potential:** With a star topology, expanding a network is easily done by adding another concentrator.
- **Cable type:** The most common cable in schools is unshielded twisted pair, which is most often used with star topologies.

A cable is the medium through which information usually moves from one network device to another. There are several types of cable that are commonly used with LANs. There are four types of cables used in networks (Kurose & Ross, 2004). Twisted pair consists of four pairs of wires that are manufactured with the wires twisted to certain specifications. Twisted pairs are available in shielded and unshielded versions. Coaxial cable consists of a single copper conductor in the center surrounded by a plastic layer for insulation and a braided metal outer shield. Fiber optic cable consists of a center glass core surrounded by layers of plastic that transmit data using light rather than electricity. It has the ability to carry more information over much longer distances. The type of cable chosen for a network is related to the network's topology, protocol, and size. Understanding the characteristics of different types of cable, and how they relate to other aspects of a network, is necessary for the development of a successful network. Wireless networks allow laptop computers or remote computers to connect to the LAN. In older school buildings where it may be difficult or impossible to install cables, wireless LANs use high frequency signals to communicate between the workstations and the server or hubs. Each workstation and server on a wireless network has some sort of transceiver/antenna to send and receive data. Wireless LANs have the disadvantages of poor security, susceptibility to interference from lights and electronic devices, and slower transmission than physical cables.

The two most common types of infrared communications used in schools are line-of-sight and scattered broadcast. With line-of-sight communication there must be an unblocked direct line between the workstation and the transceiver. Scattered infrared communication is a broadcast of infrared transmissions sent out in multiple directions that bounce off walls and ceilings until eventually hitting the receiver (Kurose & Ross, 2004). Most importantly, at the heart of most networks, the file server usually is a very fast computer with a large amount of RAM, or random access memory, and storage space, along with a fast network interface card. It is usually installed with a network operating system, or NOS, along with any software applications and data files that need to be shared. It also controls the communication of information between the nodes on a network. This requires a fast computer that can store a lot of information. File servers should have at least the following characteristics when compared to other computers (Winkelman, 2005):

- Fast microprocessor
- A fast hard drive with large storage
- A RAID (redundant array of inexpensive disks) to preserve data after a disk casualty
- A tape back-up unit such as DAT, JAZ, ZIP, or CD-RW drive
- Numerous expansion slots
- Network interface card
- Large RAM

The user computers connected to a network are called workstations. Almost any computer can serve as a network workstation as long as it is configured with a network interface card, networking software, and the appropriate cables.

The network interface card, or NIC, provides the connection between the network and the workstation. Most NICs are internal, with the card fitting into an expansion slot in the computer. Laptop computers can now be purchased with a built-in network interface card.

According to most surveys, among the three most common network interface connections, Ethernet is the most popular, followed by Token Ring, and LocalTalk (Winkelman, 2005).

A switch (or concentrator) provides a central connection point for cables from workstations, servers, and peripherals. In a star topology, twisted-pair wire is run from each workstation to a central hub. Most switches are active, that is, they electrically amplify the signal as it moves from one device to another.

Since a signal loses strength as it passes along a cable, a device called repeater is often necessary to boost the signal. They are used when the total length of the

Figure 10.2. A diagram to show the functions of networking hardware

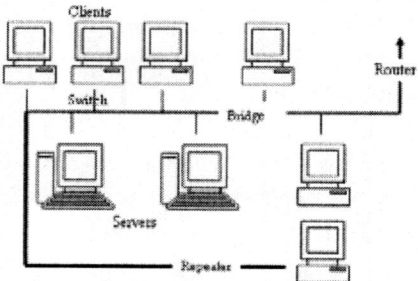

network cable exceeds the standards set for the type of cable being used. A good example of the use of repeaters would be in a local area network using a star topology with unshielded twisted-pair cabling. The length limit for unshielded twisted-pair cable is 100 meters. The most common configuration is for each workstation to be connected by twisted-pair cable to a multiport active switch. The switch/repeater amplifies all the signals that pass through it, allowing for the total length of cable on the network to exceed the 100-meter limit (see Figure 10.2).

The major advantages of installing a school LAN include (Kurose & Ross, 2004):

- Speed.
- Security.
- Centralized software management.
- Resource sharing.
- Cost.
- Electronic mail. The presence of a network provides the hardware necessary to install an e-mail system.
- Flexible access. School networks allow students to access their files from computers throughout the school.
- Online collaboration.

Disadvantages of installing a school LAN include (Kurose & Ross, 2004):

- Expensive installation.
- Requires administrative time.
- File server may fail.
- Cables may break.

Most districts fund their WANs and LANS with a combination of state technology allotment funds and state TIF funds, federal e-rate funds (funds administered by the Federal Communications Commission), local funds, and some bond proceeds (Lucas, 1997). By using e-rate, a federal program, many schools and libraries have obtained funds for improving network infrastructure at a fraction of the full cost. Some districts are also able to qualify for 90% federal funding due to the high number of students eligible for free and reduced-price lunches, which is a key program requirement that dictates the level of funding.

The Internet of the Pre-Web Age

The Internet (or "net") is an INTERconnection of computer NETworks that allows information to be exchanged between the millions of connected computers. The categories of information available on the Internet include e-mails, WWW, USENET, and so forth..

In the mid-1960s, the Internet was originated by the U.S. military's Advanced Research Projects Agency (ARPA) (Okin, 2005). In 1972, the first e-mail program was created to send messages across the network. E-mail holds the title as being the first official Internet communication tool. For almost three decades, the e-mail system existed for the exclusive use of government, research, and higher education. Throughout the 1980s, more and more people became aware of this incredible communication tool. In 1988, the first K-12 schools in the United States were connected to the system in order to utilize the e-mail capabilities. In 1990, the network was officially referred to as the Internet, which was then opened to commercial use. In 1992, the WWW was created by a research facility in Switzerland. By the end of 1994, advertising, and mass marketing found their way online, and nearly three million computers were connected to the Internet with 140 countries that could be reached by e-mails (Okin, 2005).

Like now, during the early years, myriad resources were available on the Internet and specialized software was used to access these resources. During the pre-Web age, Gopher, ARCHIE, and VERONICA were the three standard "search" tools on the Internet before the Web. Gopher, an older Internet service, has been eclipsed by the World Wide Web. Gopher uses a structure of linked directories displayed as text menus. Most of the information indexed within the Internet before 1992 was in the form of text (Okin, 2005).Gopher did not have the mixed page display of text and graphics, or the versatile linking that now characterizes the Web. Presently, users can access Gopher by using a Web browser. The URL for a Gopher resource begins with gopher://. For example, the URL for the Gopher server called AskERIC is gopher://ericir.syr.edu.

The ARCHIE database is made up of file directories from hundreds of systems. When users search this database on the basis of a file's name, ARCHIE can tell the user which directory paths on which systems hold a copy of the desired file.

The VERONICA database is a collection of menus from most Gopher sites. When users conduct a VERONICA search, they are searching menu items. During the search, VERONICA builds a tentative menu consisting of just those items that match the user's request. When the search is completed, VERONICA will present the user with a customized Gopher menu.

FETCH is a small program that makes navigating server sites and transferring files comparatively easy. FETCH is also used for uploading files to other computers so the user can avoid having to interact with the UNIX operating system on the server machines (Okin, 2005). When utilizing Gopher, users had to select the desired item from the menu instead of typing in command lines, as is required in the Command Line Interface (or CLI). This selection process brought the search one step closer to the graphic user interface (or GUI).

File transport protocol (FTP) is a method for retrieving files from a remote Internet site. The user can use an FTP client to transfer files to and from a computer to an FTP server. Most servers offer FTP capability, so the user can apply FTP tools to upload or download files from and to an Internet server. It is generally easier, faster, and more efficient to transfer files via FTP than other previous methods such as ARCHIE or FETCH.

USENET News allows users to post messages in newsgroups that any other users connected to the Internet can read (assuming they have access). Where e-mail is for person-to-person communication, USENET News is for public discussion for any and all others to read and use. There are newsgroups dedicated to thousands of topics. USENET is a great forum for getting help or information from other users. It is also great for holding discussions with people who have similar interests (Okin, 2005).

The World Wide Web

Since the early 1990s, Gopher, ARCHIE, VERONICA, Telnet, USENET, and other older Internet services have been eclipsed by the appearance of World Wide Web. The phrase World Wide Web refers to the collective set of server/host computers speaking the same network protocol. The Web, or WWW, consists of a system of pages where the information is linked together. Using a Web browser, a user can read information on the Web. After clicking on a hyperlinked word on a Web page, the browser takes the user to the next page of related information, where the source is located.

In the early years of the WWW, one popular Web browser was Mosaic, a browser developed at the National Center for Supercomputing Applications at the University of Illinois at Urbana-Champaign in the early 1990s. Many believed that the GUI-based easy-to-use point-and-click Mosaic interface helped popularize the Web.

Overall, there are two types of interfaces between a computer application and the user, CLI and GUI. CLI (command line interface) allows the user to type a text command and the computer responds according to that command. To experience the CLI interface with emulators of early line-mode browsers, the user can visit Deja Vu home page at http://www.dejavu.org. GUI (graphical user interface, pronounced "gooey"), is where the user clicks on a visual screen that has icons, windows, and menus by using a pointing device, such as a mouse.

Currently, although many browsers are available, Microsoft Internet Explorer, Netscape Navigator, and Mozilla Firefox are the most popular browsers used.

To access information on the Web, a computer must run special "client" software that can interact with the servers. The user may apply a different client program on the PC or MAC for each type of information desired. If the user wants to access the Internet from home or business, the following equipment is needed (Okin, 2005):

- A computer
- A modem that allows the computer to talk to other computers over telephone lines
- TCP/IP software that allows the computer to talk the language of the Internet
- PPP or SLIP protocol software that allows a full-access Internet connection over phone lines
- Client software for the types of information desired
- An account with an Internet service provider (or ISP)

An ISP is the party providing a user with connectivity to the Internet. Some users have a cable or some sort of wireless link to their ISP. For others, their computer may dial an ISP by phone and send and receive Internet packets over the phone line; the ISP then forwards the packets over the Internet. ISPs usually charge between $5 and $50 per month, plus initial set-up fee, depending on the services they offer. It is important to note that users may need to find an ISP that has a local dial-up number; otherwise they will pay long-distance charges to the phone company.

Many of the computers on the Net act as "servers" to distribute information (Kurose & Ross, 2004). Typically, users visit a Web site by clicking on a hyperlink that brings them to that site, or keying the site's URL directly into the address bar of a browser. Many users may wish to know more about the mechanisms that bring Web pages to a computer. Just exactly how do the Web pages find their way into a user's Internet browser? The process largely depends on the Web server.

A good example to explain this process is the Educator's Reference Desk [sm]. The user can decide on a particular Web site by typing its URL: http://www.eduref.org/. Through an Internet connection, the user's browser initiates a connection to the Web server that is storing the Educator's Reference Desk [sm] files by converting the domain name into an Internet address, and then locating the server "eduref," that is storing the information for that Web address. The Web server "eduref" stores all of the files necessary to display the pages of Educator's Reference Desk [sm] on a computer, typically all the individual HTML pages, images/graphic files, and scripts that comprise the entirety of a Web site.

Once contact has been made, the browser requests the data from the Web server "eduref," and using protocols such as HTTP, the server delivers the data back to the browser. The browser in turn converts the computer languages of the files into what the user sees displayed in the browser. In the same way, Web server "eduref" can send the files to many client computers at the same time, allowing global access to the same page simultaneously. The host or the Web server is a computer that acts as a file server. Users at remote computers (i.e., client computers) are allowed to access information stored on the server, or host computer. The phrase World Wide Web refers to the collective set of servers (computers) speaking HTTP.

URL, abbreviation for uniform resource locator, is the global address of documents and other resources on the Web. The first part of URL indicates what protocol to use, and the second part specifies the Web address or the domain name where the resource is located. For example, the URL below points to a Web page that should be reached using the HTTP protocol http://www.eduref.org/, where HTTP is the protocol while "eduref" is the domain name of the resource.

TCP/IP, or transmission control protocol/Internet protocol, is the collection of communications protocols used to connect host computers on the Internet. TCP/IP uses several sets of protocols, the two major ones being TCP and IP. TCP/IP is built into the UNIX operating system and is implemented by the Internet; making it the de facto standard for transmitting data over networks (Okin, 2005). Even other proprietary network operating systems that have their own protocols, such as Novell Netware, also support TCP/IP. Industry standards, such as TCP/IP and other protocols, help to ensure cross-platform connectivity. All of the computers on the Internet speak the same TCP/IP language.

Hypertext transfer protocol (or HTTP) is the set of language rules Web users must follow to communicate with each other.

IP (also called Internet addresses) is an identifier for a computer or device on a TCP/IP network. Networks use the TCP/IP protocol to route messages based on the IP address of the destination. The format of an IP address is a 32-bit numeric address in the format of four numbers separated by periods. The four numbers in an IP address are used in different ways to identify a particular network and a host on that network. Each number can be 0 to 255. For example, 1.129.17.240 could be an IP address (Okin, 2005). BIND, the Berkeley Internet name daemon, is the program that makes the domain name service (DNS) work. Without it, a user would be typing addresses like 207.106.15.214 instead of www.popcorns.org.

Domain names are reserved. For example, www.ed.gov.us is unique and registered to the US Department of Education. Examples of extensions include .com, org, .gov, .net, and .mil. Examples of newer extension are .biz, .info, and .tv. Each country has a regulatory body in charge of domain name registration. Examples of country extensions include .ca, .nz, .jp, and .au.

Currently, the five regional Internet registries (ARIN, RIPE NCC, LACNIC, APNIC, and AFRINIC) serve specific geographical areas worldwide. According to Internet Corporation For Assigned Names and Numbers, the number of unassigned Internet addresses is running out, so new classless schemes will be developed soon.

The regional internet registries (RIRs) are responsible for allocating and assigning IP addresses to ISPs, organizations, and end users in their geographical regions. Those wishing to obtain IP addresses will contact the RIR responsible for their geographical region. Connecting a private network to the Internet requires the use of registered IP addresses in order to avoid duplicates (Okin, 2005). Within an isolated network, such as from the school computer lab in a LAN, IP addresses can be assigned at random as long as each one is unique.

The World Wide Web Consortium (or W3C) was created in 1994 to establish universal **Web site** design rules and blue print for the future. With the mission of leading the Web to its full potential, W3C has over 350 participating organizations worldwide including universities, governments, and industry.

School Web Projects

Despite all the attention paid to Web browsers, a Web server holds Web pages and allows client programs, such as browsers, including Microsoft Internet Explorer and Netscape Navigator, to read and write them.

What is amazing is that anyone with enough technical know-how can build a Web server using completely free software. The Apache Software Foundation provides support for the Apache community of open-source software projects.

In 2000, there was a record growth of 16 million hostnames. The year 2005 continues to shape up as a historic year for Internet growth. According to the Netcraft Web Server Survey (2006), the factors in the dramatic growth include:

- Increasing use of the Internet by small businesses as Web sites and online storefronts become more affordable.
- Speculation in the market for domain names, buoyed by rising resale prices and the ability to generate revenue via pay-per-click advertising on parked domains.
- Strong sales of online advertising, especially keyword-based contextual ads that support business models for both domain parking and commercial Weblogs.

Professional technical staff has been hired in nearly all school districts to work with the schools and departments to expand a district's Web sites and ensure that each school and department can share information with other staff, parents, comments, and the public. To have school or department information displayed on the district Web site, a school representative must either call or e-mail the Webmaster to get the necessary information posted. Some districts also welcome parents and volunteers to help with the development of Web pages for district schools by providing them with user ids, passwords, and work space on the Web server.

A good school Web project has to account for backups, uninterruptible power supply (UPS), site monitoring, redundancy, server maintenance, security, and overall reliability. If a person works in a small school or office, he or she may not have the equipment necessary to host a server and provide 24/7 reliability. Most districts' technical staff assists schools in purchasing hardware and software; installing LANs, new labs, and equipment; and training school personnel in the daily operation of the labs and equipment. Districts' technical staff also build Web servers and allocate server spaces for individual schools. Many times, it is more feasible for a school to contract out to a hosting service or use the service of the district information technology office.

In the occasions when system administration is outsourced to a third-party vendor or the district information technology office, it is recommended that some basic information is gathered about the third party prior to outsourcing (*Learn the Net*, 2005):

1. How fast and robust is the connection to the Internet? Does the service provider guarantee 24-hour a day service and support? Do they have uninterrupted power supplies and reliable backup systems? Also, what kind of server will they be working with?

    IT specialists describe computer data and files in a number of ways. Ordinary modems convert computer data to audio tones/analog to transfer over the regular phone lines. The analog format is a waveform with valleys and ridges. It refers to the natural form of sound/audio. To store/playback on a computer, analog data is converted to digital data, that is, bits and bytes. This digital representation can then be stored, edited, processed, and transferred between media. A binary file is a file that can only be read with special software, such as word processors or image viewers. Binary files contain embedded codes that create bold or underlined text, for example. Text files, on the other hand, contain no embedded codes.

    As for the speed, the district's Web support office should have at least two high-speed connections (T1 or T3) to the Internet.

    The transmission of digital signals is inherently faster than tone/analog signal transfer over the communication lines. ISDN, short for integrated services digital network, is a network/telephone connection that transfers data at rates more than four times faster than a 28.8Kbps modem. ISDN "modems" connect digitally. Primary rate ISDN, also known as T1 service, delivers at a rate of 1.544 Mbps. T3 transmits at an extremely high rate: 44.7 Mbps.

Finally, bandwidth is the width of the band over which frequencies are transmitted. A band is a portion of the electromagnetic spectrum (Willard, 2001). The bandwidth is the difference between the highest and lowest frequencies. Bandwidth is used to describe the rate of data transfer. In the electronic arena, bandwidth is measured in thousands of characters moving from source to target in parts of a second. The greater the bandwidth, the greater the carrying capacity. The most popular analogy for bandwidth is the "information superhighway." Another popular analogy treats bandwidth as if it were a pipe. A pipe has a measurable capacity: a predictable volume of water can flow through a water trunk. FCC (Federal Communications Commission) is the authority to allocate portions of the band. For example, the band for VHF television broadcast is defined from 54 to 88 million cycles per second. And, of course, the band contains many "channels." FCC began licensing spectrum as if it were a scarce resource under the framework established by the Communications Act of 1934.

2. How is the Web support office organized? How many employees do they have?

Avoid one-man start-up operations. When it comes to a school or institution, a company must have professional programmers and network specialists and must offer responsive user support.

3. Does the Web support office offer full domain name service?

Some Web support offices of the school districts or organizations do not want to offer the full pathname aliases required to support different domain names. Instead of offering the district the option of a *www.myschoolname.edu* domain name, some companies will offer pathnames that look like *www.districtABC/myschoolname*. This type of URL is usually too long and also difficult to remember, but it is easier for the Web support office to maintain and easier for an Internet search engine to find a specific school district's Web pages.

4. How are Web files stored?

As computing environments have become larger and more complex, the task of managing the many resources the network has to offer has become more complex for network administrators. The user's task of finding those resources has become just as difficult. The needs to not only organize information, but to make that information easy to manage and locate, has become a serious challenge. To store files, it is a good practice to use a folder/directory hierarchy structure, which is a directory of information storage location that uses a systematic scheme to organize the information.

On Windows-based operating systems and Mac OS, directories are depicted as "folders" and "folders within folders." Moving around is accomplished by clicking on the icons.

In a multiuser environment, when the user logs in, he or she will enter the computer in the personal "home" directory. To refer to directories, most operating systems rely on what is called a "pathname." Every object has an "absolute" pathname that is valid from anywhere on the computer. The absolute pathname always begins from the root directory. There is also a "relative" pathname, which is in reference to the current directory.

5. What are the provisions for security?

The Web support office needs to monitor activity on the site 24-hours a day so as to spot suspicious activity before it can happen. Hackers have broken into password-secured areas on some servers to access application status and student grade records. The Web support office also should have a program for proactively using state-of-the-art firewalls or other security methods. To protect children from inappropriate content, many districts and schools have also implemented additional security measures to block students' access to a number of sensitive words, search engines, listservs, Web sites, and electronic groupware. Local community, parent organizations, state mandates, and grant requirements are all watchdogs of campus Web security policy.

As a provision for security, some technical departments set up intranets that are parts of the Internet or parts of the Web used internally within a district or organization. These types of intranets may be expanded and updated regularly to include more information, forms, policies, procedures, and contact information to all employees.

6. What kind of reports does the hosting service provide?

A traffic log file is simply a record of the number of times a particular file has been requested (this is also commonly referred to as a "hit"). The other basic information that can be found on a traffic log include the date and time of the request, the size of the file served, whether there were errors in serving the file, and the sites or IP addresses the visitor came from. There is a wealth of data in traffic report files as for when and how a reader can access a Web page that can help fine-tune the district's Web site. The Web support office should be able to offer detailed reports about site performances.

7. How will Web pages be updated? Does the district have FTP access?

Nowadays, the most common way to update Web pages is to edit them on a computer and upload the files to the Web server through FTP.

Most FTP tools can automatically download and display the proper descriptions of the files. Unlike ARCHIE or FETCH users, FTP users do not have to search the index file for the desired entry.

Most FTP tools now have full Drag and Drop support. Simply drag one or more files or complete directory structures onto the file view area of an FTP program to transfer them to the location on the server. Receiving files is also as simple as dragging files or directories onto a folder.

8. Does the Web server support special requests, such as CGI, so district employees or students can use forms, database searches, and image maps? Does it support *FrontPage*, *ColdFusion,* and other server-side applications?

   CGI, short for common gateway interface, is a server-side program that runs at the request of the client. Web servers that support CGI typically perform interactive Web actions. Normally, servers "serve" static files such as HTML documents, images, movies, and sounds. In CGI, clients request a program to be executed and results to be returned, as in database or search applications (Willard, 2001). All interactive form processing requires CGI.

   Server-side markup (SSM) are "tags" embedded in the Web page that get interpreted "on the fly," that is, they are processed by the server each time the page is requested. For example, a "last modified" time/date stamp, for example, producing Wednesday, 8-June-2005 10:00:16 EDT, is done with the tag <!--#flastmod file="name_of_file.htm"-->. These types of interactive pages are also called active server pages.

   If a district wants to have forms or image maps on the Web site, full access to a CGI-bin directory is necessary; this is the directory where CGI scripts and other executable programs are stored.

A Good Web Development Team

The volume and variety of information available on the World Wide Web is tremendous, and it is increasing all the time. More and more schools and education-related programs are now disseminating information through the Web.

Visitors want simple, yet interesting sites with appealing graphics and user interaction. However, if the design is too busy or the pages take too long to download, potential clients will just leave. For this reason, a good Web development team is crucial to an education Web project.

A project manager is responsible for managing the technology team's activities, especially communication among the team members. A solid plan must be detailed, straightforward, and easy to understand. Regular project updates should occur so the members may interact and discuss various tasks in depth. A hardcopy of the plan should be readily available to each member, and displayed in an easy to reach area. Project management software, such as Microsoft *Project,* can be used as an in-depth tool in the creation of the project plan. It allows users to create a calendar, Gantt chart, flow charts, and to track resources, as well as other valuable features.

All team members have a responsibility to be actively involved in the project. Most importantly, each of the members in the planning should be involved from the beginning. If not, team members may not understand the scope and the required result. Without constant communication, details will be missed and tasks could be incomplete or wrong.

If an institute uses its Web site to present information, they may only need a static site that will be updated periodically. A Web team may consist of a single skilled Webmaster. Other sites may require monthly, weekly, daily, and in some cases, up-to-the-minute updates requiring round the clock attention.

A large-sized Web development team may consist of multiple system administrators, Web application programmers, Webmasters, and project managers (Lee & Owens, 2000). Although software tools make it possible for one person to perform every task, few people have the combination of technical, artistic, and management skills necessary to fill each role well. As a rule, Web projects are best developed by teams with a range of expertise (Lee & Owens, 2000). Team members must understand each crew's role and responsibilities in order to perform well. A sample structure of a typical team for a large-sized Web project is shown.

Project Manager

The project manager is critical to a successful team. This person is responsible for the team's individual members, communication, and follow-through, and must understand the scope and expectations of the client to correctly convey the ideas to the team members. Good oral and written communication skills are essential, as

Figure 10.3. The typical structure of a Web development team

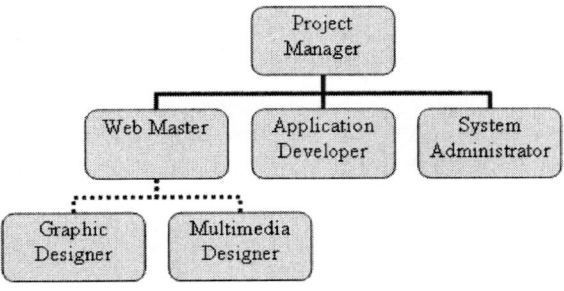

are time management and organizational skills. Generally speaking, 3 to 5 years of project management experience is a typical requirement for this position.

Webmaster

In addition to knowing HTML and a few scripts, this person must also have good written skills, should be responsible for writing, and will work closely with the client and project manager to determine the content of the site and layout. Depending on the size of the site, the Webmaster may also be responsible for graphic design. Knowledge of animation, photo editing, as well as scripting, operating systems, and the Internet server applications that run on the server and database engines is always desirable. Three to five years of experience is typical for a qualified Webmaster.

Application Developer

The Web applications developer is responsible for developing server-side functionality for Web-based applications (Kurose, Ross, 2004). This involves working with all aspects of the server and database. Common Internet programming languages include PERL, CGI, ActiveX, ASP, and Java, among others. Experience with IP networks, database development, and an understanding of the operating system are essential. This team member must be able to work with the project manager to analyze and interpret the client requirements and recommend solutions, so strong problem solving and analytical skills are essential. Depending on the complexity of the applications, the developer should have anywhere from 2-4 years experience.

Systems Administrator

A good SysAdmin can make the difference in a secure and stable environment. System administrators are generally responsible for building, maintaining, and securing the Web, application, and database servers in the Internet architecture. A Microsoft Certified Systems Engineer (MCSE) with a background in Internet information server has the appropriate skill set for system administration in a Microsoft environment. If a system environment runs on UNIX, an individual with firewall and Web server background, along with 4-6 years of network administration experience, should possess the necessary skills to complete any Web team.

Sometimes it is more feasible to outsource this task to a hosting service or use the district information technology servers and resources.

Graphic Designer and Other Multimedia Designers

Even though Webmasters often have the basics of graphic design, if resource is not a problem, graphics designers and multimedia designers will greatly enhance a Web development team. The graphic designer can assist in the creation of images, Web page layouts, and other graphical needs of the development project. Additionally, they should be proficient with the latest multimedia tools such as photo editing, paint, and drawing programs. Adobe Photoshop and Illustrator are recognized as the industry standard. Knowledge of layout, composition, and color theory as well as experience with HTML is a plus. A multimedia designer or developer uses a mixture of text, graphics, animation, and sound to produce interactive Web sites, CD-ROMS, and DVDs. They work in a wide range of sectors including commerce, industry, education, and entertainment. Typical duties include:

- analyzing client needs
- identifying the media to be used
- adapting customers' existing products or services to fit into the a proposed new multimedia system
- producing animated, audio, and video content
- installing the material at the customer site

Once a proposal is accepted, the Web pages are designed, which could include copy, sound, and animation, using appropriate software tools.

As with educational multimedia design, developing a Web project also involves skill sets ranging from project management and interface design to programming. Sometimes, budgets and schedules require team members to juggle more than one role. In some cases, teachers, principals, school staff, PTA members, students, and others are asked to act as school Webmasters, responsible for maintaining a Web site for a school.

Building an Educational Web Site

Define Your Audience

Before designing a Web site, it is important to define the target audience. Will the site be accessed by as many people as possible, or is a special group targeted? For instance, without a high-speed Internet connection, downloading a graphics-intensive or multimedia-rich Web page can be painfully slow. Currently, some people access the Web with a dial-up connection. For teachers and students with a 56-Kbps modem at home through dial-up, it can be a frustrating and slow experience. On the other hand, if the target audience is lab users through the district, it is reasonable to expect that they will have high-speed connections (Lee & Owens, 2000). That means that graphic and multimedia clips should be added to the site.

So, take the users' hardware and software into consideration. When appealing to the widest possible audience, however, the Web pages should contain small graphic files and avoid the use of advanced features such as Java. Studies indicate that 8 seconds is the optimum download time. If not, file sizes should be small enough to download in 15 seconds or less. The easiest solution is to keep the site simple and avoid fancy effects.

Web Management Tools

The most common question for a Web manager has to be "Is the Web site up?" If the answer is "no," all else fades into insignificance. Even a relatively small, static site needs good availability. System administrators often need Web management tools to ensure functionality and uptime of a Web server. Web management tools help to accomplish these tasks from keeping content current and synchronized to tracking usage and making certain the site has not been defaced.

The available uptime of school Web pages becomes increasingly important as parents, students, and teachers come to rely more and more on the Internet. And uptime becomes absolutely critical during a crisis such as detrimental weather conditions. Unless there is staff able to watch the site around the clock, the system administrators need monitoring and notification tools along with a thorough plan for correcting problems as they occur.

Among common Web management tools, there are programs that provide a single point of access for consolidated information, allowing system administrators to monitor the availability and performance of the entire infrastructure (Learn the Net, 2005). Web link checkers are programs that test HTML documents for invalid hypertext links. Some checkers automatically check a list of Web pages to see whether they still exist, or whether they have changed since the last time the program was run. Some let administrators create "spiders" that constantly crawl through their Web sites searching for more than 50 types of content problems such as forms that do not work. Some structure editor programs allow system administrators to create a graphical display of developing Web sites. System administrators can then edit and organize the links between pages, and can create new documents and links. A new remote management tool is now available that allows customers to automate routine and administrative tasks at remote sites, such as repairing, troubleshooting,

Figure 10.4. The components of building a Web site

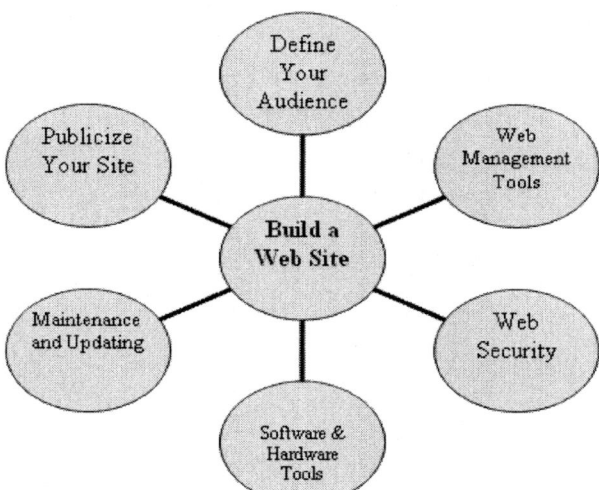

and server provisioning, while still being able to view the status of tasks through a secure Web portal.

Web Security

The first lesson many system administrators learn about Web application security is that there is no such thing as perfect security. A PC that is connected to the Internet is always vulnerable to a malicious attack whenever the PC is working. Even if a browser is not running, merely turning on a PC with an Internet or LAN connection renders the device vulnerable to attack. This gives a hacker access to the user's hard drive and desktop, and opens the door for malicious hack attacks (McNab, 2004). A better method is to install either a hardware or software firewall. The software firewall is the more common and cheaper of the two methods. It is a piece of software code that resides on the PC and is always running. The software firewall watches interactions between the PC and the Internet and blocks any suspicious activities. A hardware firewall typically is a small device that is plugged into the user's home network between the outside network connection and computer inside so that all transmissions have to pass through the hardware firewall.

Firewalls are currently considered very effective in preventing hackers from breaking into school network systems.

Some of the most basic security recommendations are also the most obvious ones (McNab, 2004):

- Keep the server computer physically secure so that hackers cannot access it.
- Secure the Web server computer and all computers on the same network with strong passwords.
- Close unused ports and turn off unused services.
- Run a virus check that monitors traffic.
- Learn about and install the latest security patches.

Implementing security is only part of the solution. Another important part is vigilance in these ways (McNab, 2004):

- Back up files often and keep the backups physically secure.
- Establish and enforce a security policy for all users.
- Use event logging and examine the logs frequently for suspicious activity.

Even if the network system has many security safeguards, system administrators need to monitor their system's event logs. Watch for repeated attempts to log into a system or for a very high number of requests against the Web server. This includes repeated attempts to log on to a particular system and an extremely high number of requests against a Web server.

Cookies do not act maliciously on computer systems. They are merely text files that can be deleted at any time. Cookies cannot be used to spread viruses and they cannot access a hard drive (Maiwald, 2003). This does not mean that cookies are not relevant to a user's privacy and anonymity on the Internet. Cookies cannot read a hard drive to find out information about a user; however, any personal information given to a Web site, including credit card information, will most likely be stored in a cookie unless it is turned off in the browser. In only this way are cookies a threat to privacy. The cookie will only contain information freely provided to a Web site.

Cookies are messages that a Web server transmits to a Web browser so that the Web server can keep track of the user's activity on a specific Web site. The message that the Web server conveys to the browser is in the form of an HTTP header that consists of a text-only string. The text is entered into the memory of the browser. The browser in turn stores the cookie information on the hard drive so when the browser is closed and reopened at a later date, the cookie information is still available.

Web sites use cookies for several different reasons (Maiwald, 2003):

- To collect demographic information about who is visiting the Web site. Sites often use this information to track how often visitors come to the site and how long they remain on the site.

- To personalize the user's experience on the Web site. Cookies can help store personal information about a user so that when the user returns to the site he or she will have a more personalized experience. The server keeps track of what is purchased and what items are searched for, and stores that information in cookies.
- To monitor advertisements. Web sites will often use cookies to keep track of what ads it lets the user see and how often the user sees the ads.

Fortunately, most attacks come from relatively unsophisticated hackers who simply look for sites that are easy to break in. System administrators' initial goal should be to protect their sites from the common exploits that comprise the vast majority of attacks.

Maintenance and Updating

Once placing the site online, the real challenge for encouraging visitors to return lies in maintaining and updating it. Poor maintenance, such as outdated content or broken links, discourages visitors.

Maintenance for a small site may take as little as 2 to 3 hours a month. On a large site, maintenance may be a full-time job (*Learn the Net,* 2005). When planning a large Web development project, working with an experienced designer will save a lot of time (Maiwald, 2003). Updating a site entails changing the content. This may be as simple as checking links to other sites to make sure they are current, or as complex as adding new capability to forms.

Starting with a well-designed site is the most effective way to prevent resource-intensive updates and maintenance. Maintenance generally means making sure that the files and file directory structures are up and running properly at all times, and all the links are functional. Since HTML documents and their related graphics components are linked in specific ways, any changes or additions made to existing documents or directories could affect or alter their relationship to one another. The most common result is that links are broken, and images or entire pages do not load properly (Maiwald, 2003). User feedback, usually via e-mail, can play a big part in flagging these types of problems so they can be resolved in a timely manner. Make sure that archived information is organized in a way that provides easy access.

Also, decide how often it is necessary to update the site and how extensive those updates will be. For example, some teachers will likely update information such as student assignments on a daily basis. A Webmaster of a school home page may update its site whenever there is update of faculty information.

It is important to analyze what site users are doing and saying by reviewing the traffic reports and user feedbacks (Maiwald, 2003). If the site is hosted by a district server computer, the district should supply detailed reports regarding this information. Many reports provide information in real time as to who is on the Web site, where they come from, which pages they access, and a lot more. Besides, a number of shareware and commercial software programs are available to people who run their own servers.

It is also important to provide a way for users to give feedback. The most common method is via e-mail. Many Webmasters provide a link at the end of a Web page. The user feedback can then be used to identify and resolve technical problems in a timely manner. User feedback, along with usage tracking data from the traffic report, should be used to guide decisions about what content to keep, replace, or improve.

It is helpful to maintain a simple documentation of the Web pages, including a brief description of each page's content, links, and graphics files. As the site grows, or if it is handed over to someone else for maintenance, the documentation will come in handy (Maiwald, 2003).

Publicize the Site

A variety of methods can be used to bring traffic to an education-related Web page. The home page, which is the start-up page for Web documents, should be on as many hot lists, or a list of frequently accessed Web documents, as possible, this increases the chances of people finding the Web site by listing the Web sites with popular search engines such as Google and Yahoo. This will ensure that the site is registered with dozens of search engines in one simple step. When registering with directories like Yahoo!, it is important to provide appropriate keywords for the Web sites by which the site can be identified (Maiwald, 2003).

To ensure that people can find the site, make sure the HTML document titles and file names are self-explanatory and that the home page accurately describes the site's purpose and contents. This increases the odds that the site will turn up in more searches.

If the content of the Web site has something valuable to offer to teachers and students, then find the appropriate newsgroups and mailing lists and let them know about it. Also, find Web sites related to this particular area of interest and ask their Webmasters to link to the site; many sites will provide this link at no cost.

Web Project Life Cycle

Most school-based Web projects follow this project life cycle (Ash, 2003):

Phase 1: Define the Scope and Vision

- **Client survey:** The questionnaire is distributed to all key stakeholders. Usually, feedback from more stakeholders is beneficial in giving a broader scope and feel for the project. It also encourages them to think through the project in a different perspective.
- **Research, assessment and design audit:** Based on creative brief feedback, the design team members do the necessary research to determine needed usability features and layout options. The design team will also review the sites that the client refers to us as "sites they like."
- **Site architecture and content:** A site map is developed to visually demonstrate how the site content and structure will be organized. This also allows team members to determine what will be needed regarding copywriting, and multimedia clips to complete other phases of the project.

Phase 2: Site Structure Development

- **Prototype design:** With the site map architecture in place, the team is now ready to develop a prototype design. For this prototype, it is common to include a proposed home page and second-level internal page that define the "look and feel" for the site. This prototype design will include only static graphic or place holders to represent what the final site might look like. They will not include any working code or interactivity.
- **Prototype refinement:** Once the prototype designs have been reviewed by the client, feedback is taken into account, and the designs are reworked until client satisfaction is acquired.

Phase 3: Site Production/Staging

- **Content collection:** Receiving content from clients on a schedule is perhaps the least predictable part of any Web project.
- **Final prototype build-out:** Upon approval of the site prototype design, the team will program the site in the HTML language. It is at this point that the site truly starts to come to life.
- **Interaction development:** Once the site has been coded in html, animations, dynamic/database functionality, and user experience features will then be added.
- **Content placement:** At this point all the content should be in house and ready to be plugged into the appropriate spots of the site.

Phase 4: Beta Launch and Testing

- **Beta review:** With all components in place, it is time for more usability testing. The site will be moved to its final home, but still remain invisible to general viewers. The team will test every page of the site in multiple browsers and on multiple computer operating systems. At this time, the client will also be able to review the site and will have time to request revisions, additions, or deletions.
- **Beta revision:** After testing is complete, any known issues or bugs will be fixed and client revisions will be completed.
- **Backend/database testing:** If the site uses a database and dynamic functionality, the backend of the site will be ran through multiple tests and will be assessed.
- **Final beta refinement:** After the backend/database testing is complete, known issues will be fixed and tested again until they pass the test.

Phase 5: Publishing/Marketing/Launch

Web site is published to the final server and goes live for all Internet users to see. The Web address will be submitted to numerous search engines for publicity purposes. This will allow Web search engines to crawl the site quicker.

Figure 10.5. Web project fife cycle

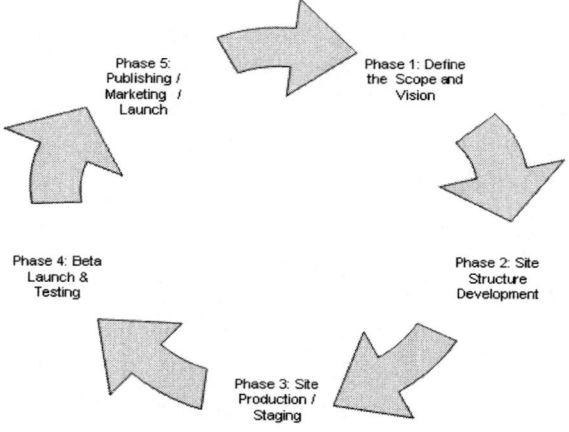

References

Ash, L. (2003). *The Web testing companion: The insider's guide to efficient and effective tests.* Hoboken, NJ: John Wiley & Sons.

Elkhart Community Schools. (2005). *District technology plan, 2006-2009.* Retrieved June 18, 2007, from http://www.elkhart.k12.in.us/content.php?id=66

Kurose, J. F., & Ross, K. (2004). *Computer networking: A top-down approach featuring the Internet* (3rd ed.). Boston: Addison Wesley.

Learn the Net. (2005). Retrieved June 18, 2007, from http://www.learnthenet.com

Lee, W., & Owens, D. L. (2000). *Multimedia-based instructional design: Computer-based training, Web-based training, and distance learning.* San Francisco: Pfeiffer.

Lucas, L. (1997). *Wide area networking guide for Texas school districts* (2nd ed.). Retrieved June 15, 2007, from http://www.tcet.unt.edu/pubs/wan/body2.pdf

Maiwald, E. (2003). *Network security: A beginner's guide* (2nd ed.). Emeryville, CA: McGraw-Hill Osborne Media.

McNab, C. (2004). *Network security assessment: Know your network.* Sebastopol, CA: O'Reilly Media.

Okin, J. R. (2005). *The Internet revolution: The not-for-dummies guide to the history, technology, and use of the Internet.* Winter Harbor, ME: Ironbound Press.

The Netcraft Web Server Survey. (2006). Retrieved June 18, 2007, from http://news.netcraft.com/archives/web_server_survey.html

Willard, W. (2001). *Web design: A beginner's guide.* Columbus, OH: McGraw-Hill Osborne Media.

Winkelman, R. (2005). *An educator's guide to school network.* Retrieved June 18, 2007, from http://fcit.usf.edu/network/default.htm

Sample Questions

1. Which Internet resource allows "live" communications between users?
   a. E-mail
   b. Listserv
   c. Electronic bulletin board
   d. Chat room

2. A high school is considering different ways to prevent hackers from breaking into the school network system. Which type of application will be the most effective?
   a. Firewall
   b. Antispam software
   c. Antivirus software
   d. Site guard

3. What is the best analogy a teacher can use to describe bandwidth?
   a. Battery
   b. Speed of light
   c. Ocean
   d. Pipe

4. What is the name for the organization that sells or gives Internet access to a person or group?
   a. Internet browser
   b. Listserv provider
   c. Service provider
   d. Gateway

5. Which of the following is automatically generated to track a user's actions over the Internet?
   a. JavaScript
   b. Spam
   c. Firewall
   d. Cookie

Answers: (1) D (2) A (3) D (4) C (5) D

Chapter XI

Web Design Tools for Educators

ISTE NETS_T, I. Technology operations and concepts

Teachers demonstrate a sound understanding of technology operations and concepts.

ISTE NETS_T, V. Productivity and professional practice

Teachers use technology to enhance their productivity and professional practice.

ISTE NETS_T, VI. Social, ethical, legal, and human issues

Teachers understand the social, ethical, legal, and human issues surrounding the use of technology in PK-12 schools, and apply those principles in practice.

Chapter objective: The teacher knows principles of Web page design and uses a variety of tools and techniques to design and troubleshoot Web pages for a diverse audience.

This chapter presents basic information about the construction of Web pages using common Web design tools. The common formats found on Web browsers are also discussed. Typical formats include HTML, Web graphics, scripts, Web compatible files (such as PDF, audio, video), and animations. Routine Web-editing processes used to create or test Web pages are also discussed.

School and District Web Pages

McKenzie (1997) observed that beginning with the mid 1990s, districts and schools launched Web sites on the Net to meet the following goals:

- To introduce visitors to the school: its mission, character, look, offerings to children, and overall spirit;
- To point to excellent information on the larger Web; identifying the best resources the Web has to offer to staff and students alike;
- To offer an opportunity to publish student works for both a local and a global audience; and
- To provide rich data locally collected on curriculum-related topics.

The Web sites of most schools meet two or three of these goals, but some achieve all four goals.

Construction of Web Pages

The following steps should be considered when constructing Web pages (Bates, 2002):

- **Step 1: Creating Web pages:** Use a text editor for typing and editing structured code of HTML and the tasks such as spell checking, tag insertion/completion. Some editors are designed for editing source code and are not a WYSIWYG (*What You See Is What You Get*) text editor, such as Macromedia Dreamweaver™ or Microsoft Frontpage™.
- **Step 2: Testing Web pages:** If Web designers want to publish a Web page, there are two additional steps to follow in order to maintain security and usability. Many districts and schools require newly developed pages to be uploaded using the processes described in Step 3 and tested on a staging server. This

staging server system is highly secure and provides a number of testing tools to manage institutional Web sites (Ash, 2003). The staging server identifies possible problems with the newly created Web pages before they are published to the production server. If a problem is identified, the staging server displays a message that is intended to help Web designers identify and troubleshoot the respective errors. In order to preserve consistency throughout the numerous institutional Web pages, some staging servers also verify whether or not the official template is correctly implemented.

- **Step 3: Moving files with FTP or Fetch tools:** Often, designers will need to move completed Web page files to and from the server. Whether images, PDF documents, or HTML documents, there are tools that will allow Web designers to upload and download these files to/from the Web server, including WS_FTP™ for Windows platforms and Fetch for Mac platform. These tools allow users to log in to the Web server with usernames and passwords. Once users are logged in, they will be able to copy any file to the desired folder on the staging server.

These three steps should be repeated until the Web pages are displayed and work properly. Because Web site design is a complex process, faculty and staff involved in creating and managing Web sites soon learn that ambitious designs require a vast investment in upkeep.

A Teacher's Professional Homepage: A Scenario

Mrs. Smith, an elementary art teacher, needs to create a set of Web pages that will function as a contact point for students and parents, as well as serve as a showcase of current students' art work. Mrs. Smith explored the training offered by the community, local colleges, and the school district. After attending some of the trainings, she had to decide which Web editors to use. Her colleagues told her that most word processing software applications, such as Corel WordPerfect™ and MS Notepad™, could be used to create "raw" HTML codes. In the mid 1990s, several software companies—Adobe Systems, Allaire Corp., Macromedia and Microsoft Corp., to name a few—introduced Web editors that would let the nontechnical person like Mrs. Smith create Web sites without writing HTML code. Mrs. Smith learned that WYSIWYG (*"what you see is what you get"*) Web editors offer the advantages of simplicity, speed, and ease of conceptualization, and the disadvantages of incomplete HTML vocabulary and user loss of control for adding or deleting tags. Thus, it is a graphical interface to a process that shows how the end result will look as it is being produced, for example, a WYSIWYG HTML editor generates HTML markup but displays the document as if viewed with a Web browser.

Today's WYSIWYG Web editors provide intuitive interfaces that shield the designer from the actual HTML codes. In addition to being easy to use, Web editors must be robust. Most Web editors support templates. Mrs. Smith likes to use templates that let Web page authors develop specific pieces of a page without concern for formatting or HTML tags. She found today's Web editors must support not only straight HTML, but also CSS (cascading style sheets), DHTML (dynamic HTML), XHTML (extensible HTML), and XML (extensible markup language). Typical professional Web editor programs include a complete package of templates, style editing, previewing, FTP, and other site management features.

After careful consideration, she decided on a Web editor for her current project to avoid the tedious task of code verification and file coordination. In developing her homepage, Mrs. Smith explored the following features:

- Inserting text
- Inserting an image
- Making an e-mail link
- Format styles
- Bullet lists
- Tables
- Background color
- Linking to another page
- Linking within pages

During Web editing, Mrs. Smith found that even minor HTML coding errors can create major problems. Her colleagues informed her that mismatched or misplaced quotation marks are one of the single most common coding errors in HTML. Because of this simple mistake, the page can break and images and other page elements may not display correctly. During the debugging process, Mrs. Smith must preview the pages with new changes through a Web browser continuously until the pages look and function as she has envisioned. She also may preview using different browsers because some Web pages can look different with different browsers.

During Web editing, Mrs. Smith checks out a couple of tutorial books from the library and uses the following list of Web sites for more information about HTML.

Figure 11.1. The basic HTML source codes of Mrs. Smith's professional homepage

Item number	Description	Actual Codes
1.	Header tags	`<html>` `<head>`
2.	Inserting a document title that can show on the browser History list	`<title>Mrs. Smith's Art Web Page </title>`

3	Inserting a document heading with special color, an image, and a e-mail link	`<h2 align=center><font COLOR="#FF8040">Welcome to Mrs. Smith's Art Web Page </font></h2>`
		 `<p align=center><img src="picture.jpg"></p>`
		 `<p align=center> <a href="mailto: mssmith@distrct.edu"> Contact me at: mssmith@distrct.edu </a></p>`

4	Insert two hyperlinks within the document	`<p align=center><a href="#ex"> Art Room Expectations</a> &#183;` `<a href="#pr"> Principles of Art</a><p>`
5	Create a line	`<hr align=center size=6 width=50%>`

6	Sets the background color to beige. Also gives instruction to the homepage including a hyperlink to another HTML document within the same server and an external Web link.	`<body bgcolor="FFFFCC">`
		 `<p> Below y is information about the art curriculum covered at Elsie Elementary School.`
		 `<b> <a href="resume.htm"> Click here</a> </b> to view a sampling of current students' art work </b>`
		 `<b><a href="http://www.nga.gov/collection/index.shtm">Click here</b> </a> to explore the world of art </b></p>`

7	A block of text that is displayed as an underlined heading and bullet list	`<h5 align=left> <a name="ex"> <u> Art Room Expectations:</a></u> </h5>`
		 `<ol>`
		 `<li> Listen and follow directions`
		 `< li > Complete projects on time`
		 `< li > Use materials properly`
		 `< li > Work area cleaned`
		 `</ ol >`

8	A block of text that is displayed as an underlined heading and table	`<h5 align=left> <u> <a name="pr"> Principles of Art:</a></u> </h5>`
		 `<table border="1"><tr> <td>Color</td> <td>Line</td></tr>`
		 `<tr> <td>Texture</td> <td>Form/Shape </td> </tr>`
		 `<tr> <td>Space </td> <td>Value</td> </tr></table>`

9	Ending an HTML document	`</body>`
		 `</head>`
		 `</html>`

- **NCSA HTML Primer:** http://www.ncsa.uiuc.edu/General/Internet/WWW/HTMLPrimer.html
- **HTML Documentation:** http://mullara.met.unimelb.edu.au:8080/home/awatkins/HTML.html
- **HTML Help:** http://www.htmlhelp.com/

When the Web editing is completed, Mrs. Smith goes through File—Save As and saves her files with short file names and with ".htm" in the extension in order for a browser to be able to recognize them as Web pages correctly. If using a regular word processor, it is important for Mrs. Smith to save files as a Web page or "text only" because the "normal" save mode of a word processor includes formatting information within the file.

Mrs. Smith found that additional special purpose Web editing tools make the job of a Web developer easier. Some Web editing tools allow Web designers to work in a drag and drop environment with a full range of HTML-oriented features to create Web sites without any programming or HTML knowledge. Some Web editing tools are template-based Web publishing software. Some Web editing tools' wizards guide users through publishing the entire Web site. Some Web editing tools conversion tools specialize in converting from non-HTML format such as PageMaker™ or QuarkXpress™ to HTML.

Mrs. Smith understands that to make Web pages, she will need the following (Bates, 2002):

- A Web space account on a Web server computer.
- A Web editor or word processor to edit the HTML code files.
- Graphics programs to edit any graphics to include.
- The FTP program to upload and download Web page files to and from the server. The FTP program will also help create directories, set permissions, and upload files. (FTP will be discussed in Chapter 10)

Now that she knows the basics, Mrs. Smith is ready to create her own homepages.

Common Web-Compatible Formats

HTML

Most Web pages are written in hypertext markup language (HTML). This is the most commonly used Web programming language whereby the documents are interpreted by the browser and/or by the server on which the files reside (Bates, 2002). Also, HTML documents can be edited using MS *Word* and a variety of other tools. Reading a Web page is a much more interactive experience than reading a print publication. With the Web, the viewer controls the sequence of pages and jumps from page to page using hypertext connected through hyperlinks. Hypertext is basically the same as regular text, with the exception that hypertext contains connections within the text to other Web documents. Synonymous with hyperlinks, anchor refers to nonlinear links within documents. The "documents" to which the hypertext connects may be local or remote, perhaps even in a different country.

Web Compatible Graphics

Graphics on Web pages help to add "information content," "style," "colors," and "navigability." The types of graphic images that are acceptable on Web pages are navigation buttons, image maps, logos, bullet points, title graphics, divider lines or horizontal rules, background images, headings, and photos. Perhaps one of the biggest mistakes Web page designers make is the misuse of graphic images. Web page graphics have to serve a function. If the function of a graphic image is only "to look good," the Web developers are unnecessarily increasing the download time of the Web pages.

Scripts

Other types of Web documents are available that can mix HTML with lines of code written in different languages, such as JavaScript, PHP, JSP, ASP, *ColdFusion,* and many more. The scripts can be embedded directly in an HTML page to respond to user events such as mouse clicks, form input, and page navigation (McDuffie, 2003). This code adds functionality to a Web page beyond the capability of HTML and most browsers.

Other Formats

Web browsers can display certain file types, such as HTML and Web-compatible graphics, as standard parts of their functions. The display of other file types may be handled by additional software, either designed to work in conjunction with the browser for the display of a specific file type (a plug-in), or a stand-alone application that the browser can launch for viewing a file requiring that application. Plug-ins (also known as players) consist of third-party software applications written by independent developers for enhanced integration with the functioning of the browser. Portable document format (or PDF) is a popular format that makes it possible to present documents intended for printing and make printable documents available to a wide audience. Some versions of the Mac operating system include the preview function to view PDF documents. Windows users are required to install Acrobat Reader or a variety of software tools to open PDF. The other main multimedia formats used on the Web are audio, video, and Flash. The filename extensions of these formats are lowercase: .swf, .mov, .avi, .mpg, .mp3, .rm, and .wav.

Web Page Tools

HTML Editor/Converter

HTML codes are document formatting codes that tell browsers how to display the document on the screen. HTML files contain the text to be displayed on the Web page embedded in its special "tag" language. Embedded within the text are markup "tags" which specify how the text is to be formatted for display, where graphics will be inserted, how links are going to connect to other pages, which background color will be displayed for the page, along with many other capabilities.

During the 1990s, HTML evolved through several stages of evolution. HTML 4.0 has been widely implemented since it became a W3C recommendation in December 1997. Newer revisions of HTML are published periodically every year. Current work is focused on extending accessibility features, multimedia objects, scripting, style sheets, layout, forms, math, and internationalization.

HTML documents are written in plain text, but with the addition of tags that describe or define the text they enclose. For example, a link is defined by the ANCHOR <A> tag placed around the hyperlinked text. It specifies the URL of the "linked to" document, for example:

Web Design Tools for Educators

Figure 10.2. Some examples of HTML tags in action

This HTML Code...	...Would Produce The Results Below:
I like <b> social studies </b> .	I like **social studies**.
<h2>Heading 2</h2>	## **Heading 2**
<p align=center>Centered text. Note the linebreak. </p>	Centered text. Note the linebreak.
<p>A new paragraph, not centered.</p>	A new paragraph, not centered.
Here's a Smiley: <img src="gifs/smiley.gif" align=top>	Here's a Smiley: ☺
Click the <a href="resume.html">link</a> to view my resume.	Click the link to view my resume.

<A HREF="http://www.terena.nl/gnrt/websearch/index.html">Web Search Tools</A>

Figure 10.2 shows some examples of HTML tags in action.

With HTML languages, most tags occur in pairs, like the tags that specify bold text: <b>....</b>. Some tags, such as the <br> linebreak, are used alone. Other tags may include optional "attributes" that affect the formatting, such as the "align=top" in the image tag.

Example of hyperlink in an HTML document:

<A HREF="http://www.google.com">Web Search Engine</A>

When the HTML document is viewed with the Web browser, the tag information between angle brackets is not visible. However, the phrase "Web Search Engine" is displayed in the format or color defined for links by the browser or the document's author. When the user selects these words, the default document "index.html" fetched from the Web server will be displayed.

Figure 10.3. A screen with HTML source codes

```
<html>
<head>
<title>University </title>
<meta HTTP-EQUIV="Content-Type" CONTENT="text/html; charset=iso-8859-1">
<meta NAME="Author" CONTENT="Miguel A. Almanza - UHD Web Technical Speciali
<meta NAME="keywords" CONTENT="University, United States">
<meta NAME="description" CONTENT="university">

<!-- TRAIL TAGS BEGIN HERE -->
<meta name="DC.Description" content="university">
<meta name="DC.Subject" content="Education">
<meta name="DC.Subject.Keyword" content="University">
<meta name="DC.Subject.Keyword" content="university">
<meta name="DC.Subject.Keyword" content="Education">
<meta name="DC.Type" content="Homepages">
<meta name="DC.Author" content="university ">
<!-- TRAIL TAGS END HERE -->

<link REL="SHORTCUT ICON" HREF="http://www.u.edu/favicon.ico">
<style TYPE="TEXT/CSS">
```

To see the HTML code that produced the Web page being read, select the Source command from Internet Explorer's View menu. The user will then see a screen with source codes (see Figure 10.3).

As explained, Web designers can develop and debug their Web pages with a Web editor. Once Web pages are completed and working, Web designers can then transfer them onto the Web server. When the Web page is "served" to a viewer, it is the responsibility of the viewer's browser to reassemble the page from its component files for viewing.

As for typefaces in Web pages, a user should be conservative with the choice of fonts, and careful not to overload readers with either too much text or too much white space. The authors recommend the use of Times and Times New Roman, which are the most common typefaces usually already installed on computers. The most common sans serif typefaces are Arial, Helvetica, and Verdana. It is recommended that users display fonts that are found on most computers used by the general public. When looking for a contemporary look, standard fonts like Helvetica or Arial are recommended. If the user desires a more sophisticated look, then fonts like Times or Verdana are recommended. (See Chapter 5 for explanation of typography).

Web Graphics Tools

A Web page, unlike a word processing document, does not actually contain the graphic as part of the HTML document. Graphics must therefore be stored in one of several specific file formats and contained in separate files (Slaybaugh, 2003). These files will initially be stored locally, then linked to the page, and finally uploaded together with the HTML page that refers to them to the Web server.

Coding Web graphics, such as GIFs, PNGs, and JPEGs, properly for short download time is also important. Here is a sample of the HTML code for a graphic image of a sun:

<IMG SRC="images/sun.gif" WIDTH="31" HEIGHT="44" ALT="The sun" VSPACE="2" HSPACE="2" BORDER="0">

In this example, the image name is a GIF, called "sun.gif," that is stored in the directory called "images" on the Web server. The file name or URL must be enclosed in quotation marks. IMG indicates the HTML coding that instructs the browser to insert a graphic image into a Web page. SRC indicates the attribute that tells which file name or URL of the graphic image the user wants to place on the Web page. WIDTH/HEIGHT are tags used to describe graphic image's dimensions, measured in pixels. Using the WIDTH and HEIGHT attributes in the IMG SRC tag preserves the layout of the pages. Also, Web pages using the WIDTH and HEIGHT attributes in their IMG SRC tags download faster than pages not using these attributes.

ALT, which also has to be enclosed in quotation marks, stands for the alternative text attribute. Alternative text must also be enclosed in quotation marks. In the event that visitors want to view text, they should turn off the "Auto Load Images" option in their browser to increase a site's download time. In the place of the graphic image, the alternative text will appear. The same text will appear if visitors are using a text-only browser.

Graphic file formats and the size of image files will significantly affect download time for a page. Only certain graphic file formats are acceptable on the Web. Thus, teacher technologists must be able to identify and use the different graphic file formats in order to place images on Web pages.

Graphical Storage Strategies

A graphic file format is a defined way of storing graphical information in a file. Once the format is defined, different applications can arrange to store and retrieve information in that format. There are currently three widely used file formats for graphics on Web: GIF, JPEG, and PNG (Slaybaugh, 2003).

Graphics interchange format (or GIF) is a format for pictures transmitted pixel by pixel over the Internet. GIF is used for graphics with fewer colors. With only a few colors, GIF images look very sharp and are very small, thereby improving download speed. The GIF specification, created by CompuServe, was put into the public domain, but Unisys claimed that it had a patent on the compression technology used. This stimulated the development of PNG.

The GIF format is suited to images composed of areas of the same solid color to allow for high compression ratios. GIF images are restricted to 256 colors (best, actually 216 "Web-safe" colors). In the past, the feature of Web-safe palette was important for display on machines that have 8-bit monitors for both Macintosh and Windows machines. Today, many machines have more colors and are not as sensitive to choice of color palette. There is a specialized variety of GIF called an "animated GIF" that provides animations of the graphics. Currently, all kinds of GIFs are universally acceptable on the Web.

Joint Photographic Experts Group (or JPEG or JPG) is a format for encoding photographs that uses fewer bytes than the pixel-by-pixel approaches of GIF and PNG. In most cases, the JPG format is used for photographic images containing continuous gradations of color. JPG images are made up of 16.7 million distinct colors, which are more colors than the human eye can distinguish and may be more than a computer can display. JPEGs are universally acceptable on the Web. JPG supports many colors; it is possible to obtain good quality and reasonable file sizes with the 40:1 compression ratios.

Portable network graphics (or PNG) is the format for encoding a picture, pixel by pixel, and sending it over the Net. PNG is recommended by the W3C, replacing both GIF and JPG. Although the PNG format is supported by many, it is not fully supported by all Web browsers and authoring applications to date.

Popular Web graphic formats usually support both transparency and interlacing of Web images (Slaybaugh, 2003):

- **Transparency:** One color (often white) is set to match the background color of the browser
- **Interlacing:** A mechanism that displays an image gradually, in increasingly finer detail until finally it is displayed at full quality

The filename extensions of these three main image formats are lowercase:

- **JPG:** .jpg
- **GIF:** .gif
- **PNG:** .png

Choosing the right file format is not only critical for the quality, but for keeping the file size under control. When selecting GIF or JPEG for graphics conversion, it is important to consider the type of image. Use a GIF format when a graphic consists primarily of line art or flat colors without gradients. JPEG format is best for photographs or images with fine tonal variations in colors, such as images with gradients or metallic images. Web editors have to be able to get their pictures into either GIF or JPEG format to be able to publish them on the Web.

Fortunately, all modern scanners and digital cameras can create files in JPEG format. Specialized image editing programs, such as Adobe *PhotoShop,* also allow users to save in a variety of formats including GIF and JPEG. In the market, there are also graphics programs, such as Macromedia *Fireworks*, dedicated to creating Web images. Other graphic formats are possible on the Web but may require either a "plug-in" or a separate, free-standing viewer application.

Whichever format chosen, the user should try to avoid making revisions to the image that has already been sized down and converted to the Web. Instead, the task should be completed with the original graphic files. GIFs utilize "lossless" compression and are generally safer for recompressing, meaning when the GIF image is compressed, no information is lost from its contents. JPEGs, however, utilize "lost" compression, which means that information is lost from its contents. Thus, a JPEG image will deteriorate if it is retouched and saved as a JPEG repeatedly.

Image Archives on the Web and Electronic Resources

Web developers can obtain graphic arts from sources, such as in-house graphic designers, using draw/paint software programs, clipart collections, commercial CDs, digital cameras, and many other origins. The Internet is also a great resource for those who do not have graphics of their own. Web search engines such as Google and metasearch engines such as Dogpile allow users to specify that they are only looking for "images" from their homepages.

To download a graphic from any Web page, first, locate an image. With Macintosh computers, point to it with the cursor and then click and hold the mouse button. With Windows-based computers, have the mouse rest right over the selected graphic and click on the right mouse button. A menu will pop up that contains a command allowing the user to "Save Picture As." Selecting this brings up the standard Save dialogue.

Imagemap Tools

Entire graphics can be made into links to other places through hyperlinks. It is possible to make parts of graphics respond to mouse clicks to lead users to more than one place from a single graphic; this is called an "image map." Imagemapper, or simple imagemap editor, is a special category of graphic editors that create click-

Figure 10.4. A clickable image map of US States from the Climate Diagnostics Center (Image used with permission from ESRL Physical Sciences Division / CIRES Climate Diagnostics Center at homepage: http://www.cdc.noaa.gov/)

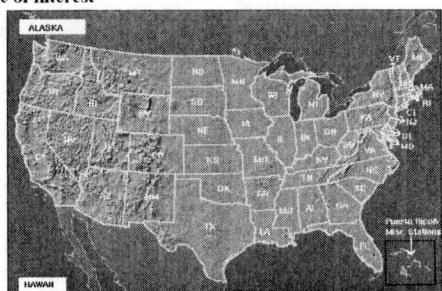

Figure 10.5. A clickable map of US States from the Climate Diagnostics Center (Image used with permission from ESRL Physical Sciences Division / CIRES Climate Diagnostics Center at homepage: http://www.cdc.noaa.gov/)

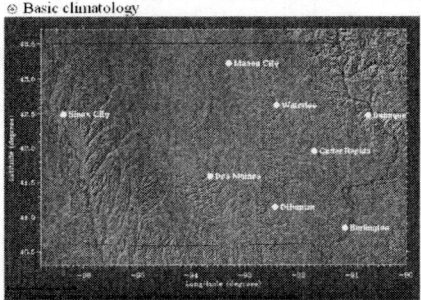

able and animated image maps (or imagemaps). Clickable maps can be based on graphical maps such as floor plans, road maps, and regional maps. In the example of the clickable map of US States from the Climate Diagnostics Center (2003), the developers scanned in existing image and overlaid "hot spots" to function as a navigation menu (see Figure 10.4).

Imagemaps provides an interesting model of a graphical interface for data retrieval. In the example of the clickable map of US States from the Climate Diagnostics Center, a click on IA on the map will hyperlink users to the state map of Iowa (see Figure 10.5). From there, users can click over a city name to view detailed climatology for a city in Iowa. In this sense, the use of clickable maps overlaps with forms as interfaces to data services.

Within an imagemap tool, an image is opened and shapes are marked out on it using the mouse. The shapes can be moved or resized at any time, and points in polygons can be added, deleted, and moved. Links can be associated with the shapes by entering URLs into the list positioned to the right of the image. When ready to save the imagemap into a Web page, usually a series of dialogs steps lead users through the process, and the page is updated with the HTML needed to implement the map. Additional useful links for further information about creating imagemages include:

- **W3C HTTPD Clickable Image Support:** http://www.w3.org/Daemon/User/CGI/HTImageDoc.html
- **NCSA Imagemap Tutorial:** http://hoohoo.ncsa.uiuc.edu/docs/tutorials/imagemapping.html

Design Issues with Web Graphics

The "resolution" is the image quality measured in terms of how many pixels are used to create an image. It is commonly referred to as "ppi" (pixels per inch). Because images are to be viewed on a screen, all Web graphics should be no larger than 72 ppi. Anything higher has no improved visual effect, and only creates longer download times. Specifically, there are two "resolutions" to consider with Web graphics: monitor resolution and image resolution. It is common for graphic designers who design graphics on high resolution large screen monitors (20 inches, 1024x768 resolution or greater) to forget that most classroom users are browsing at 800x600 or even 600x480 resolution (Slaybaugh, 2003).

Image resolution refers to the number of pixels in an image. Image resolution is sometimes identified by the width and height of the image as well as the total number of pixels in the image. For example, an image that is 2048 pixels wide and 1536 pixels high (2048 X 1536) contains 3,145,728 pixels.

A Web site that looks clean on a monitor with millions of colors could look dithered and jagged on a monitor with only 256 colors. Colors that appear bright and sharp on one screen may appear dark and dull on another. A Web page that appears well suited for a 17" or larger screen will appear cut-off on a smaller one.

However, it is important to note that reducing the file size may not necessarily reduce the size of the image. The general rule is to keep Web page size between 40 – 60 KB. Any extra graphic images on the Web page should serve a function that is directly related to the mission of the homepage.

It is also important to remember that graphic images are primarily used to enhance Web page function. If graphic images considerably increase the Web pages' download time, then the user needs to either size down the graphic images, replace them with a smaller image, or replace them with the HTML default bullets, horizontal rules, or colored heading text.

The advantage of color on the Web is that it is an added benefit with no cost. Technically, the user can produce millions of colors on a screen, provided the monitor and video display are of decent quality. The disadvantage is that there are actually only 216 Web-safe colors, meaning that these are the only colors that appear the same on all monitors and operating systems without dithering, be they PCs or Macs.

Scripting Tools

When Java landed on the world stage in the spring of 1995, it represented a new way to administer and deliver software in the network age. Java is an object-oriented, Web programming language, similar to C++. Designed for portability, independence, built-in security mechanisms, and usability embedded in small devices, it took off as a language for small applications ("applets") that ran within a Web browser. JAVA applications are executable on any java-enabled browser with the "Java Virtual Machine" (McDuffie, 2003). Thus, JAVA will run on any operating system. Java applets allow software to be administered on a single server and downloaded to multiple clients via a Web browser. When a new version of a program was ready, only the server needed updating. JAVA applications are stand-alone programs, whereas JAVA applets are code snippets that are designed to run within Web pages to produce various special effects. When someone accesses a Web page with applets, the applets automatically download with the page: All that is needed to view the effect comes with the page itself, making applets independent of the operating systems. This design feature makes applets particularly desirable for multimedia applications. An aglet is a Java object that can move from one host on the Internet to another. That is, an aglet that executes on one host can suddenly halt execution, dispatch to a remote host, and resume execution there. When the aglet moves, it takes along its program code as well as its data. A built-in security mechanism makes it safe for a computer to host untrusted aglets.

JavaScript is not Java. Developed under the Sun Microsystems brand, JAVA is used to create stand-alone applets. Applets are downloaded as separate files for a browser alongside an HTML document, and provide an infinite variety of added functionality to the Web site the user is visiting. On the other hand, JavaScript, developed by Netscape, is a smaller language that does not create applets or stand-alone applications. JavaScript resembles JAVA, but it runs on the client/user side, not the host/server (McDuffie, 2003). JavaScript resides within HTML documents, and can provide interactivity above and beyond flat HTML pages without CGI programs.

JAVA and JavaScript share a number of vocabulary and syntax constructions. While JAVA programming is beyond the scope of this book, JavaScript is much easier to learn and write. All school Web personnel need to program in JavaScript and use a JavaScript-enabled browser, such as Internet Explorer. In the market, there are code libraries and scripting tools for both JAVA and JavaScript.

Other Web scripting languages include CGI, PERL, and PHP (Willard, 2001):

- **CGI** (common gateway interface) is a standard for creating scripting programs that allow a server to pass a user's request to an application program and receive data back to send to the user. CGI developers usually create a CGI bin directory on a Web server to store CGI program files,
- **PERL** (practical extraction and reporting language) is a programming language designed for processing text, and commonly used to write server-based CGI scripts to dynamically generate Web pages or process form results.
- **PHP** is another server-side scripting language used to create dynamic Web pages. The Web page files, which have the extension ".php," include special PHP tags that are processed on the server to generate HTML codes for Web pages.

Some tools enable a Web site to have interactive database capabilities. Macromedia *ColdFusion* is a dynamic Web page technology that includes proprietary server software, a development toolset, and a special markup language (CFML). The Web page files, which have the extension ".cfm," include special tags that are processed by the server to generate the HTML code for the Web pages. Users can define database query parameters and HTML properties with familiar HTML-like tags to fit their needs. Some developers use application programs, such as *ColdFusion*, to write server-side markup (SSM) scripts, which are "tags" embedded in the Web page that get interpreted "on the fly", processed by the server each time the page is requested. For example, a "last modified" time/date stamp commonly seen on homepages, are accomplished with the tags.

There are several other types of code generators. Some advanced ASP software assist with sophisticated Web-based database management, while other tools allow simple CGI programming by using templates in PERL scripts.

Table Wizards

The HTML standard provides support for tables in Web documents for organizing the display of information on Web pages (Willard, 2001). Teachers should think of a table as a combination of "columns" and "rows." Tables can create effects similar

Figure 10.6. A sample table

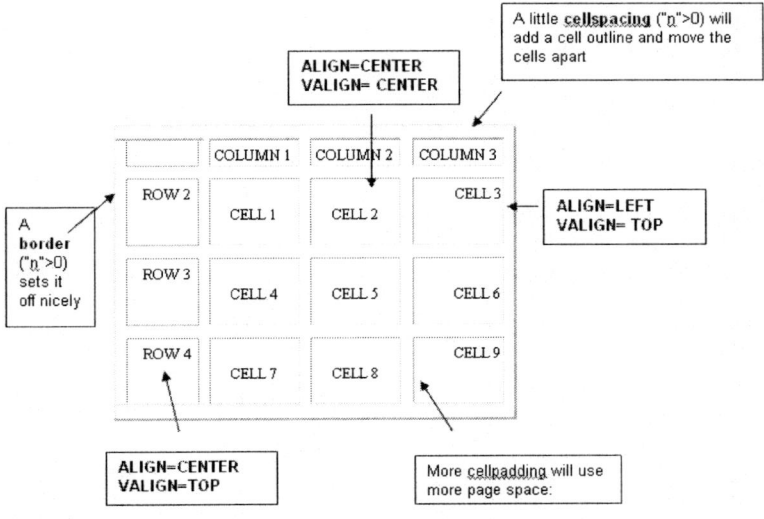

to using "frames" but without the hassle of setting up "frames." Figure 10.6 depicts a typical table:

Thus, some of the most important layout aspects that can be done with tables are (Bates, 2002):

- Dividing the page into separate sections.
- Creating menus.
- Adding interactive form fields.
- Creating fast loading headers for the page.
- Easy alignment of images that have been cut into smaller pieces.
- A simple way to allow text to be written in two or more columns next to each other.

Form Wizards

A form is simply an area that can contain form fields. Forms are a defined area of an HTML document such as a pop-up window or box into which the users input data to have the data processed, for instance, to run a search on a database or to accept login name and password. Form fields are objects such as text boxes, drop-down menus, or radio buttons that allow the visitor to enter information. The data keyed into the form is passed to a CGI script that then passes it to the relevant application. When the visitor clicks a submit button, the content of the form is usually sent to a program that runs on the server. When the process is complete, the output is sent back using CGI script again, and the results presented to the user as some new HTML generated on the fly. JavaScript is sometimes used to create magic with form fields.

Figure 10.7. HTML tags can be added between the <form> and </form> tags

```
html>
<head>
<title>My Form</title>
</head>
<body>
<form method="post" action="http://www.districts.edu/cgi-bin/formmail.cgi">
</form>
</body>
</html>
```

The <form> tag tells the browser where the form starts and ends. All kinds of HTML tags can be added between the <form> and </form> tags to achieve a number of features.

For educators who are not professional programmers, dozens of free services can be found on the Web that offer free CGI scripts for many purpose. Educators can also use different types of online form tools to quickly create a form without knowing JavaScript.

Cascading Style Sheet Editor

A style sheet is a document that describes to a computer program and browsers how to translate the document markup into a particular presentation on the screen or in print. Cascading style sheets (CSS) is a mechanism for Web authors and readers to attach styles including fonts, colors, and so forth, to HTML documents (Bates, 2002). The definitions of the styles are usually stored in the HEAD or the BODY of the document, or in a separate file. The basic format of the STYLE tag is:

<STYLE TYPE="text/css">
HTML tag.class {special formatting}
<SPAN> {special formatting}
</STYLE>

Many of the recommendations are widely implemented in major browsers. Lately, CSS are extended to cover more than simply text styles and how documents are presented on screens.

Multimedia and Other Tools

Web browsers can display certain file types, such as text, graphics, table, forms, and style sheets, as a standard part of their function. Other formats are possible on the Web, but these will require either a "plug-in," which is a mini-application that becomes part of the browser and must be downloaded separately, or a separate, free-standing "helper" application that is opened by the browser to display content in a separate window. Time and effort are necessary to download and install plug-ins, but most of the time the effort is worth it, as the other choice may be to do without the data or of lower quality.

Plug-ins are third party software applications written by independent developers for enhanced integration with the functioning of the browser (Willard, 2001). Plug-ins are loaded when the Web browser is launched and can act instantly and nonintrusively when called upon, giving the browser enhanced functionality. Some plug-ins may be bundled with browser software, while others are available for downloading. In most cases, plug-ins are free. Some Web browser plug-ins allow users to view CAD drawings via the Internet, and zoom and print in high quality. Other plug-ins play audio files such as RMF, MIDI, MOD, AIFF, WAV, and AU files.

Many of the maps and documents on the Web require ActiveX controls to enable viewing. ActiveX is a set of technologies from Microsoft that provides tools for linking desktop applications to the Web. For instance, ActiveX technology allows users to view *Word* and *Excel* documents directly in a browser. An ActiveX control is similar to a JAVA applet. It is not a programming language, but rather a set of rules for how applications should share information. Programmers can develop ActiveX controls in a variety of languages, including C, C++, Visual Basic, and JAVA.

Some Web animation software applications let Web pages come alive with exciting interactive animation with easy to use interface. Over the years, *Flash* has almost become the Web animation standard. Flash (also known as Shockwave *Flash*) is a vector-based graphic format that is proprietary to Macromedia. Its player is built into the latest versions of most browsers. Developers use the Flash program to produce interactive animations called "*Flash* movies." Macromedia *Shockwave* plug-in is used to display multimedia files such as animation created with Macromedia *Director*. Like Flash movies, Shockwave movies are intended for Web-based distribution to Web browsers.

Virtual reality modeling language, or VRML, is an Internet standard for the rendering of 3-D graphics. VRML files can be viewed with plug-ins such as Live3D.

Some multimedia streaming tools let users send video clips in the same amount of time and space that it takes to send text, and the receiver does not need to have any special viewing capabilities.

Multimedia should be used carefully on the Web for several reasons (Willard, 2001):

- Media files are usually very large and take a long time to download without a broadband connection.
- Each media format requires a software application or plug-in to view.
- Printing is not an option for most media files.
- Updating media files is time consuming.
- As part of good practice and ADA recommendation, users will need to provide more than one format for video and audio files.

Other Web Component Builders

A special type of Web component builder is LMS. Integrated Web-based learning management systems, or LMS, such as *WebCT* (now a BlackBoard subsidiary) have become more visible in K-12 education in general. As of December 2006, *WebCT* is available in 14 major world languages in over 60 countries. More and more K-12 courses use *WebCT* as a course supplement, or are offered online as distance learning courses via *WebCT* (Costello, 2003; Fraker, 2003; Westhoff, 2003). With LMS, all operations are configured via Web-based forms.

Navigation Schemes in Web Design

Web designers use these basic Web site navigation schemes:

- Text links
- Graphic images - navigation buttons
- Graphic images - image maps
- Drop-down Menus - JavaScript, CGI, and so forth.

An ideal Web site navigation scheme is consistent throughout the entire Web site, and allows visitors to find what they are searching for quickly and easily. A Web site is not a document an audience can physically hold. The Web is a much more interactive experience than a print publication. The designers have to organize the content very differently from the way one might organize them from a brochure, newsletter, or book. The Web is a much more interactive experience than a print publication. The viewer controls the sequence of pages and hyperlinks from page to page. Designers cannot assume the viewers have seen previous pages or will proceed to subsequent pages in a certain order. Each page must be able to stand on its own. A good Web site always reminds its visitors where they are and how to get to another location within the site.

Many new Web surfers understand that blue, underlined text is a hyperlink, and blue text usually indicates an unvisited link yet purple text usually indicates a visited link. If the designers elect not to use the default colors, the text links should be emphasized in some way such as boldfaced, a larger font size, set between small vertical lines or square brackets, or a combination of these. In other words, text links should be unique and should not look the same as any other text in the same Web pages.

Text links offer several advantages and disadvantages. The biggest advantage of using text links is the quick download time compared with graphics (Willard, 2001). The other advantage of text links is that some of the text can be keywords. The biggest disadvantage of text links is that they can be boring to view. The disadvantage of using graphic images as navigation buttons is that many visitors might not understand that the graphic image is a hyperlink to move to graphic images that add uniqueness, color, personality, and visual appeal to a Web site. Most Web sites use Web graphics (buttons) as a navigation scheme. However, download time is a big concern in deciding whether to use navigation buttons.

Designing American Disablity Act (ADA) Compliant Web Pages

When using an Internet browser, low vision and blind users can use screen reading software that converts text, navigation, and graphic "ALT tags" into a Braille output or a voice output through a synthesizer, screen enlargers/magnifiers, scanners that convert text into synthesized speech or a Braille printout, voice recognition software, Braille or enlarged keyboards, and Braille display. In the Alt label, developers can type in a brief description of the image. This text will be spoken to a visually impaired or partially sighted person by a talking Web browser. When the Web page with ALT tags is first opened but before the image is fully downloaded, the ALT tags will be displayed by browsers where the image will appear. When the mouse is positioned over the image in a browser running on a PC, the ALT tags can be displayed as pop-up "tip text." If users, for speed reasons, switched off the image downloading feature, the ALT tags can still be displayed by any Web browser. For all the reasons given, but most importantly the last, ensure that every image on the pages has an Alt label.

Typical adaptive technologies for physical disabilities and repetitive strain injuries (RSI) include a modified mouse (head mounted, foot operated, eye-tracking system, joysticks, etc.), and voice recognition software.

Adaptive technologies for the hearing disabled include closed captioning, show sounds that translate nonspeech audio into a visual manifestation, and telecommunications devices for the deaf (TDD). The process called "universal design" assures that a course is accessible to students and instructors with a wide range of abilities and disabilities by the Center for Universal Design (2006). Although not all courses must comply with these standards, they provide a good model for the design of accessible materials. General principles include:

- Text-based resources, such as bulletin boards, e-mail, and distribution lists, are fully accessible to students with disabilities, regardless of the assistive technology used.
- Web pages are accessible to students and instructors using a wide variety of assistive technology. Developers have to either avoid certain types of inaccessible features or formats, or create alternative methods for accessing the inaccessible content.

Web accessibility initiative (or WAI) is W3C's attempt to ensure the use of the Web by anyone regardless of disability. This public effort is to ensure usage availability to a large range of impaired users

Print Design vs. Web Page Design

When some people turn on their computer, they think they are reading a printed page on their screen. They usually want to apply print strategies to a Web layout. However, many of the rules of print simply do not apply to the Web. Web designers must organize the content on Web pages very differently from the way one might organize them for printed material. Since Web pages are not documents the audience can physically hold, Web designers cannot assume the viewer has seen previous pages or will proceed to subsequent pages on the Web site. Each page must be able to stand on its own. Thus, Web page readers always need to be reminded where they are and how to get to other places on the site.

Boosting a Web Site's Credibility

Teacher technologists want to design Web pages that look credible. Fogg (2002) conducted 3 years of research that included over 4,500 people and compiled 10 guidelines for building the credibility of a Web site. System administrators can use these guidelines to critique their own Web pages:

1. Make it easy to verify the accuracy of the information on the site.
2. Show that there is a real organization behind the site.
3. Highlight the expertise in an organization and in the content and services provided.

4. Show that honest and trustworthy people stand behind the site.
5. Make it easy for users to contact the site managers.
6. Design the site so it looks professional (or is appropriate for the purpose).
7. Make the site easy to use—and useful.
8. Update the site's content often (at least show it has been reviewed recently).
9. Use restraint with any promotional content.
10. Avoid errors of all types, no matter how small they seem.

The first basic rule of Web site design is that the site should be easy to read. To make the Web site easy to read, Web designers must always consider color contrast, legible typefaces, font size, and font style when designing the Web site and Web graphic images.

Protecting Web Sites

US copyright law states that electronic files, including Web files, are copyrighted the moment they are placed into a tangible form, even if they are not on display to the general public. Protected Web files may include the site's contents, codes, scripting, graphic images, sound, and video clips (*Learn the Net, 2005*). Online thievery can be unpleasant. The Web site administrators can take the following steps to protect Web materials from online thieves:

- Place a copyright notice on every page
- Register the site with the U.S. Copyright Office
- Save copies of the Web site
- Protect the Web graphic images
- Disable image copying

The first step toward protection is to display the copyright notice on the bottom of the home page and all following pages. This copyright notice should be followed by the year of publication and the institution's name, such as: "© 2003-2006, ABC District. All rights reserved." Web administrators can also register their sites with the US Copyright Office or save a copy of the new pages or versions to a backup media. Preserve the original dates the files were made. For extra protection, Web administrators can take screen shots of the folders that contain all of the Web files, including their file information and dates of creation. To further protect Web images, developers may also consider disabling image copying with scripting languages. However, image disabling is not foolproof because of screen shots.

Wrap Up School Web Projects

Once the school Web projects are completed, the page should be tested on a variety of browsers. This will give a good idea of how different viewers will see it. People access the Web with a wide variety of computers and monitors. All Web browsers are not the same and do not support all features (Ash, 2003). To further complicate matters, some people use text-only browsers to view the Web, while others turn off the graphics loading capability of the browsers to speed up the downloading. The challenge is to address these differences.

Note that there are different releases and platforms (Windows and Mac) of each browser. Even the best-planned Web site may look different when viewed with different Web browsers. It is common that some Web pages that look perfect may look incongruous with another browser; scripts that run smoothly with a browser may generate script errors with another browser. Ideally, designers can create separate versions of Web pages tailored to different browsers. Keep in mind, however, that developing different versions is cumbersome. Another solution is to use a CGI script that evaluates the type of browser that is requesting a particular HTML file and builds an appropriate version of that file on the fly. While this option is complex to implement, it is more efficient and much easier to maintain.

Also, users' hardware and telecommunication speed must be considered. If the Web site typically requires a broadband connection, try downloading the pages over a 56 Kbps dial-up modem connection. If a Web designer is frustrated by the experience, then the user will be frustrated also. Providing viewing options is the key to friendly user support. If Web designers make heavy use of images or animations, there are a few things they can do to accommodate, rather than frustrate viewers with slower connection lines or visual disabilities (Ash, 2003). First of all, they can develop parallel sites; a simple one that does not use the "enhancements" and one that has all of the bells and whistles. The best way to accomplish this is to direct the user with a link at the top of the home page to the alternative versions with the "ALT" tag.

Finally, as with educational multimedia design, developing a Web project also involves skill sets ranging from project management and interface design to programming. Sometimes budgets and schedules require team members to juggle more than one role. In some cases, teachers, principals, school staff, PTA members, students, and others are school Webmasters, responsible for maintaining a Web site for a school large and small. As a rule, Web projects are best developed by teams with a range of expertise. The more that is understood about each team member's role and responsibilities, the better each will perform in an assigned role.

References

Ash, L. (2003). *The Web testing companion: The insider's guide to efficient and effective tests.* Hoboken, NJ: John Wiley & Sons.

Bates, C. (2002). *Web programming: Building Internet applications* (2nd ed.). Hoboken, NJ: John Wiley & Sons.

Cascading Style Sheets. (2006). Retrieved June 18, 2007, from http://www.w3.org/Style/CSS/

Center for Universal Design. (2006). Retrieved June 18, 2007, from http://www.design.ncsu.edu/cud/

Climate Diagnostics Center. (2003). United States climate page. Retrieved June 18, 2007, from http://www.cdc.noaa.gov/USclimate/states.fast.html

Costello, D. (2003). Standards, technology and e-learning – A graduate course in education and computer science. *Society for Information Technology and Teacher Education, 2003.* Association for the Advancement of Computing in Education, Charlottesville, VA, 304.

Fogg, B. J. (May 2002). *Stanford guidelines for Web credibility.* Retrieved June 18, 2007, from http://www.webcredibility.org/guidelines/

Fraker, F. (2003). Teaching online in conjunction with a six week field experience. *Society for Information Technology and Teacher Education, 2003.* Association for the Advancement of Computing in Education, Charlottesville, VA, 333-334.

Learn the Net. (2005). Retrieved June 18, 2007, from http://www.learnthenet.com

McDuffie, T. S., (2003). *JavaScript: Concepts & techniques.* Wilsonville, OR: Franklin Beedle & Associates.

McKenzie, J. (1997). *Why in the World Wide Web?* Retrieved June 18, 2007, from http://www.fno.org/mar97/why.html

Slaybaugh, M. (2003). *Professional Web graphics.* Boston: Course Technology.

Watkins, R., & Corry, M. (2004). *E-learning companion: A students' guide to online success.* Boston: Houghton Mifflin.

Westhoff, G. (2003). Training preservice students to utilize Web-based based portfolios and select appropriate bodies of evidence. *Society for Information*

Technology and Teacher Education, 2003. Association for the Advancement of Computing in Education, Charlottesville, VA, 206-09.

Willard, W. (2001). *Web design: A beginner's guide.* Columbus, OH: McGraw-Hill Osborne Media.

Sample Questions

1. Which is the best practice when designing images for the visually impaired Web users?
   a. Build in links to show another Web page with description
   b. Convert the Web page to the gif format
   c. Use the alt feature to provide description in text
   d. Do not use any image

2. The most significant use of a table on a Web page is:
   a. To align image
   b. To wrap texts
   c. Add column to a Web page
   d. Enlarge graphics

3. The purpose of adding graphics on the content page of a Web site is:
   a. To add color to the Web page
   b. To enable the graphics to play a significant role in the Web page design
   c. To add variety to the Web page
   d. That they are required by the district

4. In order to add search functions to a Web page, a teacher is likely to include the following:
   a. GIF
   b. CGI
   c. Aviator script
   d. VRML

5. What is the best practice when a teacher uploads large number of files to a Web site?
   a. To separate folders
   b. Upload one at a time
   c. Upload all at one time
   d. Rename the files first

Answers: (1) C (2) C (3) B (4) B (5) C

Chapter XII

Web Communications and Interaction for Teaching and Learning

ISTE NETS_T, II. Planning and designing learning environments and experiences

Teachers plan and design effective learning environments and experiences supported by technology.

ISTE NETS_T, IV. Assessment and evaluation

Teachers apply technology to facilitate a variety of effective assessment and evaluation strategies.

ISTE NETS_T, VI. Social, ethical, legal, and human issues

Teachers understand the social, ethical, legal, and human issues surrounding the use of technology in PK-12 schools and apply those principles in practice.

Chapter objective: The teacher knows how to use Web pages to communicate and interact effectively with others.

Virtual Learning Communities (or VLC)

Potentially, cyberspace offers students and educators a myriad of resources for educational use within the classroom. Boetcher, Duggan, and White (1999) describe online learning communities as a "gathering of people, in an online 'space' where they communicate, connect, and get to know each other better over time." Students can participate in VLC in order to span distances and link with others with similar interests or expertise.

The Internet also has significance for professional communication among teachers. According to Becker, 16% of teachers communicated with peers outside their buildings on professional matters (1999). In late 2000, the rate rose to 33% for those who had Internet access at home and at school. Beginning educators may wish to participate in online discussion forums in order to receive support from more experienced teachers. Educators may also wish to participate in content related discussion groups to exchange teaching methods and ideas. Some teachers may also decide to participate in online distance education classes offered over the Internet or through videotape to meet the needs of special student populations: limited English, migrant worker's children, special education, and so forth. There are also virtual discussion forums especially for teachers. Teachers.net (2006) is one of the Web sites that host listserv, chat rooms, and electronic bulletin boards.

Other educators may wish to link with various experts in specific fields to gain their input on student projects. For example, a teacher may wish to link with scientists at NASA to seek aid with student science projects. Teachers may also wish to support a classroom pen pal project, or key pal project, by setting up a VLC that would allow students to exchange language learning experiences.

Effective VLC tools that teachers may use to enhance their own or student learning are as follows (Mason & Hart, 1997):

- **Synchronous chat:** In a chat room, members communicate in real time, so they are typing and reading conversations simultaneously. These can be very exciting for students in remote locations or for students paired with older students or adults, but teachers should always remember to monitor conversations. Chat rooms allow for synchronous meetings that may later be posted for those unable to attend the chat. It is also easier for the instructor to keep up with the status of team interactions and provide intermediate feedback when there is a problem. Chat may be secure if desired because rooms may be locked.
- **E-mail lists:** Mailing lists, special interest group (or SIG), or listservs all provide ways to send a particular group the same information or the same e-mail message at the same time. Teachers and students can request to be put on mailing lists for information for special topics and/or can create their own.

For example, if a class is involved in a special project of interest to the entire school, a mailing list could communicate progress to all classrooms in the school.

- **Newsgroups:** Rather than being sent information, a reader may enter a newsgroup site whenever he or she wishes to read messages or information that has been posted. Members are often allowed to post messages or articles as well. Threaded message boards within the site allow for discussions to take place and develop asynchronously.
- **Sharing files and links:** The online environment allows teachers to combine various techniques such as e-mail, threaded discussions, chat rooms, whiteboard programs, shared applications, streamlined video or audio, and interactive CD-ROMs and DVD to educate students. Most of these tools allow file sharing so that group members may upload files and make them accessible to either the public or a select few. Link sharing is a characteristic of these tools (Lee & Owens, 2002).

In sum, when students discover VLCs or other online virtual community systems within their own classrooms, schools, or districts, they will be "hooked" into using the computer for communication. Because peer interest is usually very high, students will learn from each other. However, teachers should monitor student activities carefully. Teachers may also need to infuse lessons with information about "safe" online practices for students. A good resource for the information is located at Tips for Safe Traveling (1997) archived by the US Department of Education.

Evaluating Virtual Learning Communities

Mason and Hart (1997) suggest that educators consider usage and participation rate and user feedback when determining the effectiveness of virtual learning communities. Table 12.1 shows how usage rates and other specific evaluation criteria are used to evaluate VLCs.

Table 12.1. Usage rates and other specific evaluation criteria are used to evaluate VLCs

Usage rate - What is the frequency of user visitation?
Participation rate - Did the virtual learning communities encourage the majority of the membership to be active participants? Was there regular attendance? Were some members more active than others?
User Feedback - What did the virtual learning community members think of their experience? Some researchers consider VLCs successful if they promote continuous interaction. Schwier (2001) states that the match between the purpose of the community and the importance to the learner determines the length of the VLC's survival and the strength of its influence.

continued on next page

Table 12.1. continued

Specific criteria for evaluation of VLCs are offered by Jones (2001). Identity - Successful communities are those with a clear identity and purpose and an organizational structure that encourages all of their members to participate actively. Size for the subject matter - A critical mass of members is needed to develop a rich knowledge base. Members of larger communities often do not feel integrally involved in the community. Members of smaller, focused communities are active participants because the goals of the community are tailored to their needs. Apparent value - A community is successful when people perceive value in the knowledge sharing performed by the community. Support structures - Support structures such as information centers, knowledge champions, and leadership add value to a community. Regular contribution - People in successful VLCs are self-motivated to participate in its activities. VLCs should be aligned with real-world structures, and participants should be able to express their thoughts about the subject area.

When to Incorporate Internet Experts

Computer-supported communication will bring the content expertise of other professionals and community members into the classroom. Content experts broaden the education of the student by providing real-world examples, modeling performances, and offering otherwise unavailable enrichment opportunities for students (Watkins & Corry, 2004).

By middle grades in the elementary levels, students are beginning to communicate well and are eager to acquire information on their own. Teachers can tap into this readiness by asking open-ended research questions. This type of lesson changes the teacher's role from subject matter expert to facilitator of learning as the students are guided through Web sites in search of answers. In his article *The Art of Getting Help*, Agre (1994) suggests that all students be taught how to get help before they are turned loose on the Internet. Agre feels that it is the teacher's responsibility to guide the student in the project to enable the student to seek answers on his own.

Students should also be taught the proper application of Internet reference works, indexes, and databases. Classroom teachers may need to make specialized databases and specific electronic reference works available to students, especially when projects are multidisciplinary, or dependent upon highly specialized research. In today's classroom, a teacher no longer needs to be the sole content matter expert in the classroom. Volunteer subject matter experts, such as meteorologists and historians, can work virtually with students in mentor-protégé relationships that contribute to the authentic learning experiences. This way, students have a chance to learn how knowledge is used in the world outside the school. This practice is known as telementoring. For example, Web sites such as the Electronic Emissary (n.d.) help students connect to experts from astronomy to zoology, 24 hours a day, and 7 days a week. The Electronic Emissary has been online since 1993 and on the Web since 1995. Before mentoring begins, the Electronic Emissary stresses the importance of preparing students for this type of learning:

Teachers should ensure that students are prepared before the communication with the mentor begins. First, students should have clearly conceived learning goals to gain the most from telementoring. The projects should be based on active, inquiry-based and student-centered lessons. Also, the tasks should be broken down into subtask structures before content-related communications begin with the experts. Students should also be aware of realistic and explicitly stated time and communications frequency estimates.

Once communication begins, the teacher should ensure that students have off-line as well as online assistance. That way the students are able to plan communications with the mentor before composing messages. The class should be prepared for a regular "rhythm" of message traffic; with a short enough turnaround time to maintain a bilateral flow of electronic conversation. A good telementoring project will be enhanced by multidimensional communication, utilizing intellect and emotion, balancing scholastic and personal information shared in the exchange.

To avoid problems and ensure success of the telementoring project, teachers must be aware of problems that may occur. The contexts in which online mentors work are quite different from most K-12 teaching/learning environments. Of particular note are differences in Internet accessibility and the expectations that these contrasts can create. Most online mentors have easy and frequent access to telecomputing tools throughout their workday, and are accustomed to having brief, multiturn, text-based conversations with colleagues using quick turnaround times (Electronic Emissary, n.d.). In comparison, K-12 students and teachers have less convenient access to telecommunications facilities. Whereas a mentor might expect a reply to an e-mail message within 24 hours, many K-12 students are able to use Internet facilities only once or twice weekly.

Furthermore, a lack of time is a challenge common to workers in both classroom and nonclassroom environments. As with books, most students are quick to assume everything they locate on the Internet is correct, just because it is there. The students have to be reminded that the information they find on the Web may be true or false, and that the information may come from all around the world. Eventually, students will have to learn to distinguish valid/reputable information from invalid information sites.

Teachers also have to protect their students by not easily releasing students' names and other personal information. Finally, information acquisition will require directed supervision to be sure that students access appropriate Web sites and communicate reliable contacts. Educators can activate the filtering feature provided by most search engines as a first measure to weed out adult or violent materials. A district may have a filtering device such as Network Nanny in place. If not, teachers should research possible filters. One resource prepared for parents is *Tips for Safe Traveling* (Department of Education, 1997).

Distance Education/Learning

Distance education takes place when the student and instructor are separated by physical space and/or time. In the past, correspondence courses through regular mail provide one type of "distance learning." Audio/visual transmission and instruction have existed since the 1930s. Radio and video-based course work have helped students who live in remote areas. Networked computers and videoconferencing, especially those linked into the Internet, provide additional education opportunities. In the future, newer technologies will be adapted for the needs of young learners.

The growth in the numbers of students learning online has increased the need to carefully investigate the factors that affect student learning in virtual schooling environments.

Research suggests that as programs become more efficient, program costs will decrease, thus increasing delivery capacity and perhaps increasing revenue. These long-term processes make the investments potentially self-sustainable in the long-term.

In K-12, distance education has been used primarily by advanced-placed and accelerated-paced students or for school choice, high school reform, and workforce preparation. Ethical use of distance education requires availability to diverse learning audiences and an effort to make formerly estranged student groups aware of the opportunities that distance education provides. Students likely to succeed in virtual courses have these common characteristics: self-directed, disciplined, organized, and technologically sophisticated.

The literature on virtual schools reveals that one central policy concern is that of ensuring equal access to students (Hawkes, 2004). Students in small, remote, and rural areas of the state may gain access to highly qualified teachers through electronic courses delivered at the school or to another location in the community. Electronic courses offer opportunities for students to take advanced high school courses. There is a rising need for high-level courses to challenge students and prepare them for college, and electronic courses may be one way to address this need. Students throughout the state may benefit from availability of advanced courses taught by experts who would not otherwise be accessible. Students at risk of dropping out of school because of pregnancy, high mobility, or disciplinary problems may also benefit from access to electronic courses.

Many states have discovered that most students who take electronic courses choose to take no more than one or two courses at a time. And many students taking electronic courses do so at district facilities rather than at home or off-site.

A meta-analysis published in 2004 reviewed 116 effect sizes from 14 Web-delivered K–12 distance education programs studied between 1999 and 2004 (Hawkes, 2004). According to the meta-analysis, among the benefits of distance education for school-age children are increased enrollment or time in school as education programs reach underserved regions; broader educational opportunities for students who are unable to attend traditional schools; access to resources and instructors not locally available; and increased student-teacher communication.

The meta-analysis also reported that virtual schooling, like classroom schooling, has had limited success in some situations (Hawkes, 2004). In an online environment, students may feel isolated, and parents may have concerns about children's social development.

Furthermore, students with language difficulties may experience a disadvantage in a text-heavy online environment, and content area subjects requiring physical demonstrations of skill such as music, physical education, or foreign language may not be practical in a technology-mediated setting. Finally, highly technical subjects such as mathematics and science may be too difficult to teach online. Institutions providing e-learning services must have clear and concise contracts defining expectations, obligations, and privileges for parents and students.

Good Practice of School-Based Distance Learning Systems

Instructors may build courses from scratch or, more often than not, customize commercial software. Many researchers believe that learning is inherently a social, dialogical process (Duffy & Cunningham, 1995). Therefore, the more "social presence" established in distance education courses to overcome the effects of geographic proximity the better (Watkins & Corry, 2004). Social presence is defined as the use of techniques to overcome the perceived distance between instructor and students. The fact that students may have to use the telephone to contact the teacher or use fax machines to turn in homework diminishes the occurrences of teacher-student interaction and decreases the spontaneity of dialogue. Electronic courses should be based on interaction with a teacher via e-mail or other online communication. "Canned" courses, without the ability to interact with a qualified instructor, may be helpful as supplemental materials but should not serve as the entire basis for a course (Duffy & Cunningham, 1995).

Administrators, teachers, and students need time and support to successfully transition into these new technology-based processes. Much of what is involved in instructional outcomes of distance education is based on what educators already know about superior instructional design. Given that the criteria for quality instruction are consistent no matter the medium, administrators are in an optimal position to employ evaluative criteria.

Evaluation of Instructional Web Sites and Electronic Resources for Students and Teachers

Students must learn early that information found on the Web may or may not be true, can be submitted by adults or by children, and may originate from anywhere around the world. Eventually, they must learn to distinguish sales and marketing sites from more neutrally informational sites. In general, it is difficult for younger children--through fourth grade--to evaluate the sites or write annotations. Younger students choose what they like and have trouble articulating why they like something. When asked why they liked a site, the common answer was "it had lots of information," or "it had good information." Student awareness is usually enhanced by identifying whether the information was easy to read, whether the site contained both pictures and text, and if the pictures aided understanding. Usually the favorite sites of children are those created by other children.

Part of teaching with technology involves providing the appropriate technology for the learner. A number of important characteristics of software and online materials should be considered by teachers to match technology with young learners (Roblyer, 2005):

- Is the title representative of the product?
- Is there a clear Web address URL, if applicable?
- Does it match the intended grade level?
- What is the level of difficulty?
- Will this match the course/subject area well?
- What is the type of media? Print? Multimedia? Online?
- Are there required or prerequisite skills?
- Is the material correlated with state and national standards?
- Are the contents appropriate, accurate, current, complete, free of bias, engaging and interesting, and interactive?

- Is the interface user-friendly, appropriate for special needs, clear, and concise?

Teaching students how to evaluate technology such as CD-ROM programs and Web sites is of utmost concern, particularly when trying to establish the accuracy of the information. There are additional criteria that teachers should consider when evaluating a Web site for use with students. Teachers should consider the following factors for evaluating Web sites: information is accurate and authentic, and the latest update is posted; the author(s) can be found easily and has/have "credentials", the site includes a way to contact an author(s) or Webmaster(s) through e-mail; navigation is easy, and pages load quickly; the beginning page provides organization and links; and the links are easy to identify and go to the correct site. Each page provides a way to go forward, backward, or home, and icons clearly represent the link; the requests for private information are secure; and the domain is a reliable (government, educational, nonprofit) rather than a more personal or commercial site (Roblyer, 2005).

Finally, teachers should always bookmark interesting sites on classroom computers so that they and the students can easily access them. It is important to be aware that a common culture-related bias seen in some software is that perspective of majority groups is emphasized, never minority groups. It is also important to note that there is a short cut teachers can use when determining the credibility of a Web site; this short cut is accomplished by checking the types of organizations linked to the Web site.

Netiquette at School

According to Resource Center for Cyberculture Studies (2004), cyberculture is "a collection of cultures and cultural products that exist on and/or are made possible by the Internet, along with the stories told about these cultures and cultural products." As teachers and administrators become more comfortable with technology, online learning will become integrated into the curricula of most schools. However, the openness of the Internet, which makes it so useful to all users, is also problematic. Children may locate material not meant for young eyes.

In order to counter this situation, Shea suggests that "core rules" on netiquette should be taught to all students. Shea defines netiquette as the network etiquette, a set of rules for behaving properly online. In the WWW version of the book *Netiquette*, published by Albion Books, Shea summarizes the core rules of netiquette for all Internet users as follows (2004):

- **Remember the human:** When we communicate electronically, we do not have the opportunity to use facial expressions, gestures, and tone of voice to communicate meaning as we do in other ways of communications. For this reason, it is easy to misinterpret a correspondent's meaning. Because receivers cannot know meaning through one's voice or facial features, expression should be used when appropriate through use of emoticons such as ☺.

- **Know your location in cyberspace:** When entering a domain of cyberspace that is new, users should first spend a while listening to the chat or reading the archives to get a sense of how the participants act.

- **Respect other people's time and bandwidth:** It is a courtesy to ensure that the time readers spend reading e-mails or participating in discussion postings is not wasted. See Chapter X for the explanation of bandwidth.

- **Create a professional online image:** Over the Internet, participants will be judged by the quality of their writing. Therefore, remind students that spelling and grammar do count. Also, students should know the subject they are discussing; they should pay attention to the content of their writing.

- **Share expert knowledge:** The reason asking questions online works is that a lot of knowledgeable people are reading the posted messages online.

- **Help keep flame wars under control:** Netiquette forbids the perpetuation of flames, which are series of angry letters (see Chapter I).

- **Respect other people's privacy:** Most schools and organizations forbid teachers or employees to share e-mail accounts. Failing to respect other people's privacy is not just bad Netiquette, it could result in dismissal from a job. Humor and wit that is appropriate for friends and family is out of place at work for teachers.

In their article *The Internetworked School: A Policy for the Future*, Fishman and Pea suggest that any special ground rules for primary and secondary students in cyberspace should be based on the school's existing policy on speech and behavior (Fishman & Pea, 1994).

Ethical Issues

Although the Internet contains a vast source of information, there are related ethical concerns. First, there is no control as to what people can post on the Web, so students may have access to incorrect or inappropriate materials of a sexual or violent nature.

Filtering software and firewalls may prevent some types of information from being received, but first amendment rights have been upheld. Teachers should always be vigilant with information that students can access. Fortunately, the inquiry-based format of WebQuest offers teachers a new alternative to the traditional classroom Web search activities. When implemented properly, students can follow the resource links provided on the WebQuest to access appropriate Web sites reviewed and approved by the teachers.

Expectations for older students include avoiding flaming, which expresses overly strong feelings, along with forwarding information to everyone in their address book and excluding obscene language use in electronic communications (Maiwald, 2003). E-mail communications by students normally are backed up and are deleted from the computer only after several functions are performed. If a teacher suspects Internet predators or other unethical use, it is normally easy to locate those communications to see what has occurred. Students should understand that school computers ought not to be viewed as personal diaries, and that teachers have access to many of their communications (Watkins & Corry, 2004). Teachers must help students form good judgments about their communications.

One reason to use the computer as a communicator is to ensure quick communication to save everyone's time. However, certain types of communication take up time. Spam, the term for e-mail junk mail, should not be forwarded, and chain letters should never be continued. One excellent concept that can be integrated with technology is summarization skills for quick communication. Also, correct mail addressing should be taught as a time and politeness issue. Forwarding others' e-mails without permission can be considered a breech of privacy. E-mails are seen by many as copyrighted, so permission to forward should be sought. Passing viruses and predators should also be discussed, and students should be taught never to give their full names, phone numbers, or addresses, and to report "techno strangers" to adults if anyone asks for that kind of information.

Some schools request students' parents or guardians to let schools know whether they give permission for their children's names or photographs to be on the Internet. Teachers who put students' work on a Web site must obtain the permission of students and their caregivers. For safety, students' names should still not be given. Because electronic communication is relatively new, these expectations and others have developed in the past few years. The computer as a communication and information-gathering device has opened up a whole new realm of expectations that must find a place in the curriculum.

The "digital divide" refers to a gap between those who have access to technology tools and those who do not. A U.S. Department of Commerce Report *Falling through the Net II: New Data on the Digital Divide* (1998) indicated that, although more Americans now own computers, certain groups are still far less likely to have computers and Internet access. Lack of such access affects the ability of students to improve their learning, adults to learn valuable technology skills, and families to benefit from online connection. The "digital divide" exists for many students and schoolteachers due to the fact that many may be first generation college goers or graduates in their families.

Lack of access means more than inconvenience, it means lack of educational opportunities. Research has shown that four groups do not experience equity regarding computer and technology use and, thus, in time may not reap the benefits of a technology-based economy. These four groups include students from low-income homes and schools, minority students, students with special needs, and girls (Roblyer, 2005).

Warren-Sam's (1997) booklet, *Closing the Equity Gap in Technology Access and Use*, describes three major areas in which inequities can arise: access, types of use, and curriculum. The result of not having equal access can be far-reaching for all of these groups. For instance, those learners who are not able to grow up playing and learning with computers can be less comfortable using them and may develop feelings of helplessness or negative beliefs about technology. Many fields in the sciences and mathematics rely on computers or other technology, so when students reach upper levels in high school, they may not be comfortable enough to take courses that employ abundant technology. This reluctance in middle and high school, in turn, blocks access to similar classes in college and in the job market later.

Another type of digital divide arises from physical challenges that some people face. Potential students and instructors may have mobility, visual, hearing, speech, learning, and other disabilities that could influence their participation in courses as they are currently designed. The Americans with Disabilities Act (A.D.A.) of 1990 delineates and protects the civil rights of people with disabilities. "No qualified individual with a disability shall, by reason of such disability, be excluded from participation in or be denied the benefits of services, programs, or activities of a public entity, or be subjected to discrimination by any such entity."

General principles to keep materials accessible to all students include (Edyburn, 2002):

- Text-based resources such as bulletin boards, e-mail, and distribution lists, should be fully accessible by students with disabilities, regardless of the assistive technology they use. Teachers should also try to ensure that a variety of Web pages are accessible. Software developers should either avoid certain types of inaccessible features or formats, or create alternative methods for accessing the inaccessible content.
- Care should be taken to ensure that all students, regardless of gender, have access to technology. Gender bias, like the literature of the past, may be evident when software excludes girls in its programs. Teachers should avoid stereotyping where a subliminal message is sent that women only use comput-

ers for clerical jobs. Teachers should also ensure that students in all academic achievement levels have access to technology. The lower achievers *may* have allocated computer time; however, teachers should ensure that a variety of software is used and avoid the exclusive use of the skill-and-drill type software (Edyburn, 2002). The main focus of the technology teachers should be on equal treatment for all students, whether from a multicultural perspective, a special needs perspective, or tolerance and bias.

- Vigilant teachers need to ensure that traditional biases and inequities that have been evident in the education system in the past do not infiltrate the classrooms or the realm of educational technology. For example, teachers should not create unequal situations in their classroom by assigning homework related to computer work that would create unequal grading situations for students who do not have easy access. The most important point is to ensure that all students have equal work time, higher-order thinking activities, and "play time" on the computers.

References

Agre, P. (1994, February). The art of getting help. *The Network Observer, 1*(2).

Becker, H. (1999). *Teaching, learning, and computing, 1998: A national survey of schools and teachers.* University of California at Irvine: CRITO.

Boetcher, S., Duggan, H., & White, N. (May 26, 1999). *The nature of online communities: What is a virtual community and why would you ever need one?* Retrieved July 21, 2006, from http://www.onlinefacilitation.com

Department of Commerce. (1998). *Falling through the Net II: New Data on the Digital Divide.*

Department of Education. (1997). *Tips for safe traveling.* Retrieved May 3, 2006, from http://www.ed.gov/pubs/parents/internet/tips.html

Duffy, T. M., & Cunningham, D. C. (1995). *Constructivism: Implications for the design and delivery of instruction.* In D. H. Jonassen (Ed.), *Handbook for research on education.*

Edyburn, D. (2002). *What every teacher should know about assistive technology.* Boston: Allyn & Bacon.

Electronic Emissary. (n.d.) Retrieved May 3, 2006, from http://emissary.wm.edu/

Fishman, B., & Pea, R. D. (1994). The internetworked school: A policy for the future. *Technos: Quarterly of Education and Technology, 3*(1), 22-26.

Hawkes, M. (2004). *Criteria for evaluating school-based distance education programs.* Retrieved May 3, 2006, from http://www.ncrel.org/tandl/eval4.htm

Jones, M. (2001). *Research issues in the design of on-line communities.* Retrieved May 3, 2006, from http://www.cc.gatech.edu/~asb/workshops/chi/99/participants/jones.html

Lee, W., & Owens, D. L. (2000). *Multimedia-based instructional design: Computer-based training, Web-based training, and distance learning.* San Francisco: Pfeiffer.

Maiwald, E. (2003). *Network security: A beginner's guide* (2nd ed.). Emeryville, CA: McGraw-Hill Osborne Media.

Mason, J., & Hart, G. (1997). *Effective use of asynchronous virtual learning communities.* Creative Collaboration in Virtual Communities Conference. Sydney, Australia: University of Sydney.

Resource Center for Cyberculture Studies. (2004). Retrieved May 3, 2006, from http://www.com.washington.edu/rccs/

Roblyer, M. D. (2005). *Integrating educational technology into teaching* (4th ed.). Upper Saddle River, NJ: Merrill, Prentice Hall.

Schwier, R.A. (2001). Catalysts, emphases and elements of virtual learning communities: Implications for research and practice. *The Quarterly Review of Distance Education, 2*(1).

Shea , V. (2004). *Netiquette.* Retrieved May 3, 2006, from http://www.albion.com/netiquette/book/index.html

Teachers.net. (2006). Retrieved July 3, 2006, from http://www.teachers.net/

Warren-Sams, B. (1997, June). *Closing the equity gap in technology access and use.* Portland, OR: Northwest Regional Educational Lab.

Watkins, R,. & Corry, M. (2004). *E-learning companion: A students' guide to online success.* Boston: Houghton Mifflin.

Sample Questions

1. When discussing the accuracy of the information presented on different Web sites, it is most important to check which of the following:
   a. How often the Web page is updated
   b. The reliability of the source.
   c. The title of the Web page.
   d. The number of visitors.

2. What is the most important factor when evaluating electronic instructional materials?
   a. The relevance of the material with lesson objectives
   b. The presentation feature of the electronic instructional materials
   c. The user-friendliness of the electronic instructional materials
   d. How updated are the electronic instructional materials

3. A high school science teacher has contacted an online expert to meet her students virtually during her science class. Which of the following is NOT on the list of items for her to show the online expert before the virtual meeting?
   a. Lesson objective
   b. List of questions
   c. Weekly diary
   d. Students' names

4. Which of the following is a culture-related bias seen in some software?
   a. Fails to take a strong stance on the need for cultural diversity
   b. Emphasizes the perspective of majority groups, never minority groups
   c. Tries to persuade students to adopt racist attitudes
   d. Simulations teach inaccurate views on dealing with racism

5. A high school student consults his teacher about desirable options for online distance learning courses. What will be the most desirable feature for online courses?

   a. The distance learning courses have to be unsupervised
   b. The distance learning Web site allows students to access previous courses
   c. The distance learning Web site provides good visual aids
   d. The distance learning Web site allows interaction with teachers and other students

Answers: (1) B (2) A (3) D (4) B (5) D

About the Authors

Irene Chen received her EdD in instructional technology from University of Houston (1998). Currently, she is an associate professor in the Department of Urban Education at the University of Houston Downtown. Dr. Chen has diverse professional experiences. Previously, she was an instructional technology specialist, learning technology coordinator, and a computer programmer/analyst. She has taught numerous graduate and undergraduate courses in instructional technology and curriculum and instruction, and delivered many K-12 in-service training and professional development activities for university staff and faculty members.

Jane Thielemann is an associate professor of education in the College of Public Service at the University of Houston-Downtown, where she teaches graduate and undergraduate courses in reading, language arts, and educational psychology. She received an EdD from the University of Houston Main Campus, and has been a member of the faculty at UH-D for 15 years. As a teacher, consultant, and author, Dr. Thielemann has written numerous articles on teacher education, minority student enrollment in higher education, and business-education partnerships. She also has authored a textbook for teacher certification, *Preparing for Teacher Certification in English, Language Arts and Reading, grades 8-12* (2006, Eakin Press, Austin, TX.) She currently resides in Clear Lake, Texas.

Index

A

absolute address 31–32
acceptable use policy (AUP) 60
achromatic colors 118
Advanced Research Projects Agency (ARPA) 13, 236
  ARPANet 13
aesthetic principles 145–148
  golden ratio 146
  Rule of Thirds 147
age appropriateness 66–72
alley. *See* gutter
ALT tag 278
analysis, design, development, implementation, & evaluation (ADDIE) model 162–163
anchors 263–264
animation
  concepts 108–109
  frame reduction 114
  new techniques 109–112
    Flash animation 110–111
    virtual reality (VR) animation 111–112
  software 107–112
antialiasing 118
antivirus tools 57–58
applets 272
ARCHIE 236
arithmetic and logic unit (ALU) 5
artificial intelligence (AI) devices 3
assistive
  technology 279

B

back projection 196
black and white pictures 119
Boolean expression 14–15
brightness 118

C

call sheet 196
camera-ready state 134
card-based systems 213–215
  HyperCard 213
cascading style sheets (CSS) 260, 275
  editor 275
casting 196
central processing unit (CPU) 5
charts 32–37
clip 196

coder-decoder (CODEC) 183
color theory 148–152
  additive colors 148
    red, green, & blue (RGB) 148
  color space 151
  color wheel 149–151
  complementary colors 150
  meaning 150–152
  mixing 149–150
  subtractive colors 148
    cyan, magenta, yellow, & black (CMYK) 148
  Web-safe colors 271
command line interface (CLI) 237
common gateway interface (CGI) 272
compression 218, 223
  standards
    MP3 217
computer
  functions 4
  screen
    capture 104
constants 27
contrast 118
cross-cutting 196
cut 196
cyberculture 293

D

data
  projector 221
defragmenter 56
desktop publishing 121–137
device drivers 59
digital
  audio workstation (DAWS) 216
  cameras 97–101
    features 97–100
    picture composition 100–101
  divide 17–20, 295–297
  literacy 88
  scanners 102–103
directory
  file structure 9–10
dissolve 196
distance education 290–293
distribution boxes 216
dithering 113, 118
document cameras 221
dolly shot 196
domain name service (DNS) 239
dot
  pitch 118
dots
  per inch (dpi) 103, 119
drawing tablets 104–105
draw programs 92–95
dynamic HTML (DHTML) 260

E

editing 197
electronic
  database management system (DBMS) 39–49
    filters 44–46
    forms 46–47
    queries 44–46
    reports 48
  spreadsheets 26
equal access 290, 296
establishing shot 197
extensible
  HTML (XHTML) 260
  markup language (XML) 260

F

"fair use" guidelines 15, 224
fade 197
fast motion 197
feature film 197
FETCH 236
file
  compression 58–59
  format converters 59–60
  management utility system 56
  size reduction 112–114
fill 118
filtering software 295
firewalls 295
firewire 191, 193
footage 197
frames per second (FPS) 107

full
  motion 197
  shot 197

G

Gopher 236
grade appropriateness 66–72
graphics
  editing 105–106
  formats 106–107
  from clipart collections 96
  from the web
    dowloads 96
    image archives 96
  literacy 33, 141–143
  storage 267–269
  user interface (GUI) 237
gutter 130

H

hanging indent 131
hierarchical structure. *See* tree structure
hierarchy 39
highlights 118
histogram 118
hue 118
hypermedia 80. *See also* hypertext
hypertext 80, 206
  markup language (HTML) 263
    editors 264–266
    tutorial Web sites 262
  transfer protocol (HTTP) 239

I

image
  capture 104
  maps 263, 270, 277
inclusive design. *See* universal design
input/output (I/O) devices 6
insert 197
instructional
  design (ID)
    models (IDM) 162–163
  software
    drills and practice 78
    educational games 78
    problem solving 79
    simulations 79
    tutorials 78
  systems
    design (ISD) 162
interlacing 113, 268
Internet
  addresses (IP) 239
  service providers (ISP) 13

J

jaggies 118
jump cut 197

K

kerning 123, 129
key frame 196
kiosks 215, 221–224

L

"lock it down" 197
lighting 152–156
line of sight 188
Linux 9
local area networks (LANs) 60, 232–235
long shot 197
low-angle shot 197
luminance 118

M

macro lenses 197
macros 38–39
media
  acquisition 169–170
  literacy 141–143
  maintenance 170–171
medium shot 197
memex machine 206
mix 197
mixing console/desk 216
montage 197
morphing 197
multimedia 206–225
  authoring
    programs 206–215

dissemination formats 220–224
project
  design teams 167–169
  director 168
  evaluation 219–220
  executive producer 169
  life cycle 166–167
    alpha testing 167
    beta testing 167
  management 163–166
  production crew 167–169
    art director 168
    audio/video specialists 168
    audio technicians 168
    camera operator 167
    content experts 167
    developers 167
    graphic artists 168
    instructional designers 167
    lead programmer 167
    program authors 167
    project manager 167
    script writers 167
    sound engineers 168
    testers 168
    video specialist 167
    writers 167
musical instrument digital interface (MIDI) 181, 216

N

negative space. *See* white space
netiquette 17, 293–294
newsgroup 287

O

offset lithography. *See* offset printing
offset printing 124, 134–136
operating systems (OS) 7–10
  basic input/output systems (BIOS) 7
  errors 10
  history 8–9
  networking 8
  system resources 7

P

"pack & go" feature 220
"pan and scan" 197
page layout programs 122, 123
paint programs 91–92
pan 197
point of view (POV) 197
presentation software 207–213
print tiling 133
probeware 54–55
productivity tools 25
project studios 215–216, 216
properties (props) 198
prototype 163–168

R

random access memory (RAM) 5–6
read-only memory (ROM) 5
regional internet registries (RIRs) 240
relative position 31
resolution 119
retake 198
reverberation 181, 182
rough cut 198

S

sampling rate 183, 196
saturation 119
scripts 258, 263, 272–275, 281
server-side markup (SSM) scripts 273
sharpness 119
shot 198
shutter speed 198
slideshows 224
software 11–13
  authoring programs 11
  electronic reference software 12
  instructional software 12
  productivity software 11
  sources 12–13
Spam 295
special effects 198
still
  capture 104

stock
  footage 198
  photography 105
storyboard 164–169, 185, 191, 200
streaming audio/video 194–195
style sheets 133
synthesized sounds 181

T

take. *See* shot
teacher
  productivity software 25
  technologists 2
telementoring 289
templates 124, 133
text
  composition 125
  flow. *See* text wrap
  wrap 130
thumbnail 119
tilt 198
tracking 129
transmission control protocol/Internet
    protocol (TCP/IP)
  network 239
transparency 268
traveling matte shot 198
tree structure 9
trojan program 57
typeface 125–129, 133
  sans serif 125–126
  serif 125–126
Type II software applications 80
Type I software applications 80
typography 125–127

U

uniform resource locator (URL)
    236, 238, 239, 242
universal
  design 72–78
    process 19
  serial bus (USB) port 6
UNIX 9
up angle. *See* low-angle shot
user navigation 144–145

V

VERONICA 236
video
  production phases
    postproduction 189–195
    preproduction 184–187
    production 187–188
vignette 198
virtual
  learning
    communities (VLC) 286–290
      evaluation 287
virus hoaxes 57
visual
  communications 89–115
    animations 89
    graphics 89
  effects 198
  literacy 32–33, 141–143

W

Web
  accessibility initiative (WAI) 279
  browser 237–240
  design
    tools 258–281
  development team 244–247
    application developer 245
    graphic designer 247
    project manager 245
    systems administrator 246–247
    Webmaster 245
  directory 15
  graphics
    tools 266–267
  page
    construction 258–259
    scripting 263
  projects 240–244
    life cycle 252–254
  sites
    , educational 247–252, 258
    evaluation 292–293
    protection 280–281
WebQuest 295

what you see is what you get (WYSIWYG) 134, 260
what you see is what you print (WYSIWYP) 134, 135
white space 132
wide area network (WAN) 231–232
Word macro viruses 57
word processing 122–123, 127–134
World Wide Web (WWW) 13, 237–240
worm programs 57

Z

zipping. *See* file compression
zoom 187–188, 198

Looking for a way to make information science and technology research easy? Electronic Resources are designed to keep your institution up-to-date on the latest information science technology trends and research.

Information Technology Research at the Click of a Mouse!

InfoSci-Online
- Instant access to thousands of information technology book chapters, journal articles, teaching cases, and conference proceedings
- Multiple search functions
- Full-text entries and complete citation information
- Upgrade to **InfoSci-Online Premium** and add thousands of authoritative entries from Information Science Reference's handbooks of research and encyclopedias!

IGI Full-Text Online Journal Collection
- Instant access to thousands of scholarly journal articles
- Full-text entries and complete citation information

IGI Teaching Case Collection
- Instant access to hundreds of comprehensive teaching cases
- Password-protected access to case instructor files

IGI E-Access
- Online, full-text access to IGI individual journals, encyclopedias, or handbooks of research

Additional E-Resources
- E-Books
- Individual Electronic Journal Articles
- Individual Electronic Teaching Cases

Resources have flexible pricing to help meet the needs of any institution.

www.igi-online.com

Sign Up for a Free Trial of IGI Databases!